In the late fifties, a depression s
Opry was going through hard t
though, and pop stars like Geor
over to country music because we had modernized our sound enough that it began to appeal to more and more people. George was one of the nicest kids I had ever met – sincere and enthusiastic about country music. Thanks to people like him, country music survived its depression beautifully. We need more men in the industry with the character of George Hamilton IV. He is a man of real class.

Chet Atkins (musician and producer, Nashville, Tennessee)

My friendship with George Hamilton IV goes back a good many years. I remember the first time we had him with us on a Billy Graham Crusade, and he won all our hearts through his simple, direct and heart-warming songs. George Hamilton IV is as unique as his name and one of the most refreshing, wholesome personalities you could ever meet. His gentleness and genuineness have endeared him to countless numbers of people around the world – I do not believe he has ever met a stranger!

Cliff Barrows (Billy Graham Crusades Choir Director, Greenville, South Carolina)

In a business where careers are built on superlatives, and stars burn out way too early, it's downright startling to see what George Hamilton IV has accomplished in 40 years of being 'a very nice guy'. Over the years we've had a lot of success together, and no one can accomplish that without his kind of talent – but how can someone do that and still be 'a very nice guy'? The dictionary says that 'nice' means 'requiring precision or tact, subtle, delicately sensitive, minutely accurate, fastidious, refined, discriminating, pleasing or pleasant, attractive, kind'. Having known George for over 40 years, and having lived with him through clichés like 'awesome', 'greatest' and 'fantastic', it's so comfortable to settle down into more mature language, and to recognize quiet strength when you see it.

Who needs hype when you're talented and courageous enough to be 'a very nice guy'?

John D. Loudermilk (singer/songwriter, Nashville, Tennessee)

It's hard to believe that nearly half a century has passed since teenagers like George Hamilton IV and I had our first pop chart successes. (Take it from me, not many young rock-'n'rollers and teen balladeers have survived from those seemingly carefree days!) Over the decades our busy paths have crossed infrequently, but, when we have met, George's kindly, Christian persona has shone brightly. It's been great, too, to share Christian platforms with him from time to time at events like Dr Billy Graham's 'Mission England' and 'Mission Scotland'. It's a privilege to commend George Hamilton IV's exciting, heart-warming story.

Sir Cliff Richard, OBE (singer/songwriter, London, England)

Among the greatest resources that I have in my life is my friendship with George Hamilton IV. George is a man of integrity, honesty and all the good virtues that mark the character of a man with whom one can be comfortable. As a writer of songs, I – along with many others – appreciate the respect George gives to the lyrics. His ability to do more than justice to a melody is legendary, of course. After working together for a good many years, I consider him certainly among my top five most beloved and respected friends.

Arthur 'Guitar Boogie' Smith (singer/songwriter/instrumentalist/ TV host, Charlotte, North Carolina)

GEORGE HAMILTON IV

AMBASSADOR OF COUNTRY MUSIC

Paul Davis

HarperCollins*Publishers*
77–85 Fulham Palace Road, London W6 8JB
www.**fire**and**water**.com

First published in Great Britain in 2000 by
HarperCollins*Publishers*
This edition 2001

1 3 5 7 9 10 8 6 4 2

A catalogue record for this book
is available from the British Library.

ISBN 0 00 710105 8

Printed and bound in Great Britain by
Omnia Books Limited, Glasgow

To

My dear wife, Hazel

Our wonderful children and grandchildren,
Anita and Ed McGirr (and Nathanael and Rachel),
Wes and Sue Davis, Laura and Paul Ewers

Our faithful parents, Helen and Tom Davis,
Rose and Walter Scott

Our loving church, Leighton Christian Fellowship,
England and worldwide

All our friends in the world of music

ACKNOWLEDGEMENTS

Thanks to Adelaide and George Hamilton IV, Lillian and George Hege Hamilton V, Sue Marshall, Al Moir, George Beverly Shea, Pat Boone, Jerry Arhelger, Cliff Barrows, Arthur Smith, Wes Davis, Sir Cliff Richard, Bill Latham, Joy and Samuel Purdy, Laura Ewers and Hazel Davis.

CONTENTS

FOREWORD
BY GEORGE HAMILTON IV

Two roads diverged in a wood, and I –
I took the one less travelled by,
And that has made all the difference.

Robert Frost, 'The Road Not Taken'

WHEN I FIRST MET Paul Davis, on one of my early trips to England, he was the editor of a wonderful Christian music magazine called *New Christian Music*. Paul introduced himself to me and I remember seeing him frequently on our concert tours in England. He, his wife Hazel and their children used to attend a lot of our concerts at the Fairfield Halls in Croydon. It seemed as if any time we appeared on the south side of London, he and his family were there!

What I most remember is how Paul was always so supportive and encouraging. I soon found out that he was a Christian, and if there was ever a man who 'walked his talk', it's Paul Davis! He's a true silent witness in the way he lives his life. It also became apparent to me that Paul is a big fan of country music. Paul's number one motivation in life is to share his faith, and I think he sees country music as a powerful tool for this – as a means of sharing faith in a nonthreatening, nonpreachy sort of way.

Looking back on it all, I believe Paul saw me as a possible silent witness myself, if I was motivated to make more use of my platform in country music to tell others about what I believe. He encouraged me, way back, to do just that. It was Paul who in 1988 suggested that I do my very first tour of British churches. I was shocked when he suggested it. I remember well my response.

'Well, Paul,' I said, 'I don't know how I could afford to do that. With the band, motel rooms, travel expenses and all the things that cost money in doing a country music concert tour, I can't see how the churches could afford to pay even the expenses of a tour like that!'

Paul explained to me that what he meant was doing a tour on my own – solo-acoustic, just me and my guitar, keeping it simple so that it would be feasible for the small churches. This frightened me. I'd never even considered getting up in front of a church congregation in Britain, or anywhere else. Since I'd had a few hit records and had gained some sort of notoriety, I'd never thought of performing with just my guitar and trying to hold an audience for an hour or so by myself. Paul kept after me about it, however, and finally in the summer of 1988 I did my first country-gospel church tour, 'Songs and Stories' – just me and my guitar, singing and sharing. To my great surprise, it was a blessing to me (and to the audiences, I hope)!

I was inspired to do more of that. It was all Paul's doing – his inspiration and his idea. We went on from that to 'A Country Christmas – A Service of Lessons and Carols' (Christmas, country-style) and that seemed to go over really well with people. We continued with 'Easter in the Country', 'Thanksgiving in the Country – A Harvest Festival in Story and Song', and then 'This Is My Story, This Is My Song', which told the life story of Fanny Crosby, the great blind hymnwriter of the 1800s. Paul and I are now working on another presentation on the life of Ira Sankey, the famous gospel singer of the Victorian era. You might say he was the George Beverly Shea of the late 1800s, and he toured with Dwight L. Moody, who was the Billy Graham of the late 1800s!

I have to say that Paul Davis, through his encouragement, support and faith, has probably inspired me more than anyone else to put my music 'on the front line' when it comes to sharing my beliefs. It was because of Paul that I became more and more involved in Christian music and in singing and sharing.

I view this biography as a labour of love on Paul's part. The stories and anecdotes about my life which I've passed along to Paul have been given in a spirit of love and hopefully in a positive way. This project is intended to detail the journey of life from a spiritual perspective, as well as outlining what has been a hectic and exciting existence so far! As I often say in my church concerts, these are 'the confessions of a reformed backslider and one-time baby Christian on a musical journey towards spiritual adulthood'. In a way this book is the journal of 'a pilgrim's progress' – and it's about a 'work in progress'. After all these years, I'm still learning. Let's get something straight, right up front: I'm not a preacher. I'm a confessor, and if I started confessing *all* my sins, this book would be bigger than *Webster's Dictionary*!

In closing, I want to say, 'Thank God for music' (and for all the fine folks it's introduced me to). Music is a bridge-builder in a world of walls. Here's to more bridges and fewer walls.

George Hamilton IV

INTRODUCTION
AMBASSADOR AND FRIEND

A man that hath friends must show himself friendly:
and there is a friend that sticketh closer than a brother.

King Solomon, Proverbs 18:24

AMONG THE WELL-KNOWN specialists of twentieth-century popular music, no one has enjoyed a more enviable reputation in both the country and gospel music fields than George Hamilton IV. His popular, easy-listening, country style (mixed with a sprinkling of folk) has been enjoyed by enthusiastic fans all over the world. A fellow hit-maker and peer of note, Pat Boone, has said of George:

> Before there was television, there was a recording industry. Indeed, before there was a music 'business' there were troubadours. These were gifted individuals who travelled their countries, and in some cases the world, like musical 'Johnny Appleseeds'. They cross-pollinated the cultures, planting musical seeds of happiness that took root and flourished everywhere the troubadours went. George Hamilton IV is a modern-day, classic troubadour. He has planted musical seeds of happiness and love. Goodwill has sprung up in his footprints. Long may he live and sing, and beautify the Earth!

In the 'dog eat dog' world of show business, that is praise indeed.

Throughout the second half of the twentieth century, George IV's name became synonymous with excellence in his particular field. A trailblazer, and something of a role model, he set for himself ever-rising standards that other aspiring performers have tried to copy. George Hamilton IV remains unique, however – a legend among his peers, successors and fans alike. Many have been amazed by his depth of humility and patience. He never ceases to exhibit delight and dedication in, as he puts it, 'meetin' and greetin' and shakin' and howdyin'' with so many people. Long after most stars would have made their legitimate excuses and slipped out through the back door of the stage, George IV would still be there talking to anyone and everyone!

I am not alone in finding him a loyal friend as well as a great singer and performer. He has been uniquely dubbed the 'International Ambassador of Country and Gospel Music' for the past five decades. George also has the rare talent needed to communicate powerfully in the area of story-telling, poetry and teaching. He takes great delight in recounting simple, life-changing truths. He is intelligent and gracious both on and off stage. Fully dedicated to his wife and family and to his Christian faith, he is a worthy role model for any young person to follow. His worldwide success has even led to him being the subject of a 'Trivial Pursuit' quiz question!

It all started with young George as a wide-eyed child in the North Carolina town of Winston-Salem. There, sitting on his railroading grandfather's knee, he would listen to the famed Grand Ole Opry broadcasts on the radio from distant Nashville, Tennessee. Little George never dreamed that one day he would not only visit Music City – as Nashville was known – to see and hear the greats of country music, but would also stand tall with the best of them, sharing the world-renowned stage at the Opry. In the United Kingdom he is one of the few American country music stars to have become a household name (although he is sometimes confused, even by the national press, with George Hamilton the movie star).

A keen supporter of evangelist Dr Billy Graham, George IV has appeared as a guest soloist at many of his worldwide meetings. Dr

Graham's friend and co-worker, gospel singer George Beverly Shea, said this about George IV:

> The dictionary describes an ambassador as 'a minister sent to a foreign state as a representative on a mission'. George Hamilton IV has fulfilled his mission. I want to honour him with the much deserved title of 'The Musical Ambassador for Christ'. George IV has selflessly and devotedly strived via his musical gift to bring lost souls to the Lord Jesus, bridging the gap between heaven and earth. I am delighted to call him my friend and brother in Christ!

Big in personality and high in integrity as he is, it is appropriate that George is a tall, well-built gentleman. When he speaks or sings his voice has a distinctive, deep and plaintive ring to it, complemented by his Southern drawl. His unique quality of enunciation and tone is immediately recognizable on all his recordings. Even in advancing years, the sophisticated George conducts himself with considerable dignity. Smartly dressed and well spoken, his manner could never be mistaken for aloofness or ego. Without hesitation or solicitation, many of his associates (some close and some not so close) happily testified to me that George sacrificially gives quality time and dedicated effort to ordinary people in all walks of life. Truly, he has earned his reputation as a 'Southern gentleman' of integrity and faith.

Outside the USA, the exposure given by George to Christian music as a whole, thanks to his ambassadorial role, should not be underemphasized. It continues to strengthen the foundations of a thriving Christian music industry and touring circuit. After half a century of constant personal appearances and the burdensome rigours of being on the road, George's zeal has not been dampened. In his comfortable living room a trophy case and shelves display an overflow of music industry, church and fan awards of every shape and size.

He lives with his wife Tinky in Franklin, Tennessee, on the outskirts of Nashville, and continues to follow an active country and gospel music concert schedule. Deservedly riding high on the heritage of his father, George 'Hege' Hamilton V also carries the

Hamilton banner onwards. George and Tinky are blessed with a close clan of loving family and friends, and Tinky is pleased that George has used his God-given talent to be a witness to so many people around the world.

On a personal note, I would like to express my thanks to George. It is to his credit that I found him to be a man who walked his talk when it came to going the extra mile! Unsolicited, he gave of his time, hospitality, energy and substance in great abundance during my research for this book.

The International Ambassador
The Ambassador was a voice, a persuasive voice,
That travelled the world-wide through.
His songs flew on the beams of morning light,
And spoke to folk with a gentle might,
Telling them how to be true.
The International Ambassador's sound
Traversed over land and sea,
Wherever a human heart may be,
Telling His story and singing His song!
In praise of the right and in blame of the wrong.

Paul Davis, Wes Davis

CHAPTER 1

IRON CURTAIN DRAMA

> George Hamilton IV is a modern-day, classic troubadour ... Goodwill has sprung up in his footprints. Long may he live and sing, and beautify the Earth!
>
> **Pat Boone** (singer, Los Angeles, California)

IT WAS A WARM summer day in 1982, and George Hamilton IV had been specifically invited to Warsaw in Poland to take part in a prestigious country music television special. The Cold War still maintained its threat and the tall, easy-going singer was a most unusual invitee to the dour capital of this once proud Central European state, held since 1947 in the tight grip of Communist domination. American country music stars had never before been given even a passing whiff of an invitation into this bastion of socialist experimentation, located – both geographically and culturally – deep behind the Iron Curtain.

The usually unassuming George IV was feeling pretty proud of himself that day, and well he might. Folk back home in the USA and in England (and, indeed, in Poland) had repeatedly told him that this was the first time an American country artiste had been invited to Poland to do a television programme. He was going to be co-hosting the programme with a local singing star. Arriving at the uninspiring airport, he was chauffeur-driven through miles of bleak, grey streets to the plush Warsaw Intercontinental Hotel. He was the 'honoured guest' of a Communist state seeking to create a favourable impression. The country boy from North Carolina did realize faintly that he was being treated with an undue abundance of official warmth and formal hospitality, all part of the state's first-class treatment. Looking back now, far more aware of what was actually going on in Poland in 1982, George considers this over-the-top treatment to be more than a little incongruous, if not absurd. He failed to appreciate it fully at the time, however.

Rising enthusiastically early on the morning of the television tapings, George peered curiously through the window of his comfortable hotel bedroom into Warsaw's historic Victory Square, basking in the freshness of the early morning sunshine. He was surprised to spy a gathering of people down in the square, as it was only just after dawn. His deeper interest stirred, he took a closer look. Why were people gathering at such an unearthly hour?

He noted that the gathering consisted of all kinds of age groups. Each group was bringing armfuls of beautiful flowers and laying them down on the dusty tarmac, forming the bunches into a universally recognizable shape. As the volume of blooms increased, George easily determined that there in the street was the unmistakable, growing shape of a flower-bejewelled cross. Intrigued and not a little puzzled, George stared at the scene as a lump formed in his throat, his eyes moistened and his open mouth dried up. If anyone had asked, he knew he would not have been able to articulate the reason for this sudden rush of emotion. 'What on earth are those folks doing down there?' he silently asked himself. 'It's crazy ... fancy getting up at this insane hour to be in the street with flowers! Why the flowers? Why the cross?'

The flow of ordinary, everyday people continued down in the square, apparently unstoppable. George, however, had other things to do besides watching the scene below his window. He already had his mind fixed on the day ahead and the taping of the television programme. This was to be a pioneer venture and he was proud to be playing 'Hillbilly Ambassador for Uncle Sam' in this far-away land. One of the great joys of his life has been to blaze new trails for American country music.

The 'big star' treatment of the previous day continued as he was whisked off to the television station in grand style. Once there, George was delighted to be using home-grown, Polish musicians and singers. It was an adventurous example of a positive, bridge-building initiative across the previously impenetrable

Iron Curtain. In the studio, political rivalry between East and West paled into irrelevant insignificance, convincing George yet again that music was truly an international language. He had already seen the art form building relationships in many diverse situations. Country music, which is folk music of a sort, has always been an all-consuming passion for George. 'It's the "music of the people" wherever they live – East or West,' he says. 'Music touches everyone's heart!'

Since his arrival in Poland, George had experienced no problem communicating, either in music or in words. He was surprised to find that the Poles were highly familiar with many of the songs he had recorded in America. Amazingly, they could also accompany him in English. He felt very ignorant. These young Polish people seemed to know rather more about his Western culture than he knew about theirs.

It turned out to be a wonderfully satisfying day. He sang classics such as Hank Williams' 'Jambalaya', and many other country songs which he never dreamed people in Poland would know – but they did, to his delight. He was in good voice and the audience was most appreciative. Proud of the result, tired but content, he returned in a chauffeured car to his plush hotel. The setting sun warmed the previously uniform-grey Warsaw vista.

'A good meal would finish the day off well,' he thought, as he sauntered down to the hotel restaurant, mouth watering in anticipation. Settling into the peaceful surroundings of the hotel coffee shop, he sat down to enjoy a good meal, topped off with a cooling ice-cream sundae. Smiling to himself, he mused on his success and continuing good fortune. 'Can life really be that bad behind the Iron Curtain?' he thought, admiring the affluence around him. 'I could be in a hotel anywhere in the world, sitting here eating this sundae amongst all these salesmen, tourists and diplomats!'

What he had not realized back then, of course, was that outside that cosy hotel ordinary citizens were enduring severe food shortages. The Polish people were experiencing great difficulty in obtaining even the basic necessities of life. Those privileged to be in that hotel occupied an isolated island of prosperity in the midst of an ocean of hunger, need and hurt. His hosts' excellent treatment of him as their honoured guest had dulled whatever awareness George may have had of how things really were in the country at large. Nothing was going to interrupt the euphoria of his day. Besides, he was really enjoying his ice-cream sundae.

His introspective, self-centred thoughts were rudely interrupted by the shock of a loud, echoing gunshot. It was followed by shouts of displeasure and screams of panic in the square below the hotel. One by one, white-faced, clearly shocked customers began to dart over to the coffee shop's lushly curtained window. The lanky, blue-jeaned singer had always been naturally inquisitive. He too wanted to know what was behind all the commotion. Reluctantly leaving his delicious sundae, he joined the crowd at the window and craned to see what his fellow guests were looking at.

The scene in the square below, made disturbingly surreal by the wash of colour from the deepening sunset, caused his eyes to open wide in unbelief. He gasped in astonishment. Ordinary Polish citizens of every age had gathered in their hundreds around that strongly symbolic cross of flowers. All were carrying candles. Through the gathering dusk, George could see that the thinly covered cross of the morning had grown into a huge, multicoloured construction. People must have been bringing flowers all day long.

What had started as a peaceful, candlelit demonstration was rapidly turning into a scene of abject horror, however. As George and the other hotel guests watched in silent and deepening alarm, army trucks full of soldiers dressed in full riot gear began to flood into the square. George noted that some carried automatic rifles with fixed bayonets, while others carried clubs or truncheons. Menacingly, these ruthless custodians of the Communist culture began to move towards the assembled crowd. 'Hey, there are kids down there! It's not just men and women … there are little kids down there!' The clipped words burst out before George could stop himself, as he expressed his anger aloud to nobody in particular. There were indeed young children taking part in the demonstration, holding lighted candles and praying alongside the adults.

What happened next shocked the Hillbilly Ambassador from 'Music City USA' to the core. The sight would be indelibly etched on his mind, still disturbing many years later. The tough-looking soldiers proceeded to manhandle and beat the peaceful family crowd, roughly bundling them onto the waiting trucks. Some tried to run away, but not many. Like sheep before their shearers, most of them remained passive and seemed willing to accept arrest at bayonet point. As he watched from his safe vantage point inside the hotel, the tearful George witnessed these innocent people being driven away into the night – who knew where?

'What's going on out there?' he exclaimed in an agitated tone. Turning round, he repeated his question to the smart young waiter who just minutes before had served him with that ice-cream sundae.

'What does it look like?' The waiter spoke sternly, in good English. Looking without fear directly at George, the angry waiter's eyes suddenly swelled with tears. George never forgot that look. It was clear to him that he was an unwelcome, self-indulgent, American alien that day. The waiter's distaste for George was undisguised. He disliked the show-business personality and all that he stood for.

'Well,' replied George, trying to inject a conciliatory note into his voice, 'well, it looks like those people are being arrested down there.'

With disgust in his voice, the young Pole replied, 'That's right! For praying and singing hymns on the streets of Warsaw. For making a cross of flowers on Victory Square.'

'Good Lord! What's going to happen to them?' George blurted out his words, barely able to hide his shock. The curt reply numbed the singer into silence.

'The ones who come back will be fined two months' salary ... that's a lot of money in this country right now. And some of them will not be coming back.'

Right there and then, overlooking Victory Square in downtown Warsaw, it dawned on George Hamilton IV that he needed to grow up. This middle-aged, hugely successful product of the privileged, capitalist West had finally come to realize, in a very forceful way, that he was still an unduly pampered baby Christian. He had never been faced with adversity or challenge of this order.

It brought back to mind another incident he had witnessed in a little church in Czechoslovakia in 1974 – a group of young Christian people who had also been willing to put their lives at risk and 'carry their crosses' as they witnessed for their faith. He turned away from the waiter, saddened and lost in thought. He had a lot to learn.

The outspoken singing preacher, Hovie Lister of the Statesmen Quartet, used to joke that God never intended Christians to sing the blues or wear a long face. The Statesmen recorded for RCA Victor, the same label as George Hamilton IV. George laughingly recalls their spirited back-up vocals on Stuart Hamblen's 'Open Up Your Heart And Let The Sunshine In' with George Beverly Shea singing lead. The realities of everyday life, however, sometimes dictate differently from such idealistic philosophy. Seasons inevitably change from sunshine to rain. King Solomon's famous wise words, put to music and sung by the likes of Pete Seeger, Vern Gosdin and Sheila Walsh, are well known to George:

> To every thing there is a season, and a time to every purpose under the heaven:
>
> A time to be born, and a time to die; a time to plant, and a time to pluck up that which is planted;
>
> A time to kill, and a time to heal; a time to break down, and a time to build up;
>
> A time to weep, and a time to laugh; a time to mourn, and a time to dance;
>
> A time to cast away stones, and a time to gather stones together; a time to embrace, and a time to refrain from embracing;
>
> A time to get, and a time to lose; a time to keep, and a time to cast away;
>
> A time to rend, and a time to sew; a time to keep silence, and a time to speak;
>
> A time to love, and a time to hate; a time of war, and a time of peace.
>
> Ecclesiastes 3:1–8

From time to time, everyone gets the blues! Life's journey has its storms as well as its sunshine. Over the years George IV has tried to cultivate a caring attitude and an acute social conscience towards those in need. 'If we look around us,' he says, 'there are many poor people who need our love, help and care. Instead of us moping around with a long face, listing all our own problems, I think we should be out there looking to give a helping hand. "Someone Is Looking For Someone Like You" (written by Gail Davies) is a peppy song that speaks good common sense along those lines. It talks to me about not feeling sorry about myself, as sometimes we are all inclined to do!'

George attests that the primary catalyst in 'turning his head around and warming his heart' (as John Wesley once described the experience) was his early visits to Eastern Europe. 'I'm sure that the Lord meant for me to go there to make me realize what a spoiled brat I'd been in my youth and how much I'd taken for granted. The freedom to worship that I enjoyed should have been treasured all the while.' George considers that he had every reason to know and live the truth, but back in the so-called 'Bible Belt' of North Carolina where he originated, he had it altogether too easy when it came to religion. 'I coasted along thinking that I was okay! Just having my name on the church roll was all that I thought was needed. How shallow I discovered that philosophy to be in 1974 when I visited Czechoslovakia for the first time.'

George was not the first country musician to tour over there behind the Iron Curtain. A British group, the Jonny Young Band from the Medway region of Kent, preceded him in 1973 as guests of a Czech band, Jiri Brabec and the Country Beat, who also played host to George a year later. Nonetheless, George recounts, 'They tell me that I was the first American country music artiste to tour in the Eastern bloc. I don't know if it's true, but that's what they say!' When George made his first visit, 1974 was a different time and Eastern Europe was a different place from the way it is now at the start of the new millennium. Things were primitive, restricted and sometimes dangerous. Everyday life for everyday people was undoubtedly tough over there at that time.

It was a crisp, dry, sunny Sunday morning when George attended his first church service in Prague. The experience remains vivid in his memory. 'I don't know why, but it didn't occur to me that I wouldn't be able to understand anything that would be going on in church that morning!' he remembers. 'Naturally, it was all in the Czech language … I guess, being a spoiled American, I just assumed it would be in my *own* language! That's evidence of how self-centred, immature and ignorant I was. Jiri Brabec took me to the Moravian Church at 5 Halkova Street. There I met Bishop Adolf Ulrich and his wife, Maria. That was really the spiritual turning point for me. I came face to face with Christian young people who loved God so much that they would willingly give up their chance of "upward mobility" in order to be a member of that church.'

Arriving early at the old, grey, soot-dyed church, George met the welcoming minister at the heavy timber door before the service commenced. Adolf Ulrich was the only Moravian minister to be decorated by the Allies in World War II. To George's delight, he discovered that the Bishop spoke reasonably good English, so they could at least have a meaningful conversation. Taking his seat in the front pew, George looked around the dimly lit church. Although it was not winter, there was still a damp chill to the drab building. 'Man, it must sure get real cold here in winter!' George thought to himself as he took in the scene.

The lines of rough-hewn, narrow pews slowly filled with work-weary people dressed in layers of hand-patched clothes. How different it was to the plush, theatre-like churches back in the USA. Even the smallest churches there were carpeted and supplied with smart hymnals. That morning in Prague, the congregation shared a few tatty hymn books, but most would sing the songs from memory. The worship service that followed was clearly alive spiritually – that much was obvious to George, even if he could not understand the words that were being said. He certainly appreciated the catchy, sacred music they sang. Some of the lilting melodies were very familiar, stirring up nostalgic memories of services back home in North Carolina.

Suddenly, to George's surprise, the minister asked him if he would sing a song for the congregation. Nervously at first, but gaining conviction as he proceeded, George sang 'Amazing Grace' and 'How Great Thou Art' – in English, of course, because that was all he knew. To his utter amazement, as tears welled in his eyes and his heart began to pound, everyone in the congregation began to sing along with him. 'They knew the songs well and sang along in Czech,' George recalls with real wonderment. 'It was very deeply meaningful and an intensely moving experience.' The tall American felt himself close to losing his composure as he sang on. The level of emotion in that drab building behind the Iron Curtain was far removed from anything he had experienced in the Bible Belt churches back home.

He continued singing – nobody seemed to want to stop – and looked out at the radiant faces of the young people in the uncomfortable wooden pews. Then the hardened professional was struck by an unusual thought. 'They're like lighthouses ... these are very special young people!' An old, familiar saying floated into his mind, something he had heard as a boy and which had seemed of no consequence at the time, but now had a clear ring of truth: 'The eyes are the window of the soul.' It was true. Those Czech youngsters manifested a spiritual maturity and a deep commitment that he could not hope to match. 'This young Czech group looked to be about the same age as I was when I made my first record in 1956, my first year at university, at the age of 19. These young people were about that age, but that's where the similarity ceased. They weren't like me at all at that age – and they were much more mature and committed than I was in 1974 at the age of 37, too.'

The absorbing service over, George took the chance to talk further with the elderly minister. He explained to his American visitor that young people who were committed Christians in Communist Czechoslovakia had a heavy price to pay – for example, they would be barred from education and forbidden to go to college. The State system saw their faith in God as a barrier to Communist progress. 'Without university training,' the minister said, 'the future looks very bleak for my youngsters. In all likelihood, they will spend their lives in some sort of low-paying manual labour or menial job. There is nothing wrong with manual work, of course. Even our Lord was a carpenter. Yet I regret that if my young people have any aspirations about being a doctor or lawyer or something of that sort, they can just forget it ... but it is a cross they gladly bear, because they love the Lord and have publicly taken a stand for him.'

Looking back today, George assesses these words in the context of the direction of his life: 'The words of this wise man of God had a profound effect on me. I guess, all of a sudden, I started wanting to grow up as a Christian.' Without even realizing it, those young Christians of Prague were a living sermon to George. 'Someone once said that the greatest sermon of all is a life well lived. Those young people spoke volumes to me about dedication and commitment. Amidst all the excitement, promotion and hype of the show-biz world that I visited in Eastern Europe, God providentially allowed these messengers to cross my path. The result is a legacy that I value highly. Having met these young people, I was deeply challenged about where I was placing my treasure – I was too concentrated on the world here and now, and not at all aware of the life to come. There is, of course, great vanity in everyone's success, even mine!'

Other elements were already working on George's conscience, and he continued to mull over the problem. Slowly, between 1974 and 1982, he came to realize that throughout his life he had been steadily avoiding his own personal responsibility as a Christian. The visit to Poland in August 1982 brought it together for him. 'I realized that I needed to do serious business with God and sincerely recommit my life to him. I was already a Christian believer, but not living in the light I had received. Up until 1982, I was certainly not living out my Christian beliefs in everyday life. Eastern Europe was the turning of the tide in terms of my Christian commitment. I do not say that I have fully made it yet, and may never perfectly do so! But my direction is now sure.

'I remember hearing Johnny Cash on television once, confessing how he had been a Christian since the age of 12. However, he, like me, had been a backslider for much of his adult life. I loved his transparent honesty because it was such a humble, truthful statement that he made. The Lord has used other events in my life to quicken my conscience too, to make me embarrassingly aware of my immaturity as a Christian. On many occasions, here in the West, I've been influenced by Christian friends who have gently led me along towards a more committed faith – Paul Davis in the UK, and in the USA all the folks on Dr Billy Graham's team, including Cliff Barrows and Bev Shea, as well as people back in Charlotte, North Carolina, such as Arthur Smith, Grady Wilson and Leighton Ford. These are a few of the many people who have encouraged me. Each one, in their own way, has helped me along without necessarily even realizing it! Just what they were, what they stood for, what they believed and, most importantly, what they lived has been an eternal influence on this pilgrim.'

CHAPTER 2

GROWING TALL

In a world where most things are store-bought, love and family are two basics that are still home-made and home-grown!

George 'Hege' Hamilton V (singer/songwriter, Nashville, Tennessee)

'I MIGHT AS WELL clear this up once and for all!' The somewhat bashful, slow-talking George Hamilton IV was speaking to me, the DJ. George was guesting with me on my BBC radio show being broadcast from Luton, England. 'I've been guilty, Paul, of going along with an early promotional writer's inaccuracy!'

'What's that, George?' I enquired, raising my eyebrows.

'Well, my friend, people ask me, "Why are you 'George the Fourth'?" My standard answer has always been that my father, grandfather and great-grandfather were all called George, and the name was passed down ... That's true, but it *skipped* a generation!'

So let's get the record straight for this book, as George explains: 'In the mid-1800s, after George Hege Hamilton I moved to the mountains of Beaver Creek, Ashe County, North Carolina, he had four children – William, Elvira, Rufus and George Hege Hamilton II. They all lived and died in Beaver Creek, and this is where the line was interrupted. George Hege Hamilton I's eldest son, William, had a son named George J. Hamilton. George Hege Hamilton I's *youngest* son, George Hege Hamilton II, named a son Will (probably after his older brother William). That Will Hamilton, my grandfather, named his son George Hege Hamilton III, in honour of his father and grandfather. To put it simply: George I fathered George II, who fathered Will, who fathered George III, who fathered George IV, who fathered George V...'

There was therefore one generation skipped as far as the name George Hege Hamilton is concerned. The unusual middle name, Hege (pronounced hegg-ee), came from the German last name of George I's mother, Anna Maria Hege. The name appears in the King James Bible, in the book of Esther: '...unto the custody of Hege the king's chamberlain, keeper of the women...' (2:3).

George IV recalls the Hamilton ancestry with great interest. The Hamiltons owned hundreds of acres of land in the Beaver Creek area, stretching for several miles from St Mary's Church to the mountain top where George IV's brother, Cabot, presently lives. Probably because of his vast landholdings, George Hamilton I's name appears on land deeds and other documents as 'George Hege Hamilton, Esquire'.

'The story I heard from my parents, grandparents and from research that my brother Cabot did,' says George, 'was that George Hamilton II was a storekeeper there in the valley at Beaver Creek. The Hamiltons owned a cannery, a mill and general store, including a post office. George Hamilton II was also the post master at Beaver Creek, on the edge of what is now West Jefferson, North Carolina. The other brothers, I believe, were farmers.'

Rufus Hamilton, a son of George Hege Hamilton I, married Laura Agatha, who was a devout Episcopalian. She insisted that 'the Hamilton boys' of Beaver Creek should either get a Moravian minister there to start a church, or she would proceed with the Episcopal Bishop of North Carolina to try to get a mission church founded herself – and thus she came to raise their children as Episcopalians rather than Moravians, a step away from tradition, since the Hamilton family had come to the mountains as Moravians (the Moravian Church was originally formed in Czechoslovakia in 1457 as the first organized Protestant denomination). Apparently the Hamilton brothers procrastinated on the matter of the church, and Laura Agatha got tired of waiting. She wrote to the Episcopalian Bishop, who came to Beaver Creek and founded a church there on land eventually given by the Hamilton brothers. Rufus and Laura Hamilton were the primary givers and builders of the church, but Rufus's siblings William, Elvira and George II, and even their father George I, who was apparently still living then, all participated and were early members of this Episcopalian church.

The church was originally called St Simon's Episcopal Church, but was later renamed St Mary's, the name it still carries today. In the 1970s Ben Long III, a talented fresco painter who studied in Italy under the masters there, offered to paint a fresco on the interior walls of the church founded by the Hamiltons. People now come from all over the States and from overseas to see this fresco, entitled 'The Mystery of Faith' and depicting the crucifixion and the ascension. Rufus and Laura are buried beside the church, and George IV's son George Hege Hamilton V married Lillian Frances Patterson there on 17 November 1990.

Will Hamilton (son of George II) fathered six children – George Hege Hamilton III, William, Sidney, Montford Transou and sisters Dot and Em. When George IV was born to George III and his wife Mary on 19 July 1937 in the Old City Hospital of Winston-Salem, North Carolina, his birth certificate named him 'George Hege Hamilton IV'. He did not use the 'IV' in his name, however, until he signed his first record contract. Orville Campbell, the astute owner of Colonial Records, instructed George to sign the legal papers with his full legal name. When he saw the 'IV' after George's name, Mr Campbell considered that it might become a hilarious 'gimmick' for a country singer to be called by such a lofty-sounding Roman numeral!

George IV was raised in his birthplace of Winston-Salem, which is in the Piedmont section of North Carolina, part of the picturesque foothills of the beautiful Blue Ridge Mountains. In the 1700s there was a small Moravian village called Salem (meaning 'peace') where originally all the inhabitants lived communally. Young people left their families at a certain age and lived and studied together (although the men and women were segregated) until they married. It was an exclusively Moravian village, and the inhabitants pooled and shared all their resources. Nearby was the town of Winston, an industrial town which was also the county seat of Forsyth County, North Carolina, and contained the courthouse and other civic buildings. Winston and Salem were so close in proximity that eventually, as they both expanded, their town boundaries overlapped. Thus they became incorporated as one town and took on the joint name of Winston-Salem.

'Winston-Salem was by no means a village – it was a good-sized town,' says George. 'When my parents were growing up, it would have been considered at the very least a small city. It was the home of R.J. Reynolds Tobacco Company, the largest manufacturer of tobacco products in America, making Winston, Salem and Camel cigarettes, Prince Albert smoking tobacco, and so on. Prince Albert Tobacco was the sponsor of the Grand Ole Opry radio programme's *Prince Albert Hour*. Winston-Salem was also the home of Hanes Knitting Mill, which was both then and now the number one manufacturer of cotton hosiery and undergarments in America. There was also Wake Forest University, a world-renowned institution. When I was growing up as a child in the thirties and forties, I believe the population was around 200,000 people. So, Winston-Salem was no "small town"!'

The Hamiltons can trace their family tree back an awesomely long way. George IV knows a good deal of fascinating family background, both from research and from memories handed down over the generations. Far back in the family ancestry, recorded documentation first mentions a Gavin Hamilton in America in 1685, although today's Hamiltons do not know for sure if he arrived that year or if that was when he first acquired land. Before the move to North Carolina, Gavin and his descendants resided in Carroll's Manor, Frederick County, Maryland. There was a Moravian community on the estate of Governor Carroll, where the Manor House still stands, and George IV delighted in visiting it in 1998.

More than 200 years ago, the Hamilton family, originally of Scots and Irish descent, travelled south from Maryland to North Carolina. They were part of an adventurous group of Moravian pilgrims seeking a new environment to settle. To spy out the land, Moravian Bishop Spangenberg initially went to Carolina on horseback. Once there, he surveyed an area of wilderness under a land grant from the King of England. The area became known as the 'Wachovia Tract'. The pious settlers followed the Bishop and settled into three communities, Bethabara, Bethania and Salem, the latter being the largest and later merging with Winston.

Horatio Hamilton, the great-grandson of Gavin Hamilton, was born in 1756 and later married Lucy Peddycourt from Carroll's Manor Moravian Settlement in Maryland. Horatio and Lucy came down to North Carolina in 1774 as founding members of the first English-speaking Moravian congregation, Hope Moravian Church, on the banks of the Muddy Creek near what is now Clemmons, North Carolina. They had a son named Samuel.

Samuel and Anna Maria Hege were the parents of George Hege Hamilton I, who was born in 1813. They were members of Friedberg Moravian Congregation, a separate community sited south of Winston and Salem. (Incidentally, in November 1999 George Hamilton IV began his 'Moravian Country Christmas Tour' at the Friedberg Moravian Church, just a few steps from where Samuel and Anna Maria are buried.) The first George Hege Hamilton was actually raised by his grandfather, Horatio. Anna Maria died soon after bearing a stillborn infant daughter, and her husband Samuel was killed on a runaway horse in Salem later the same year.

George I moved to the mountains of North Carolina as a young man. He was probably able to purchase cheap land due to the hard life in the mountain territory. Few were willing to battle with the tough winters and hard ground in order to eke out a living. Of course, he was sole heir to both Horatio and Samuel, so he no doubt inherited some money – with which he bought hundreds of acres in the Beaver Creek area of Ashe County, North Carolina. Always keen to spot a musical link, George IV surmises that, since his kinfolks' place was only about 15 miles from country singer Doc Watson's front porch at Deep Gap, close to Boone, Doc's mountain ancestors and the Hamiltons must have known each other. Country singer Del Reeves' kin also lived just over the mountain in Sparta, North Carolina.

Circumstances in the mountainous frontier proved even worse than first perceived, and such extreme conditions tested everyone. Tough as he was, it was too much for George I's grandson Will, George IV's grandfather. Eventually Will reluctantly decided he had had enough, and Will and his wife, Ella Transou Hamilton, made an exodus from the wild, wonderful Beaver Creek mountains. 'They moved to Winston-Salem, where my grandfather Will became a "railroad man" for Southbound Railroad. There was a Moravian congregation in the railroad community of East Winston called Fries Memorial Moravian Church, which they joined. That's how my father, George Hege Hamilton III, was born in the city of Winston-Salem and how I became a "citybilly" instead of a "hillbilly".'

George Hamilton IV was the first child of Mary Lillian and George Hege Hamilton III. His parents were informally and affectionately known as 'Sis' and 'Hege'. The troubled thirties saw America steadily climbing out of the economic depression that had started in the mid-twenties. Politically, the nation was hopefully clinging on to its isolationist policy. Meanwhile, however, the stormclouds of war were gathering in Europe and the Far East, threatening to disturb the New World's peace and growing prosperity. To some, it truly seemed that the end of the world was at hand. On one otherwise unremarkable Sunday morning in 1941, the inevitable happened. War came to the New World, and everything was changed.

That fateful morning, a tired Sis Hamilton was cooking the family's Sunday lunch as four-year-old George IV came skipping past her, heading for the backyard. Just at that moment came the dreadful news announcement on the radio that Hawaii's Pearl Harbor had been bombed by Japanese aeroplanes. It was an earth-shaking catastrophe, one that was to affect every aspect of life, as the Hamiltons were soon to discover. George IV's uncle (Sis's brother) Buck Pendry was a radio operator aboard the USS *Bagley* stationed in Pearl Harbor. Buck became a witness and survivor of the Japanese bombing – his ship was in dock right on the shore and luckily just below the hill that the 'Zero' bombers flew over on their way to bomb the harbour, so it was one of the few ships spared.

The family supported each other staunchly through all that followed. They were a close-knit group and George's grandparents played a huge part in his life. Both his grandfathers were railroad men based in Winston-Salem. 'I'd always heard that my maternal grandfather Pendry was from Yadkin County. Nobody knows much about him. He was a bit of a mystery man. I don't know much about how he and my grandmother met. I always called her "Mama Pendry" and I always called my paternal grandmother "Nanny", as did my brother Cabot. The Pendry and Hamilton families both lived in East Winston, because their menfolk were all railroad men. That's obviously how my mother and dad met. Their fathers were both railroad workers – they might have been friends, though I don't know that for sure.

'I never met my mother's father, Grandfather Pendry, also named William like my paternal grandfather. Grandfather Pendry was killed in an accident at Barber Junction. It's said that he fell off the back of a train. I heard that there was a new, "green" engineer who either unexpectedly put the brakes on or lurched forward! My grandfather fell off the train, and then the train backed over him. He was brought back to Mama Pendry's house in a basket. Now that always sounded ghoulish to me, but it wasn't a picnic basket – it was a large wicker basket like the kind they used for laundry back in those days. It was quite a shock, though, and it stuck with them for the rest of their lives. So Mama Pendry became a young widow with two small children, my mother Mary Lillian, nicknamed "Sis", and her little brother William, nicknamed "Buck".

'My grandmother always told me that her father (whose last name was McGraw) kept horses at his livery stable. As a little girl, she remembers him delivering materials for Reynolda House, which was the mansion of the Reynolds family, the founders of R.J. Reynolds Tobacco Company. My great-grandfather either worked for Lentz Transfer and Storage Company or was on assignment to them when a shipment of Greek marble arrived in Winston to build Reynolda House. As a small child, Mama Pendry rode the wagon with her daddy carrying the marble out to build the mansion.'

Mama Pendry also told George IV that when she was a child the real 'Buffalo Bill' came to Winston with his Wild West show. Her father boarded Buffalo Bill's horses and livestock at his livery stable. She could clearly remember meeting Buffalo Bill in all his splendour, with his buckskins and his big white stetson. She also recalled that the Lone Ranger actor, Clayton Moore, came through Winston and her father took care of the legendary horse Silver overnight at his stable.

Years later, while living in Charlotte in the seventies, George had a chance to meet Clayton Moore himself. The actor came through town as the celebrity guest of some grand store opening. George says he will never forget that the hero looked just like he did in the movies. 'How impressed I was that he looked so much like I'd always pictured the Lone Ranger in my mind! Memories flooded back of radio shows, films and the later television series. My mother had her own horse, called Missy. My first son, Peyton, now owns a stable and is a horse-trainer in South Carolina, and my daughter Mary also owns her own horse. She has been a rider since an early age, winning many a blue ribbon at competitions and contests. I guess we all got our love of horses from Mama Pendry!'

Grandfather Will Hamilton was to remain a railroad man at heart right up to the day he died. The local train station was an imposing concrete building that fuelled George IV's boyhood dreams of far-away adventure. 'Like many country singers, I've got a "thing" about trains. It's sad nowadays to see America's train stations boarded up and abandoned.'

In the twenties, his grandfather Will loved the country-blues music of Jimmie Rodgers, the yodelling 'Singing Brakeman'. Country music was evolving as a commercial art form at that time, having always previously been essentially a home-grown commodity. Jimmie Rodgers was the world's very first country music superstar, and his records sold millions during the Depression, an enormous achievement in those days. 'Comparatively, in proportion to the population as it was then,' declares George IV, 'Jimmie Rodgers' record sales would have equalled those of Elvis Presley or the Beatles in their heyday.' Rodgers was signed by the RCA Victor record company, and George IV's grandfather could never have guessed that his grandson would one day also record for the same prestigious label.

Well before the advent of grandson George IV, grandfather Will was an avid listener to the legendary Nashville radio broadcast from the Grand Ole Opry – though never in his wildest dreams did he expect the new baby to become a star of that very show. Almost as soon as George IV was born, his grandfather Will's musical influence on him began to take effect. The baby grew very familiar with the warm surroundings of Granddaddy and Nanny Hamilton's house. It was conveniently just two blocks from the parents' home and naturally the doting grandparents were always volunteering to babysit. As a baby and a toddler, there is no doubt that the future country music star was thoroughly spoiled!

'Will, are you teachin' that baby those hillbilly songs again?' Nanny would shout knowingly from the steaming kitchen. 'If you're not careful, Will, we'll have a yodeller on our hands!'

Granddaddy Will, sitting contentedly on the old, wooden rocking chair in the front parlour, bounced the baby gently in tempo with the song coming from the Victrola phonograph. 'Clap your hands, son, come on, sing along with the music!' In response to his wife's laughter, he would say gently, 'Oh Ella, there's no harm done. This child just loves Jimmie Rodgers! Come and see, Ella … look at those smiles … he gets real tickled when the yodellin' starts. Come see for yourself!'

Three-piece, black suits were very much in vogue back then, and baby George was fascinated by the big, shiny gold railroad watch dangling from his Granddaddy's waistcoat. A man of few words, Will carried himself with great dignity. Unlike many of his rougher work colleagues, with his starched white shirt and black tie, Grandfather Hamilton's demeanour was quiet, loving and unimposing. If you passed him casually on the street, he could easily be mistaken for a doctor, a preacher, a banker or even an undertaker. But George's best memories of his grandfather are all musical: 'My greatest recollection is of him bouncing me on his knee to the fiddle and guitar sounds of the Grand Ole Opry.

Other times, we'd listen together to the plaintive vocals of the old, scratchy Jimmie Rodgers 78s he'd spin. That old, wind-up Victrola was never silent – the sounds of "My Carolina Sunshine Girl", "The Desert Blues", "T for Texas" and other favourites were always echoing around my grandparents' house.'

Those bright, sunny days inevitably clouded over from time to time. The ageing railroad man often fell sick when George IV was a boy, and Granddaddy Hamilton passed away when George was still quite young. They were great buddies, so the separation was painful, even if the memories left behind were sweet. 'I remember some railroad men singing "Life's Railway To Heaven" at my granddad's funeral,' recalls George. He learned later that gradual hardening of the arteries had eventually led to his grandfather's death. During his increasingly recurring bouts of ill health, Granddaddy's bed would be set up in the living room by the warm fire. George loved to visit and climb on top of the old patchwork quilt. He would sit there for hours, listening with wide eyes and bated breath while his grandfather, still sharp of mind, wove together adventurous tales about the old pioneers on the wild frontier.

Nanny Hamilton never totally got over the loss of her beloved and colourful spouse. Taller than Will and less withdrawn, Ella was always much more extrovert than her husband. She was forever demonstrating the love she felt for her grandson. George surmises that it was her deep love of life and zeal for living that helped her to survive well into old age. Lovingly stored memories of Nanny and Granddaddy Hamilton cheered many a lonely hour in George's later life.

As the family breadwinner, George's father was forced to spend long hours on duty, which often irritated his pining spouse, awaiting his return to the family home. 'Hege, are you havin' to work again?' she would say. 'Those young sons of ours don't hardly see you! I swear that job's turnin' you into a regular workaholic.' But she knew that he was simply doing his best to support his wife and family.

The full name of George's father was George Hege Hamilton III, but, as George recalls, he always went by the name 'Hege'. 'He used to sign his name "G. Hege Hamilton". I don't remember him ever using "the III". Having come up through the hard times of the Depression and having had to get a job while he finished high school, he never got a chance to go to university. He had to get a job and help support his own family. My father always had a great respect for the work ethic. He put a lot of stock in my getting an education and being able to make a living doing something worthwhile – which for him was trade. I don't ever recall him *remotely* suggesting that I ought to make a life out of show business. Not that he discouraged it, but his main interest was that I get an education first.

'My father was born in the East Winston railroad community of Winston-Salem. Most of the men in that area worked on the railroad – East Winston was very close to the Union Station in Winston where all the trains were based. My mother's father was also a railroad man, of course, and that's why they happened to live in the same neighbourhood.' Economic depression forced every family to adapt to the pragmatic realities of unemployment. In those troubled days, breadwinners were under immense stress. Earning a living and providing for a family was a strenuous, sacrificial task that bit deep into family time.

In his teens, George's father worked part time on weekday afternoons at the local drugstore, after classes at the high school in Winston-Salem. His boss was the pharmacist Mr M.C. Goodman (nicknamed 'Goody' Goodman) who invented a winning headache powder formula. It later became known as 'Goody's Headache Powder' and became such a thriving, big-business enterprise throughout America that it later sponsored the famed Grand Ole Opry radio broadcasts.

Hege Hamilton was Mr Goodman's first 'Goody's Headache Powder' employee. Before this step up, however, his somewhat unflattering job title was 'Soda Jerk'. As George recalls, 'My father worked at the soda fountain. He was what they call a "soda jerk" in America – somebody who literally "jerks the sodas", pouring soda pop, making milkshakes, chocolate sundaes and banana splits. The drugstore was a place where teenagers would hang out and socialize after school. Then Mr Goodman started making and selling his own patented headache remedy, which worked faster than aspirin. This headache remedy became pretty popular around Winston-Salem, and most of the people coming into the drugstore for medicine were coming for that!'

One afternoon while the store was quiet, Mr Goodman approached Hege, who was busy rinsing the dishes left by his latest customer. 'You know, Hege, these headache powders are really catching on,' he said. 'People are starting to call them "Goody's Headache Powders". I think I'm on to something here! I'm thinking about selling the drugstore and going full time into the headache powder business. Would you like to be my first employee?'

When George's father finished high school at 16, therefore, rather than going on to university, he joined Goodman's growing company as its first employee. The company grew by leaps and bounds and as the local headache remedy invention took off nationwide, ever bigger business expansion was proposed. 'By the time my father died, he was the Vice President and General Manager of Goody's Manufacturing Corporation, with over 100 employees in Winston-Salem and all sorts of salesmen out on the road.' The headache powder packets were proudly labelled with the simple slogan, 'Goody's – They Are Good'. In time, the company became one of the top three headache powder producers in America.

In his spare time, Hege was kept busy as the superintendent of the local Moravian Sunday School. Prematurely bald, he would joke that 'grass don't grow on a busy street'. Few were willing to cross him, however, as he was tough and strong. A great sports-lover, George's father was never happier than when he was on a sports field enjoying a game of baseball or American football. Physical competition thrilled him, but to his disappointment his son never matched his interest in sports. 'A great athlete? That I was never to be – unlike my dad; he kept in good athletic shape until the day he was called home!'

Many decades later, a nostalgic George Hamilton IV wistfully recalls the long-lost days of his youth, his dearly missed parents and the happy home they nurtured. 'I remember my mother and father telling me stories about how they used to roller-skate to high school with their friends. That seems incredible to me because it was several miles from East Winston to Reynolds High School on the west side of town. My mother told me that my father used to sing occasionally with the Reynolds High School Dance Band – The Re-Bops. He liked Russ Columbo and Bing Crosby. As a kid, I can remember hearing him singing not only in the shower but also in the car. I remember that a lot of the 78 records around the house were by the pop crooners and big bands – my parents' courting and early married years were in the heyday of Louis Armstrong, Tommy Dorsey, Duke Ellington and the like. I don't recall that my dad even *liked* country music!

'My mother told me that my father's high school nickname was "the Sheik". In those days, the term "Sheik" alluded to Rudolph Valentino, meaning someone who was handsome, charming and a real ladies' man. My father and mother graduated from Reynolds High School and got married soon after. Mama Pendry (my mother's mother) wasn't all that thrilled when my mother and father started courting. She was still grieving over her husband's untimely railroad death some years before. She resented my father a little for, as she put it "stealing Sis away from her" and leaving her alone – she still had my mother's younger brother Buck to raise. So, my father and Mama Pendry didn't always get along too well.

'My father was very athletic. When I was a little boy, I can't remember a weekend that we didn't tag along with him to a softball game. The commercial league's local teams were sponsored by companies as an advertisement for their businesses. My dad played on teams sponsored by Barqs Beverages, Fritts' Garage and his own company Goody's Headache Powders. He loved sports. Every season of the year, there was some kind of sport that he was involved in. He was very good himself, very aggressive and competitive. I just never was much like that. I wasn't very aggressive, I didn't like competition and I was just not very good at sports.

'Some time after I became a member of the Grand Ole Opry, my father got to know Chet Atkins and since both shared a love of golf, they would play a round together from time to time. When Chet was on tour and came through Winston-Salem, my father would set up a golf game for Chet and later Chet occasionally took my dad along with him on pro-am golf tournaments. They got along really well. Also, quite a while after I joined the Opry, my father was probably instrumental in hooking up Goody's Headache Powders as a sponsor. For many years now, Goody's has been associated with the Opry and the Nashville Network. I'm sure this was partially due to my father, who by then had grown to love country music and its performers through my involvement and Chet's friendship.'

The modest Hamilton family home was leased for 95 dollars a month. A simple, brick-built building with two bedrooms, it was located on the edge of town, just behind the old Baptist Hospital, and close enough for the boys to walk to school. Although the house was not expensive or luxurious, it was practical, comfortable and, most important of all, it was a happy home. The Hamiltons were certainly not wealthy. Hard-working they may have been, but they did not earn enough money to be snobs. Life in those days was basic and sober for most households. The nation was slowly climbing out of the Great Depression – only to be faced with the worries of war.

As a young boy, George loved to spend his days outside with his friends, splashing, paddling and fishing, or climbing the majestic trees which graced the North Carolina countryside. Many days he would return home tired and dirty, sometimes in tears if he had fallen out of one of those great trees. He revelled in outdoor, country pursuits – much more fun, he thought, than competing on the sports field. Music, however, was always his first love and his sports-mad father understood that his growing son's aptitudes and interests were always going to be different from his own.

'I had a happy home with loving parents,' George says. 'My mother was the family live wire! She was always independent in spirit, full of outrageous comments and character that would often embarrass my father. Dad was serious, quiet and businesslike in comparison, yet he would laugh out loud at my mother's special ways – "Your mother, son, should be in on the stage!" he would say, puffing on his pipe.' He never realized that it would be his son who was destined to fly high in the show-business skies. A pretty redhead, Sis Hamilton would joke that redheads were 'fiery and fun-loving'. 'It's not true that blondes have the most fun,' she would say. 'Let me tell you all that redheads do!' George says proudly, 'She was all that! As a high-school girl, she was a good looker too. Later on in life she put on a little weight, but ladies back then were not as paranoid as they can be over such things nowadays!'

Mr and Mrs Hamilton III raised their two sons with loving discipline. George and his younger brother Cabot were generally well-behaved, polite young lads. Inevitably, though, even the best raised children cause some embarrassment to their parents. At the age of three, George's angelic halo slipped a little after the family arrived at a friend's house for dinner. As it was the Christmas season, the Hamiltons had brought a gift for the friend's child. Thinking the process through with some logic, George waited patiently all evening for his own gift to be given. As the evening drew to a close and the visitors were preparing to leave, toddler George realized that he still had not received a present. Overcome by the injustice of the situation, young George threw himself to the floor with a 'terrible twos' tantrum, much to the horror of his cringing parents!

George and his little brother Cabot (born five years after George) shared a great enthusiasm for anything to do with trains. The railroad tracks were always a rich source of imagination and adventure. Nothing was more exciting than a visit to the station... 'Come on George! Get a move on!' The early morning peace was rudely disturbed as a pyjama-clad Cabot urgently tried to wake his brother. 'Come on! Get up, you lazy head! This is the day we get to visit the train station with Mama Pendry! Come on! Maybe if we get lucky the engineers will feed us candy like last time...' Hastily the two brothers washed, dressed and then sped to the breakfast table. Gulping down their cornflakes, they chattered excitedly about the day in prospect. Later, reaching the train station with their puffing grandmother in tow, the two brothers watched goggle-eyed as the massive trains rolled by, great iron monsters pulling into and out of the station with their noisy jets of steam, full of important-looking people, passing through the Hamilton home town on their way to important destinations.

'We were all railroad fans back then,' recalls George, 'even though as a little fella I was kinda scared to death by those massive, noisy steam engines!' The smart soldiers and sailors shouldering their kit bags and going to war, the briefcase-carrying, cigar-smoking businessmen, the dreamy couples cuddling in the train seats – all held a fascination for the impressionable youngsters. Eventually, pressured by their worn-out grandmother, the two boys would meander home from the station, kicking stones, the smell of the sooty trains still strong in their nostrils. Back home, their patient mother would listen smiling as they conjured up stories about the strange characters they had seen that day.

George has never lost his fascination for trains. 'It's interesting – throughout my career, I've always had a "thing" about trains. I guess it's all because I'm the grandson of railroad men! I'm grateful to have had several hits with train songs, including Gordon Lightfoot's "Steel Rail Blues", Ray Griff's "Canadian Pacific" and, of course, John D. Loudermilk's "Blue Train" and "Abilene". What haunting lyrics!

> 'I sit alone, most every night, watch them trains pull out
> of sight.
> Don't I wish they were carryin' me back to Abilene?
> My Abilene.'

George's musical influences were threefold: country, western and Southern gospel. 'I don't recall any sort of pushing or urging to get into music as a career from anybody really. It was just something that I took a liking to and somewhere along the line began to imagine myself being a professional country music singer.'

George's paternal grandfather William Hamilton could lay claim to being a 'real' hillbilly – coming from genuine 'mountain stock', he grew up amidst the fiddle tunes, square dances, hoedowns and barn dances of the Blue Ridge Mountain community of Beaver Creek. 'Grandfather came from mountain folk, so he was a hillbilly spiritually, I guess, despite physically being a railroad man in East Winston. So that makes me a "hillbilly once-removed"! My country, mountain and folk music influences, plus my interest in trains, train songs and Jimmie Rodgers, all came about through my grandfather Will Hamilton.

'Then my maternal grandmother, Mama Pendry, used to take me to see the singing cowboy films at a theatre in Winston-Salem. She would often take me to the Saturday afternoon picture shows and we'd see Gene Autry, her particular favourite, as well as Roy Rogers, Tex Ritter and Johnny Mack Brown. She instilled in me a love for that western movie music.

'Thanks to my Uncle Sid and his wife Elma, I also heard a lot of Southern gospel quartet music. They took me to the 'All Night Gospel Sings' at Reynolds High School auditorium. The host of those shows was a man named Wally Fowler, who later discovered Patsy Cline in Winchester, Virginia. He was doing a Grand Ole Opry Talent Search and met Ginny Hensley (the name of the young Patsy Cline). He got her a prized audition at WSM Radio, Nashville.'

At the age of 12, George's passionate love of country music grew hotter with the sacrificial purchase by his parents of his first guitar. The instrument hardly ever left his hands to begin with, but constant practising made the sensitive tips of his fingers red and raw. Mistakenly, he thought he had gained complete mastery of the beast when he had learned three chords! He was encouraged to practise further by the sight of professional performers. The radio station WAIR (Winston-Salem) aired an entertaining show with the smooth-tongued Dave Cox and his band, the Carolina Troubadours, at the break of day on Saturday mornings. Happy to sacrifice precious sleep in support of her son, Sis Hamilton would rise before dawn to drive the star-gazing George IV to the radio station, where he could watch enthralled as the 'pickers and grinners' did their live show.

Today, a grateful George muses over the sacrifices his mother made all those years ago. 'Looking back now,' he says, 'how many mothers would do that for their sons? When I began to show an interest in the guitar, she bought me one, at some expense. Then she would take me to the live Saturday morning radio show on WAIR that featured country musicians singing and playing at the crack of dawn. I remember my mother driving me up there so I could go and sit and visit with these musicians and hear them play. I was sort of star-struck by that. My mother went out of her way to help me hang out with these people and be around them. My father never discouraged that – but he was still very concerned that I get an education!'

Back then, country music was considered to be solely for the working class – for farmers, hillbillies and blue-collar workers. Culturally, it was certainly not an art form supported by bankers, lawyers and other such 'uptown' urban people. 'My mother didn't care what people around may have thought,' George remembers with pride. Sis Hamilton was never one to be overly concerned about public opinion. She had a mind of her own and formed her own convictions. 'She was a deep-thinking, devoted homemaker, and she made no secret of her love for country music as well as old-fashioned family values!'

One of the more unusual things she did was to scribble out Bible verses on sheets of paper and hang them conspicuously on the door of the refrigerator. 'Be sure to read those Scripture verses, boys,' she would say. 'I put some new ones up today, so check 'em out. That way, kids, you'll get yourselves some precious wisdom – that'll set you up real fine for the times ahead!'

Their mother was more like a big sister to George and his brother. While other housewives were busy with sewing bees and bridge clubs, Sis would much rather roll up her sleeves and make mud pies with her boys. Other kids from the neighbourhood loved to go to the Hamilton house to play. George's mother would always be ready to bake cookies and build tents for them to play in. During a rowdy game of cowboys and Indians, complete with twig bows and finger guns, one of George's schoolfriends slumped exhausted next to him in the blanket wigwam. 'Your Mom sure ain't like most Moms,' he panted. 'She sure is mighty friendly and part of the gang!' They peeped out of the wigwam to see Mother Hamilton hiding behind a bush in splendid Gene Autry matinée mimicry.

The fast-growing George inherited his parents' hard-working ethos. Morning and evening, the wannabe-hillbilly-singer would diligently earn some sorely needed pocket money. The job of newspaper delivery boy, however, had its problems. Very skinny and somewhat frail, George suffered from glandular fever off and on throughout this period and hauling newspapers twice a day in all weathers just wasn't always possible. Once, when he was very ill, George remembers lying in bed, unable to fulfil his daily newspaper delivery duties. He gazed out of his bedroom window – and there, moving up and down the dusty streets, was his mother pulling his own little red wagon piled high with newspapers. Anxious that George shouldn't lose his much needed earnings, she was doing the job for him! It never occurred to her that it might be considered by the neighbours to be unseemly or unladylike.

'That's my favourite memory of her,' says George quietly. 'I was so sick that I don't remember her ever asking me if it would be all right for her to carry my paper route. But I remember looking out the window that day and seeing my mother walking down the street with the little red wagon. If one can imagine a mother delivering newspapers to her neighbours for her son, well that pretty much says it all about Sis. She couldn't care less what the neighbours thought! That's the kind of individual she was – conventions meant little to her because she was never locked into a routine. Mother was a real Bohemian. She just didn't care what anybody thought and she followed her heart. She was the one who first picked up on my dream of wanting to be in country music. She probably did encourage it more than I realized at the time. She was always more inclined towards "artsy things".'

George grew to be more like his mother than he would care to admit. Many decades later, his wife Tinky would often jokingly refer to some 'home truths' about George's likeness to his mother – to his secret delight. 'George, you've got a lot of your mother in you! Reading these press reports, it seems you're perceived to be quieter, more controlled and dignified than you really are … "Gentleman George" is a sedate, dignified tag, but in reality I think you've got a common streak up your back a mile wide!' Tinky loves to joke about George's 'hillbilly heritage' too.

Mixed in with all his mother's qualities, George also inherited his father's sometimes painful, introverted shyness. Always rather insecure, self-conscious and awkward, the pre-teen kid nevertheless suddenly came alive with the purchase of his first guitar. 'It seemed as if the lights went on for me! I found something that mattered to me and seemed to make an impression on others too, which pleased me. Music gave me something to offer at teenage get-togethers…' After that, 'Don't forget to bring your guitar, George!' was a suggestion he loved to hear. Hayrides, class dinners and youth fellowships at the church now took on a different dimension for him. Folk songs like 'On Top Of Old Smokey', and the Guy Mitchell numbers 'Truly, Truly Fair' and 'The Pawnshop On The Corner In Pittsburgh Pennsylvania' became his most-requested party pieces.

George never saw the legendary 'hillbilly Shakespeare' Hank Williams in person, but he did ensure that he heard the star regularly on radio broadcasts. The first 78 records he ever bought were Hank's 'Long Gone Lonesome Blues', 'Wedding Bells' and 'Mind Your Own Business'. That skinny, country superstar really connected with young George from North Carolina, and that yellow MGM record label with the lion motif figured largely in his star-struck dreams.

Hank Williams' impression on and legacy to the mainstream of popular music has never been surpassed by any country artiste before or since – an amazing fact when you consider that his career lasted just six years. As radio announcer Grant Turner remembers, 'Hank Williams blazed like a meteor above the firmament of his fellows. His songs stirred the hearts and souls of America's working millions. He suddenly departed without time for a word of farewell, on New Year's Day 1953, at the age of 29.' When he died, Hank Williams had already become a legend. He was the undisputed king of country music during the late forties and early fifties. It was Hank's songs and records that first spelled out the importance of 'country' to mainstream American music audiences. Some sad, some happy, his songs racked up millions of sales not only in the rural South but throughout the USA. Classic songs like 'Your Cheatin' Heart', 'Cold, Cold, Heart', 'Jambalaya' and 'Hey, Good Lookin'' were destined to become standards.

Today, the Hank Williams catalogue of self-penned songs ranks as essential material because of its constant usage by world-famous vocalists and instrumentalists. Few balladeers have had Hank Williams' gift for communication, and he could condense all the hopes and heartaches of life into a simple song. He sang from experience, from his own endless ups and downs. It is said that Hank gloried in the good times with a full-blooded gusto. He enjoyed the fancy cars, the custom-made clothes and all the legitimate and illegitimate trappings that came with stardom. But even at the height of his fame, he never forgot the poorer times and places of his earlier life.

Hank became an exclusive MGM recording artiste in 1947, the very year MGM Records started in the recording business. His first recording for them featured the rock'n'roll-style hit 'Move It On Over'. From that time on, he turned out success after success, including 'Lovesick Blues' which became one of the biggest hits in the history of country music. In addition to love ballads, novelty numbers and blues laments, Hank also recorded country hymns and story ballads, and even humorous narrations under the name of 'Luke the Drifter'. No matter what the style, he always turned in a remarkably relevant, vital and vivid performance in his light, haunting voice.

There was another facet of Hank Williams' art which also drew the admiration of many – his talent for performing sacred and inspirational music. Sacred music had always been a part of the country field, and like all country-orientated artistes, he never strayed far from that sacred repertoire. Hank wrote many of his gospel songs himself, including 'Jesus Is Calling', 'Ready To Go Home', 'Last Night I Dreamed Of Heaven', 'Are You Building A Temple In Heaven?', 'Are You Walkin' and a-Talkin' With The Lord?' and 'Going Home'. Others were written by men who played important roles in Hank Williams' career, including Fred Rose and Roy Acuff. You might say that, despite his waywardness, huge success and wealth, Hank tried to remain a simple and faithful Christian pouring his heart into his gospel songs.

Old-time country music artist and cowboy movie star Redd Harper, a contemporary of Hank Williams, once declared that it was obvious to anyone who ever met Hank Williams that he had 'the deepest hunger for God', and his secular songs revealed this just as much as his gospel repertoire. It is an apt description of Hank's plaintive and heartfelt style. The great guitarist Billy Byrd, from Ernest Tubb's Texas Troubadours band, best described Hank's special beat as 'tick-tack guitar'. To George IV's mind, Hank was the first 'rockabilly' – 'Hank cleverly fused rhythm to country music,' he says. More than any other performer, Hank Williams made a deep and lasting impression on the young lad with his first guitar.

George always enjoyed the fast songs, but his real favourites were the sad ballads. 'The first song I remember mastering on my cheap guitar, other than "Old Smokey", was "Wedding Bells". I loved those sad ballads. But, always contrary, the country songs that I started to sing *weren't* sad. They were all fun songs, more along the lines of Little Jimmy Dickens and Tommy Collins!' Whatever the style of song, George just loved to play and sing. Was it really possible that something which was so much fun could develop into a career? It seemed too much to hope for.

CHAPTER 3

DOUBLE LOVE

When the nights draw in and the temperature drops, what better than to put another log on the fire, and sit back and enjoy the music of George Hamilton IV!

Larry Adams (journalist and broadcaster, Kent, England)

'MOTHER, I'm saving up my money from my paper route 'cause I want to go to Nashville!' Out of the blue, the 12-year-old George informed his bemused mother of his plans while she rinsed the breakfast dishes in the kitchen. 'I need to go and see the Grand Ole Opry for myself.'

'Don't be silly, George, you're only 12 and it's hundreds of miles!' his mother retorted with finality. The young boy's face fell.

In the light of this not unexpected response, George IV was utterly amazed when later that day he was told that his mother had consented to the trip after all, having discussed it fully with his dad. In those days America was a much safer and more peaceful place than the violent country it can be today. It was not so strange, therefore, that the boy was allowed to go all the way to Nashville alone. Excitement flushed his face as he contemplated that 450-mile Greyhound bus trip. It would take a long time, for sure. The road systems back then had yet to see the wholescale innovation of high-speed highways, and even the city-to-city and state-to-state roads often meandered slowly, mile after mile.

The great day finally came. George's parents took him, beaming with excitement, to purchase the ticket at the bus station. With a simple paper note pinned on his neat sports jacket plainly stating his name and address, he boarded the bus at suppertime in Winston-Salem. His now rather nervous mother addressed the driver, who was wiping the windscreen: 'Please sir, I'd be most grateful if you'd kindly keep your eye on my boy ... he's going to Nashville!'

Turning to her, the driver smiled and nodded reassuringly. 'Yes, Mam! I'd be glad to. He'll be okay with me.'

The exhausting journey took all night. The Greyhound seemed to stop at every country town along the two-lane, rural highway. For the bug-eyed youngster, each stop was a romantic adventure as he disembarked to play the colourfully lit jukeboxes in the small cafés. Songs by Eddy Arnold, Hank Snow, Carl Smith, Red Foley and Hank Williams echoed around the bus stops – much to the annoyance of the other, older passengers. Between stops, sitting up front right behind the driver, George thrilled at every turn of the road. As they passed through mountains and valleys, he pestered the poor driver to death with his incessant chat. These days the buses carry signs forbidding such distracting tactics! This driver was understanding, however, and while George bent his ear all the way to Nashville, he in turn told the impressionable young boy about seeing UFOs in the sky above the road late at night. Those 450 miles were packed full of wonder and excitement.

Nashville, the capital of country music, beckoned to George through the darkness. It was the culmination of a dream. Six o'clock dawned as the bus duly rolled into its destination. He had not slept a wink all night. The young adventurer checked into the modest YMCA, which cost one dollar, 50 cents a night. Conveniently situated, the YMCA building was right across the street from the old National Life Insurance Company building, the home of WSM Radio's Grand Ole Opry.

The star-studded Friday night show took place in the upstairs studio of that building and on Saturday morning they rehearsed the 'Prince Albert' NBC radio network portion of the show. George's spartan corner room in the YMCA gave him a good vantage point. Wide-eyed, he watched his country music heroes climbing the concrete steps opposite him on their way to the rehearsals. Red Foley, Minnie Pearl, Ernest Tubb – it was a star-spangled parade of one great personality after another. George could barely contain his excitement: here were his record-cover heroes in the flesh! Later, he managed to gain entrance to the building and was given permission to watch his heroes rehearse. The sponsor of the show, Prince Albert Smoking Tobacco, was part of the Reynolds Tobacco Company based in Winston-Salem, and that special local connection had afforded him a complimentary entrance ticket.

It was at this Saturday morning rehearsal that George met up with the great guitarist Chet Atkins for the first time. Chet was just a young man then, but he was already making an impact on the country music scene. The young visitor from the hills of North Carolina caught sight of Chet standing in the WSM studio hallway, apparently aloof and bored. Plucking up courage, George blurted out what he later thought must have been the dumbest question of all time: 'Excuse me, sir, er ... aren't you Mr Atkins?'

The stupid question seemed to scratch the ice, but not break it. The tall guitarist smiled quizzically, then responded positively to the boy's question. Clearly on his guard, Chet did not appear altogether friendly. George learned later that he had misunderstood Chet's attitude. Basically, Chet was very shy and not at all unfriendly. At the time, though, both stood looking at each other in an embarrassed silence, two shy people waiting for each other to take the conversation further. It was not to be, however: Chet was being urgently recalled to his rehearsal.

After the rehearsal, George was walking away down the hallway when a loud voice suddenly caught him by surprise. 'Hey, kid!'

George spun around. Who could be calling him with such urgency? To his amazement, a shadowy figure was walking rapidly towards him down the dimly lit corridor. It was Chet Atkins. 'I'm gonna get a haircut,' he said. 'Do you wanna walk down with me?'

Perhaps the star was not unfriendly after all; perhaps that dumb first question *had* broken the ice. Chet was a quiet individual whose invitation to the barber shop was his own way of extending the hand of friendship to a stranger. It was obvious that George was a starry-eyed fan in awe of all the Nashville celebrities, and Chet was willing to show some friendliness towards him. The youngster could not believe his good fortune.

What a thrill it was to chat with such a famous personality face to face! Shyness gone, George asked an endless stream of questions about his heroes, Hank Williams, Red Foley, Hank Snow and the rest, while the amused barber at the Hermitage Hotel clipped away at Chet's hair. Outside, the conversation continued as they made their way back up the hill to WSM's studio. Before they parted company, George's heart skipped a beat as Chet asked him a final question. 'George, how would you like to come backstage at the Grand Ole Opry, if I can get you in?'

'Gee, sir, there's nothing I'd like better!' George replied excitedly. His best dreams were coming true – the long journey was paying off with unbelievable bonuses. Little did he know it then, but a decade later George would be one of the select few to become part of Chet's 'clan' when he rose to be RCA Victor's head honcho.

'Meet me at the stage door at seven o'clock, then, and you can go in with me.'

Such opening doors were not all down to chance, however. Back home in Winston-Salem, George knew a guitar-playing engineer called Tom Collins, who worked for Western Electric. Tom also had some business involvement with Chet Atkins in evolving what was called the 'Bigsby Tremolo' for Chet's Gretsch guitar. The 'Bigsby Tremolo' was a little lever device attached to the guitar which stretched and bent the notes. That Winston-Salem contact with Chet Atkins, George was convinced, was surely helping him develop his relationship with the star instrumentalist. 'Looking back,' he recalls, 'I'm sure that it was Tom who put me in touch with Chet as a young man. He let Chet know that I was coming to Nashville and to kind of look out for me.

'There was also another helpful man named David Cobb. As an announcer on WSM Radio, he was very kind to me and helped me to get backstage at the WSM a couple of times. One of Dad's employees at Goody's was a salesman named Brian Burdette, based in Nashville. He was a friend of David Cobb and gave me the introduction. So there were several people who were very helpful when I first started visiting Nashville on that Greyhound bus.'

Back at home, Sis and Hege Hamilton listened in stunned silence to their babbling young son on the other end of the telephone. Had they not been convinced that their son was not prone to making up stories, it would have been hard to believe what they were hearing. Poor brother Cabot just sat there envious of George's adventure. Even his new jigsaw puzzle seemed to have lost its appeal. Meanwhile, in the poorly lit phone booth of a Nashville café, George hopped from one foot to another as he told his story. He could barely contain his enthusiasm – never mind what his parents thought, *he* could hardly believe the events of the day so far. 'Oh, Mom, you should have heard those wonderful singers!' No detail was excluded from his breathless account, even down to how much Chet had tipped the barber. 'Oh, Mom, this has been like a dream come true ... thanks for letting me come!'

Needless to say, George Hamilton IV was at the stage door that evening well before the appointed time. Chet took him backstage and into an Aladdin's Cave. Expensive white western-style suits studded with rhinestones and sequins ... high-heeled, pointed cowboy boots ... large white stetsons ... everything sparkled, and George was dazzled. He found himself face to face with celebrities who had always seemed to him to be larger-than-life heroes – Ernest Tubb, Hank Snow, Marty Robbins, Carl Smith, Ferlin Husky, Webb Pierce, Little Jimmy Dickens, Minnie Pearl, Roy Acuff – they were all major stars to him. What struck him most about that evening was these people's warm approachability. Not a single one of them acted in a cold or arrogant way towards the star-struck youngster.

He floated on air from one glamorous star to another that evening, shaking hands and telling each one how big a fan of theirs he was. He was also presumptuous enough to tell them that he too was a singer and wanted to be like them one day. Everyone humoured the boy with all the appearance of genuine respect, but Ernest Tubb took more than a passing interest. 'Ernest Tubb was to have a major impact on me,' stated a grateful George in later years, 'and not just musically. I never met Hank Williams, of course, so instead of Hank, Ernest was to become the major country music influence on me.' Sincere and down to earth, Ernest was a fine role model for an aspiring star.

In the years that followed, trips to Nashville in the fall became a regular occurrence for which George patiently saved the nickels and dimes from his pocket money. He was now committed, hook, line and sinker, to realizing his dream of becoming a country and western singer.

One crucial day in his early teens, he managed to get into the WSM Radio studios with his humble guitar for a special talent show called the Junior Grand Ole Opry. 'I had taken my guitar with me to Nashville to try and get on the Junior programme,' remembers George. 'It was broadcast from a studio in the National Life Insurance Company building where WSM Radio used to be downtown. It was in the same studio where they did the Friday Night Opry and the Prince Albert network show, before they moved it down to the Ryman.' With his guitar in hand, in its worn cardboard case, George was hopeful of an audition.

'Wait here at the back!' The announcer Louie Buck spoke with such authority that George immediately stopped in his tracks and stood still, awaiting further instructions. Then came the news: 'We're full today, but we'll see if you can be fitted in later.' Being shy, polite and not at all pushy, George remembers how he just sat back and consequently missed his precious chance. 'Apparently, they *did* have room for me that day after all. They looked around for me, but didn't see me because I was all the way at the back of the rehearsal hall. So I didn't get on.'

It was his good fortune, therefore, that Ernest Tubb happened along. 'Hey, are you a singer, son?' Ernest spoke in his slow Texan drawl, eyeing George's little guitar.

'Well, yes sir! I'm a country music singer and ... and I hope someday to be a professional like you, Mr Tubb!'

Ernest's response was to invite the youngster to sing on the 'Midnight Jamboree' radio show at the Ernest Tubb Record Shop down on Nashville's Lower Broadway, near the old Ryman Auditorium. George was astonished. Every Saturday, after the conclusion of the main Grand Ole Opry show, Ernest would do a live 'Jamboree' broadcast. It was the next best thing to being on the Opry itself. George Hamilton IV was a green novice from North Carolina, just an aspiring kid with no record company or track record in performance. Now he was to appear on the famous WSM Radio! The invitation was all the more amazing because Ernest did not even ask the boy for an audition. His obvious ambition was apparently enough to convince Ernest to give him the opportunity.

The 'Midnight Jamboree' appearance was brief but enjoyable, and was held in the crowded, confined space of the record shop. The main feature of the show was to showcase Ernest and his Texas Troubadours and their product, but the star was known, for his big heart and it was not unusual for him to promote a newcomer. George was thrilled to gain such a prized position and he performed impeccably.

After the show, at one o'clock in the morning, Ernest announced to everyone that he was going to the Princess Theater for an all-night, fundraising telethon to raise money for poor people with health problems. The announcement was delivered in true show-business style by the seasoned veteran: 'It's gonna be a *great* show! There's me, the Texas Troubadours, Chet Atkins, *Governor Frank Clement* of Tennessee, and the *Great Gildersleeve*, the famous radio comedian ... we're *all* gonna be there! Why not come along?' This was a general announcement to the radio audience, but then he looked over at George and nodded a personal invitation in his direction.

They went out into the cold night and, to George's surprise, he was beckoned over and ushered into the largest Cadillac he had ever seen in his life. It was a fancy vehicle, just fine for a major country music star, but of a grandeur never seen on the modest streets of George's home town Winston-Salem. Ernest kindly placed George's little cardboard case holding his cheap Serenader guitar in the trunk. The humble instrument joined Ernest's own expensive, hand-tooled leather case – the one that held the expensive guitar with 'Ernest Tubb' emblazoned in pearl on the neck. The trunk surely held the chalk and cheese of guitar quality that night!

George IV just could not believe his luck. Sitting there in that limousine with a musical legend, he was on the edge of his seat with excitement. How proud he was when they disembarked at the theatre and he heard Ernest introducing 'little old George' to the Great Gildersleeve, the radio personality. 'Let me introduce you to my friend, George Hamilton – he's with my backing group and I'd like for him to have a song spot!' It was a truly invaluable break for an untried novice.

Realizing the enormity of the task and the occasion, George suddenly felt a million miles from home. A little later, stepping tentatively onto the floodlit stage and approaching the mike with his battered guitar, George looked nervously to his left and right. There in the wings he spied his heroes, Ernest, Chet and a few others, smiling at him and waiting to hear him do what he said he could do, waiting for him to launch into his song. As he struck up the first chord, however, George's mind went suddenly blank and his tongue stuck to the roof of his mouth. He had forgotten the words.

Looking down at his feet and biting his lip, George began to feel very shaky indeed. The Texas Troubadour Billy Byrd realized the poor boy's predicament and covered up for him by playing the longest instrumental break George reckoned he had ever heard. With his head lowered in embarrassment, the tall newcomer stood stock still behind the mike. What was he to do? Then from behind him came the calm, kindly voice of Ernest Tubb. 'It's okay, son. Take your time – you'll get it!' He nodded encouragingly from the wings.

George's pounding heart felt as if it was about to explode. The stage lights were on, the cameras were rolling, and all the attention was on him. Even the State Governor was sitting expectantly in the front row. Eventually, after several skilful instrumental turnarounds from a supportive Billy Byrd, the evasive words popped back into George's mind and he managed to make it through the song. Acutely embarrassed, he left the stage in tears. Surely his goose was well and truly cooked! George certainly felt as if he deserved a rebuke, and he was expecting a lecture from Ernest Tubb, the person he believed he had just let down. He was overcome by a sense of failure and self-condemnation. 'I sure was embarrassed for that kind Mr Tubb! After all, he'd put me on the bill with all those professionals...'

Then came the confrontation he was dreading. There before him stood the tall figure of Ernest Tubb. Yet he showed no anger or embarrassment. 'Son, don't worry!' he said, his voice gentle as he patted the youngster's shoulder. 'I'm forgetting my words all the time!' George's eyes spilled over. He knew that what Ernest had said was untrue. He knew that it was said simply to re-establish his self-confidence. What a lesson he learned that day! Looking back, George declares with a smile, 'I sure am glad that no one has dug up those old television tapes, either for broadcasting or blackmail purposes!'

Riding back to the YMCA, young George was heartbroken, struggling to hold back the tears. As the Cadillac pulled up outside the hostel, Ernest turned calmly to the anguished youngster. The look on his face was full of sympathy. 'Son, don't worry about tonight. You did great down at the record shop. I think you also did fine on TV. You may have forgotten the words, but you picked up okay. It ain't a disaster! Listen, if you love country music, you stick with it – always be sincere, practise hard and you'll do real good!' He smiled broadly and sincerely, and George felt hugely comforted. It wasn't the end of his hopes. There was still a chance for him to do what he loved. Years later, when he was a great star in his own right and recording for RCA Victor, George Hamilton IV insisted on doing a tribute album to that great country gentleman.

Country music was not to be the only love of George's life. There was time for other things too, and it was not too many years before the stage-struck teenager was also a fair way to becoming love-struck. There were some awkward moments along the way, however, especially as the lanky youth was shy and not all that sure of himself. Now, of course, George can look back on these crises and laugh, but they were all too real at the time!

It all started when he was just eight years old, sitting in class in the third grade. George became aware of a pretty girl with pigtails who sat in front of him – Jane, the daughter of the local minister, Rev. Ralph Bassett of the Fries Memorial Moravian Church. George did not normally pay much attention to girls, but she was special somehow. Then he blushed as the object of his admiration sidled up and handed him a little folded note as he sat stiffly at his wooden desk. He opened it up, and his heart skipped a beat:

I love you! Do you love me? Circle yes or no.
Jane

Up until then, young George Hamilton IV had never thought about whether he loved *any* girls except his Mom! Hypnotized, he stared at the rough note and thought very carefully over the question. Finally he circled the 'yes' and handed the note back to Miss Jane Bassett. His first romance, it seemed, had begun.

'Would I be marrying this girl?' He pondered the question as he wandered excitedly home from school that day. As George remembers it now, it was one of those rare days when the sun shone brightly, the sweet-scented flowers waved in the warm breeze and the birds twittered in the leafy trees. In a word, it was heaven. George had never felt better. Could their friendship last a lifetime?

They did become good friends and he visited Jane a few times at her home, where her mother would give them cake and ice-cream. A couple of weeks later, however, the 'life-long romance' came to an abrupt end. One of Jane's girlfriends came skipping up to George in the school hallway and laughingly destroyed his dreams. 'Jane doesn't love you any more and doesn't wanna go steady with you anymore!' she announced.

'Why?' asked George, suddenly shattered.

'Jane says you're too serious! She says she's tired of ya, George!' The reply was curt and final.

Thus the tentative relationship was not to be the start of a life-long marriage, after all – but it did make George think about the opposite sex in a romantic way for the first time. Jane Bassett and her family moved away in due course, as her father went to minister in Pennsylvania. As it does for most people, however, the memory of George's first 'romance' sticks out nostalgically and somewhat humorously in his scrapbook of recollections.

George continued to notice pretty girls from a distance and maybe, he admits, he flirted a bit – but he did not attempt to get too close. Nothing of a 'going steady' nature was to develop on the dating front as he concentrated for the time being on more boyish pursuits of fishing and tree-climbing with his pals. 'Guys are so much less trouble than gals!' As the next few years drifted by and George left his pre-teens behind, the only girls he had anything to do with were those at the youth fellowship of his local church. Carolyn and Peggy Holder, Judy Jones and Ann Highsmith were the four who caught his eye most, he says.

While he was a junior at high school, he spent most of his time in the company of two friends called Larry Foltz and George Agee. They would ride around in Larry's father's car, which gave the teenagers a feeling of independence and importance. (Prudently, the Hamilton family only had one car, which was always in use. George was not permitted to borrow it, much to his annoyance.) Full of youthful bravado, the teenage boys would describe their car excursions around town as 'ridin' around', heading for whatever seemed exciting. Sometimes they went to a movie, sometimes they hung out at the local hamburger joint. Real adventures, of the storybook type, rarely occurred in that sleepy part of North Carolina. Looking back, George considers that their teenage antics were the Winston-Salem version of the *Happy Days* television show!

George's two pals were really good-looking guys who seemed to attract endless girlfriends. Larry's special girl was Kay Watts. They were all somewhat worried about George IV because he was very shy and inhibited about many things, girls in particular. One day he was lazing around at home, country music blazing from the phonograph, when the phone rang. It was Larry with an urgent invitation.

'Hey, George! Kay's meeting me uptown after shopping and we're going to the movies. Kay's friend Tinky Peyton is gonna be with her at the shops. Why don't you come along and make a double date?'

George was stunned into silence for a while. Suddenly the pressure was on! He had seen Tinky in the school hallway and remembered thinking how attractive she was, but he had never had the courage to ask her out. Larry's voice interrupted the silence. 'Are you still there, George?'

'Yes, I ... I'm still here, Larry!' It would all be too embarrassing. He couldn't face it. He searched hurriedly for an excuse. 'I've got some, er, some studying to do tonight, Larry.'

'Oh, come on, George, that can wait!' Larry was persistent.

Then to his surprise, George found himself saying words he would never have uttered in less pressured, more rational times: 'Okay, I'll be there.'

When George met up with Tinky that evening, he was smitten by this pretty girl wearing a cashmere sweater, bobby socks and billowed skirt. The romantic Hollywood movie that evening was *Three Coins in the Fountain*. 'What on earth can I say to this girl?' George asked himself desperately as they sat through the film. His eyes were on the screen, but his mind was drifting and dreaming. The sweet sounds of the Frank Sinatra theme tune echoed around his brain as they left the cinema. The movie had been pure Hollywood escapism, but now he was trapped!

The four teenagers strolled off to the bus station because Larry was without a car that day. Kay's aunt had promised to pick them up in her car and give them all a ride home. Sitting self-consciously on the bus station seat next to Tinky, George could not think of a single thing to say to her. He had never been good at small talk. Suddenly, he could stand it no longer and jumped up. 'I'm gonna have to go home now. My mother's expecting me for dinner!' he blurted to the startled trio. Before his stunned friends had time to react, he was gone, hopping onto one of the city buses and heading home via Ardmore.

His acute shyness had got the better of him, much to the annoyance of Tinky. She felt deeply offended. Was it something she had said? 'Well,' she said sharply, 'I guess that's the last I'll see of George IV!' Larry and Kay were the ones lost for words now.

Rather like George's disaster on stage at the Princess Theater, the debacle at the bus station did not spell the end of his romantic aspirations. There was still hope for him and Tinky, and a chance to mend things came by in due course.

Although never a keen sportsman, George IV was always eager to see his school succeed on the sports field. 'We had a great coach in John Tandy; he was a fine motivator of students. He tried to get everyone excited about the school football team, including the cheerleaders. Guys like me, who weren't athletically inclined, he involved in what he described as being "managers".' A manager was essentially just a 'water boy', carrying water and towels for the football players or rendering basic first aid if someone was injured, but 'manager' was a more dignified and encouraging term of reference. George and his buddy Larry were both managers and were able to feel part of the team, travelling on the team bus from school to school.

When the annual 'Home-Coming Dance' for the football team rolled around, it was traditional to escort one's best girlfriend to the event. The girls were expected to wear flowers on their party dresses and the football players would parade around the field in open convertibles while their escorts sat proudly next to them, smiling as sweetly as they could. Even the managers were expected to have escorts, and this was George's opportunity.

George plucked up all his courage and telephoned Tinky, in humble, self-effacing Clark Kent mode (he hoped), to invite her to be his escort for the great occasion. 'Oh, hi Tink! This is, er, George ... um ... George Hamilton ... I was kinda wondering, would you like to be, er, be my escort at the ... the Home-Coming Dance?'

He did not have to wait long for the reply. 'Oh sure, George!' exclaimed Tinky. 'I didn't expect to hear from *you*! You don't need to be shy – I'm glad to be your gal for the Dance!' If nothing else, George Hamilton IV had a way of surprising her! She had never expected to hear from him again after the hurried bus station exodus, but she was developing rather a soft spot for the hesitant George.

The Home-Coming Dance was a much more successful occasion than their first date, and Tinky and George started to go out on a regular basis. George progressed to his senior year and he and Tinky, aged seventeen and sixteen respectively, saw more and more of each other. George was beginning to fall for this live-wire brunette. Universally popular, she had a bubbly personality that made her well liked and very good company. Her real name was Adelaide, but she had been called Tinky since her childhood, when she had been nicknamed after the feisty fairy Tinkerbell in *Peter Pan*.

New Year's Eve of 1954 found Tinky and George once again on a double date with Larry and Kay, taking part in a 'scavenger hunt' party. A list of items was assigned to party members to find, and the first back with all the items would be the winners. Larry and Kay went to a neighbour's house to ask for an old dishcloth, leaving Tinky and George to chat. It was the opportunity for George to express his seriousness about her. 'Tinky, I've kinda grown fond of you,' he told her. 'How about you and me going steady?' Always afraid of rejection, he was worried about what her response might be. He was mighty relieved when she smiled, nodded and planted a kiss on his cheek.

As the months passed, he came to realize quite clearly that she was the only one for him. When he went off to the University of North Carolina to study English, Tinky stayed behind in Winston-Salem as she had another year to complete in high school. George missed her terribly and made every effort to return home as often as he could at weekends.

In the spring of his first year at university, George started making records. By the summer of 1956, the year of Tinky's graduation, he was booked to transfer to Washington DC's American University as well as to join the *Jimmy Dean TV Show*. Tinky, in turn, made plans to go to a ladies' college in Greensboro, North Carolina. This concerned George. They would be hundreds of miles apart, separated by slow roads and rail systems, to say nothing of primitive telephone communications. 'I was keenly aware that Tinky was special to me and that we wouldn't be seeing much of each other for a while,' George explains. 'My fledgling career was finding its feet by then, yet I didn't want it to interfere in our budding romance. I certainly didn't want to leave her in the dust as my career started to take off!'

Tinky's parents never admitted to George what they thought about this long-legged guitar picker and singer going steady with their daughter. George confessed he found this surprising, because the couple's fathers were business associates of sorts at Goody's Headache Powder Company. Tinky's father was in Sales, a department over which George's father had responsibility. On one occasion, due to economic cutbacks initiated by policy decisions taken over his head, Mr Hamilton was put into a terrible predicament. He was faced with the unenviable and embarrassing task of firing Tinky's father. George recalls how his poor father had to execute company policy as the 'hatchet man': 'That hardly made him popular with staff at the time, or with Tinky's parents!' Clearly, feelings and tempers ran hot. It was not the best foundation for the two lovers, but when the heat had cooled, George desperately hoped that Tinky's father would appreciate that *his* father had simply been doing his job. To their credit, Tinky's parents always treated their girl's beau graciously, despite the trauma of the firing.

Originally from Virginia, Tinky's parents were the 'Old South' personified in George's eyes. Tinky's grandfather Dr Watson was a professor at the University of Virginia and her family came from a rich line of Virginia aristocracy, proud descendants of Thomas Jefferson and Robert E. Lee. Centred in the area surrounding Charlottesville, Virginia (home of the University of Virginia), the family included university professors, doctors and lawyers. The beautiful campus in Charlottesville was actually designed and built by Thomas Jefferson, architect of the Declaration of Independence and later a President of the United States. Today the campus boasts a building named after Tinky's grandfather Dr Watson, who had been Virginia's State geologist and travelled to the North Pole with Admiral Robert Peary on his first expedition in 1909.

Almost all teenage girls have posters on their bedroom walls of the latest music or movie stars, and Tinky Peyton was no exception. Unlike her college mates, however, she actually knew the personality adorning her walls: he was her childhood sweetheart. She was always amused to overhear her friends commenting on the handsome singer with a number in his name. By Christmas 1957 George's single 'A Rose And A Baby Ruth' had blasted into the pop charts and other hits were on the way, such as 'Why Don't They Understand?', written by England's Joe 'Mr Piano' Henderson.

Earlier that year, at Thanksgiving, the couple had committed themselves to each other for life. The decision was a rational one, and the subject was maturely approached, as George recalls. 'It wasn't so much "popping the question" as if it was a hasty decision taken on the spur of the moment – rather it was two people, much in love, sitting down and committing themselves to each other and planning their future accordingly as a couple.'

To their great disappointment and pain, however, the couple's decision caused great friction with the Hamilton parents. Always wanting whatever was best for George, they were concerned about his studies and his career, which by then already included the demands of television shows and concert tours. 'How on earth, son, could you be responsible for a wife and family at this time?' asked George's father sternly. 'Why not finish your education first? It's just not fair on Tinky. Besides, George, you're far too young to be getting married – you're only 20!'

Mr Hamilton was deadly serious, and was not bashful in making his strong misgivings known to George, never mincing his words. George remembers the pain of standing up to his father. 'I must have loved Tinky a whole lot because I self-assuredly stood up to him! The arguments became very heated, especially at night when I arrived home late with the family car. He would be there waiting for me. "What time do you call this, George?" he'd say. "You didn't keep your word. You said you'd be in at midnight, and this is one o'clock! Don't you think you're getting too serious with this girl?"'

The angry questions would come out, one after another, time and again. 'Besides, George, you don't even have a proper job!' That was a favourite line of argument.

'But Dad,' George would tearfully respond, 'I'm making good money as a singer!'

'No, George! That's not the same as a *proper* job. You're a student and you should recognize that! How can you expect to take on the responsibilities of a wife?'

Reaching a stalemate, Father Hamilton would stomp off to bed. George's worried mother remained aloof, as best she could, as she listened to the arguments in bed. One thing she did understand was that her son was uncompromising on this issue. She believed that her husband was right, however, and in the morning she would turn up the pressure. 'George, your father is quite right. You should listen to his advice, son.'

'Oh Mom, you may think Dad's right practically speaking, but the one thing I know is that I'm in love with Tinky – I'm determined to marry her! I'm sorry, Mom, but I'm gonna marry Tinky. I don't care what anyone else says.' On reflection, George now admits that he was somewhat arrogant in being so dismissive and thinking his parents hopelessly old fashioned and out of date.

Nevertheless, between Thanksgiving and Christmas, George got cold feet about marriage. The concern of both his parents and his manager must have been working on him subconsciously, even as he defended his intentions. His manager Connie B. Gay was more worried that his diary should be kept clear for touring. 'Don't forget, George,' he advised, 'those teenage girls who represent the majority of your fans want you to be *single*! It's all part of your "teenage idol" image!' George's business contacts who marketed him as a 'teen balladeer' feared that being married would blow the whole of his budding singing career. After all, he was being hyped in magazines aimed at adolescent girls. His status, they said, would fall if he was to become a married man.

It was no wonder that George got such cold feet and harboured second thoughts about an early marriage. He was being bombarded with anti-marriage counselling from pretty much everyone, including family and business associates. Tinky had been confidently expecting to receive an engagement ring at Christmas, but instead George gave her a television set. She was taken by surprise and deeply hurt, although she did her best to hide her feelings. 'Where's the ring?' she asked silently, fighting back tears. Tinky and George had already visited the jeweller's store and picked out a ring. She had been so sure that he would make Christmas Day 'The Day', and she had even kept her nails carefully manicured so that she could show off the ring that would make her the future Mrs Hamilton IV.

George had let his girl down with an unwarranted bump. It was no wonder that in the early months of the New Year she dated a couple of other young men. George's integrity and faithfulness had come into serious doubt as far as she was concerned. Returning to Washington DC, George faced his touring schedule with mounting enthusiasm, but he knew deep down that Tinky was not just going to sit at home and wait for him to make up his mind about her. The worry of it all eventually tipped the scales for him.

In the spring of 1958, against all adverse advice, George popped the question. 'I'm sorry that I let you down, Tinky,' he told her. 'Do you still love me? Is it possible we can still make a life together?'

'Oh, George,' she said in return, 'you know I love you and I always thought we had a future together!'

The next thing they knew, they had set the date: 7 June 1958. Once the wedding date was set, all criticism from George's parents ceased and it was support all the way. There were no more arguments or talk of how stupid it was for him to marry.

George and Tinky discussed the idea of eloping to Hawaii because it would all be so much easier, but Tinky's heart was really set on a big white wedding in church. Eventually the great day dawned and Adelaide Peyton, dressed in a white and pink organdy wedding gown trimmed with seed pearls and lace, glided down the aisle of the First Baptist Church of Winston-Salem to meet her fiancé, who stood proudly at the front of the church beside his father, who was acting as best man. It was a delightfully happy wedding, co-officiated by the ministers from Tinky's and George's churches. Afterwards the couple left to spend their honeymoon in a plush hotel in Bermuda.

Tinky was only 19 and George just 20 when they married, and a little over a year later they were parents. The down-to-earth realities of marriage and the burden of parenthood were suddenly upon them. 'We were in love,' declares George, 'but looking back now, we were very young when the storms started to hit!'

CHAPTER 4

YOUNG HEART-THROB

Always bear in mind that your resolution to succeed is more important than any other thing.

Abraham Lincoln (President, United States of America)

BY THE TIME he came to marry Tinky in the summer of 1958, George's singing career was already on an upward curve. The previous few years had been hectic and exhilarating as he forged a place for himself on the music scene. As the new millennium gets underway, George Hamilton IV finds it hard to believe that the first of his many hit records made its appearance way back in the Cold War fifties, while he was still just a teenager.

Inspired by what he heard and saw in Nashville on his regular visits, country music was the only topic of conversation the young George was interested in when he returned home. 'I was pretty much nothing and nobody until I discovered the guitar and music. Suddenly, it gave me a reason for being. I found that there was something I could do that people seemed to like and appreciate. It gave me confidence and made me feel like I had some sort of worth. Under my high-school yearbook picture – I think in jest – was the phrase, "Grand Ole Opry, here I come!" I'm sure it was a joke, because my classmates felt I was obsessed with the Grand Ole Opry and that was their way of teasing me.'

Before long (despite the teasing) George had formed a country music band with some buddies. Always a bit of an outsider, George never really felt he fitted in at school. He was never a sportsman or a major academic, and he was certainly not known for his outstanding popularity with the girls. He did find a like-minded friend in Jim Gay, however. Jim was in the year above George and his first love was country music, which he played on the piano. In an effort to sound more authentic, Jim decided to learn to pluck and strum on a guitar. 'You should go and talk to that tall kid, George the Fourth!' someone suggested, and thus was struck a partnership that soon became an enduring friendship.

In a funny twist to the tale, Jim bought George's beloved but battered Serenader guitar from him for the princely sum of eight dollars. A number of years later, Jim returned the guitar to its original owner, in honour of the memories it represented. The gesture demonstrates the high regard in which George is held by his friends. Jim could have commanded a high price at auction for the instrument.

Taking their name from that much loved guitar, Jim and George formed a band called the Serenaders, inviting another friend called Henry Heitman to join them. With Henry on double bass, Jim on piano or accordion and George up front on rhythm guitar, they embarked on an adventure that enthralled them for the rest of their high-school years. They relished the prospect of entertaining audiences in and around their home town, and went about the whole business with gusto.

In 1953/4, the Serenaders cut their first record in the back room of the Starling-Thomas Music Company for the prized fee of one dollar per song. Young Cabot Hamilton played drums along with the original trio band. Among the songs minted were Roy Acuff's 'Beer, Wine and Whiskey' and 'Sleepin' At The Foot Of The Bed', a hit by Little Jimmy Dickens. George and his band began to acquire a good local reputation, playing apparently spontaneously at get-togethers and ball game intervals. In time the Serenaders started to receive firm professional bookings. They printed their own business cards, offering 'music for all occasions' – an enterprising move which attracted a wide variety of engagements. As the boys loaded their instruments into the trunk and set off to play at another birthday party, prom or social, little did their guitar-picking lead singer realize that this was just a prelude of things to come.

Winston-Salem may not have been the life and soul of the party in show-business terms, but it did boast a UHF channel television station, WTOB. A particular favourite with George was the Saturday evening country music show headed by Johnny Young and the Rhythm Boys (not to be confused with the previously mentioned Jonny Young Band from Kent). Also appearing on WTOB were the headline act Dwight Barker and the Melody Boys. With the performers clad in rhinestone-studded western clothes, high-heeled cowboy boots and the obligatory stetsons, this was Winston-Salem's modest answer to the Grand Ole Opry. George was thrilled when, as a raw 17-year-old, he was invited to join them as a singing guest. It was modest, no doubt about that, but it was undeniably a step up the ladder.

'I started appearing on a Saturday night television show called *The Hoedown Party*, with Dwight Barker and the Melody Boys. That's where I met people like Dewey Adams, Felix Johnson and Bruce Eller. They were true country musicians, not high-school buddies who did it for a lark or a hobby. We started playing some shows around Winston-Salem together too. I think it was these guys who probably played on my first demo tape which was sent down to Orville Campbell at Colonial Records in Chapel Hill.'

By that time, of course, George was going steady with Tinky Peyton. She and her schoolfriends were typical of the teenagers of the day – Fats Domino, Little Richard, Bill Haley and the Comets were their adolescent musical tastes. Looking back, a bewildered George remembers in some disbelief (and with just a hint of criticism), 'In those days, such music was called "rhythm and blues". Before that – and it's kinda hard to believe now – it was actually called "race music"! The now-familiar term "rock'n'roll" had yet to be coined by the legendary DJ Alan Freed. Still, *my* enduring interest continued to be country music, not the "popular" stuff.'

Tinky's high-school friends were consequently somewhat bemused by her shy, skinny, awkward boyfriend. It seemed to them that he could only spark into life when he was offered the chance to 'pick'n'grin'. Country music was emphatically not the fashion in Reynolds High School in 1954–5. The Platters, the Ames Brothers, Guy Mitchell, Fats Domino, Joni James, Pat

Boone, Teresa Brewer, Sam Cooke, Little Richard, the Four Aces, Eddie Fisher, Perry Como and Andy Williams were all the rage, and Hank Williams' songs and George IV's regular trips to Nashville became the subject of much teasing by his peers. 'There goes George, the long-legged hillbilly!' they would laugh, but to the aspiring singer it was like water off a duck's back. Country music was now well and truly his major love. Tinky found herself forced to take a crash course in the genre later on, when it turned out that she was stuck with a country 'nut' for life!

In the whole high school, only four pupils played the guitar – Jim Gay, Buddy Cagle, Charlie Hemrick and George Hamilton. Buddy Cagle went on to find success with Imperial Records. As a youngster he lived in the local children's home, where George would visit him after school. While other kids practised their American football skills, Buddy and George would practise guitar chords. George remembers his strumming partner with affection. 'Buddy Cagle loved and knew every early Marty Robbins song. He even managed to imitate Marty's yodel! He went on to do some great country music recordings.' Charlie Hemrick was also befriended by George as a fellow guitar picker. He sang on the local radio and became George's 'local hero' for a time.

George and his little group of partners in music were out on a limb together, bucking the trend. What was so enthralling about country music? George Hamilton was a typical, middle-class, suburban boy. Winston-Salem was not a country town – it was a good-sized city. The Hamilton family house was modest, but it was by no means a farmhouse or a country shack. His background simply did not fit the typical 'country boy' mould. Country music, moreover, was not for 'cool' high-school kids; that much was clear. In his darker moments, despite the love affair he had going for country music, the old question haunted George's mind: 'Isn't this music earmarked for hillbillies, farmers and rednecks?' What was he doing? Was he barking up the wrong tree?

As it turned out, it was not that long before George received some welcome reassurance that he was right to stick to what he loved to play. The teenager had a part-time job as a soda jerk at the Biltmore Dairy Bar, and Tinky visited him there regularly. One day, she took a sip of her soda pop and said casually, 'Hey, George, have you thought about entering the Key Club Follies talent show competition this year? If you're gonna do something, you'd better do it fast – entries have to be done by next month!' The Key Club Follies was an annual high-school event. With his eyes on fostering support for his talent, George took little persuasion to be involved.

On the night, George and his guitar, accompanied by Henry Heitman on bass and Jimmy Gay on piano, mounted the stage for their spot in the talent show. They sang 'Wedding Bells' and 'Kaw-Liga', both of which were Hank Williams classics. Almost before they had finished, the 2,000 students in the audience erupted into applause. Against the odds, the band had brought the house down.

All at once George Hamilton IV, the untrendy loner with no interest in parties, drinking, sports or dancing, found himself accepted in quite a special way by his peers. 'George sure is cool!' His new reputation spread quickly and he was suddenly in great demand. He had found his niche. Classmates now lapped up his vocals and his band's novel country music at every opportunity. Invitations for the Serenaders to provide home-grown entertainment steadily increased during George's senior year.

In early June 1955 he graduated from Reynolds High School and laid plans to study English at the university at Chapel Hill, North Carolina. Meanwhile, Tinky was fairly convinced that her boyfriend's weird taste in music would prove to be nothing more than a passing schoolboy whim. A university education would surely do away with all that, and her George would settle down to a career in teaching, or something just as respectable – *anything* but country music! How wrong she was…

WTOB's show *The Hoedown Party* employed a couple of enterprising engineers who helped George make a demo tape of songs, including 'Out Behind The Barn' and 'Satisfied Mind' (hits for Little Jimmie Dickens and Porter Wagoner respectively). The engineers knew a man called Jimmie Skinner, who in turn knew

Orville Campbell, the editor and publisher of the Chapel Hill weekly newspaper. Orville was also the owner of Colonial Records, a small local record label. His biggest claim to fame was that he had discovered Andy Griffith, the great character actor of Broadway and Hollywood fame. To George's knowledge, Orville Campbell was the only person in North Carolina making commercial recordings. And whether Orville knew it or not, George IV was determined to be his next recording artiste. This was his chance, and he seized it with both hands.

Jimmie Skinner kindly offered to make the initial contact and delivered the demo tape to Campbell. He was not exactly overwhelmed, however. In fact, he was distinctly underwhelmed. Still, Jimmie was a friend. 'Tell the kid to come by and see me sometime,' Campbell told him. His remark was delivered half-heartedly, but George took him up on the invitation during his very first week at university. To his surprise, Orville Campbell received him kindly despite his initial lack of enthusiasm, and did not attempt to throw cold water over his youthful aspirations. 'Why don't you try writing songs, George?' he suggested. 'If you're gonna be a recording artiste, you'll need some original material. Chapel Hill doesn't boast too many songwriters – there's room out there for you, son, so get writin'!'

A contract with Colonial Records was sealed by George's signature, witnessed by his father. Suddenly, George Hamilton IV was a professional. Inspired by Orville's helpfulness and solid advice, George recorded a couple of his own humorous song creations on 12 March 1956, at UNC Radio and TV Department's Swain Hall. The songs, 'I Got A Secret' and 'Sam', were laid straight onto 12-inch acetate and released on 5 May. The modest offering only gained regional circulation, but it was a start.

Some of George's spare time in his college days was spent singing in Jim Thornton's show *Saturday Night Country Style* on WTVD in Durham. The town was just eight miles down the road from where George was living, and in latter years hosted the Sugar Hill record label which helped kick off the career of Ricky Skaggs and – much later – took superstar Dolly Parton back to her country roots. One Saturday night a camera operator George barely knew came up to him, saying he had some advice for the singer. George listened patiently. 'George, you ought to meet the guy who works down in the Art Department,' the cameraman told him. 'He writes folk songs. His name is John D. Loudermilk.'

'What a weird name!' George exclaimed, pulling a face. 'Besides, I didn't know anyone *wrote* folk songs – I thought they were handed down from generation to generation!'

Nevertheless, despite his doubts George dutifully sauntered down to see this folk-song gentleman with the odd name. After brief introductions, Loudermilk handed him a new song he had written entitled 'A Rose And A Baby Ruth'. In all truth, George was totally unimpressed both by the individual and the song. The song's writer may well have had the same initial thoughts about George, a skinny singer with wild dreams of becoming a country music star!

Johnny Dee (as Loudermilk was known) was raised in the Salvation Army community of Durham during the Great Depression, after his family hit hard times. The Salvation Army inducted John into their music ranks at an early age. First he picked up the rudiments of the piano from his mother, and then he learned how to master the brass, percussion and string instruments. He also learned to sing in the Salvation Army quartets and choirs, later appearing on local radio and television. Johnny's job in the WTVD Art Department was to draw weather sketch pictures of clouds, sunshine and rain. There were no computerized graphics in those days and even the weather report had to be sketched by hand. In his spare time he played classical guitar and wrote folk songs. Yet 'A Rose And A Baby Ruth' was anything but a folk song. It was about a love-sick teenager who could only afford to give his sweetheart one single rose and a 'Baby Ruth' candy bar.

One day, as George was eating breakfast in the university's Alexander dormitory, a phone call came through for him. It was Orville Campbell. 'Son, would you drive by the newspaper office?' he said. 'I've found a *great* song for you! I want it to be your first nationally released record.' He sounded very excited and George wondered what this great song could be that was going to set him on the ladder of fame at last. Well, he was in for a shock: when he arrived at Orville's busy, untidy office, he was presented with a tape of 'A Rose And A Baby Ruth'. Apparently, John D. Loudermilk had not been satisfied with George's lukewarm reaction to his song and had taken it straight to Orville Campbell, who loved it. 'I guess that was the quiet genius of the man!' George admits now. 'Mr Campbell recognized the potential that I had failed to see.'

At the time, however, George stifled a groan and Orville simply stared at him and smiled. 'Kid,' he said, 'you don't sing so good, but anybody with as much determination as you've got deserves a chance. I'm gonna give you one with this "teen ballad".' He outlined his plans in his thick Southern drawl, speaking with a contagious confidence. 'We're gonna make a hit record for you ... and another thing – I want you to use that stupid Roman numeral at the end of your name. It'll make a great gimmick. Besides, it'll look good on my Colonial Records label to carry such a distinguished-sounding name!'

George was hungry enough for success to give it a go, regardless of his personal misgivings about the soppy, adolescent song. After all, what did he have to lose? Knowing George's deep-seated desire to remain 'country', Orville Campbell added a final comment with a broad grin. 'You can do a hillbilly song on side two if you like!' And so George Hamilton IV was hooked.

His self-penned, humorous ditty 'If You Don't Know I Ain't Gonna Tell You' became the flip side of 'A Rose And A Baby Ruth'. The two songs were recorded on 18 June 1956 and the single was released in July under the name of George Hamilton IV and the Country Gentlemen. The Gentlemen were Joe Tanner (lead guitar), Henry Heitman (bass), Dennis Beam (drums) and the Blue Notes (backing vocals).

John D. Loudermilk was absent on National Guard camp duty at the time of the recording and he was none too pleased when he finally heard the tapes on his return. The sound was not as he had envisaged it. In his frustration, he made his feelings abundantly clear. 'You guys *ruined* my song!' he stormed. Orville Campbell was left with a very discouraged singer and a highly disgruntled songwriter on his hands, but he went right ahead and released the record.

To everyone's surprise, the newly released single started kicking up a little dust, initially just in North Carolina. Orville Campbell, always an astute businessman, had apparently struck gold. Then Buddy Deane, a Baltimore radio DJ who also had a successful television dance party show, took an interest in the disc. In a voting slot on his radio show, 'A Rose And A Baby Ruth' scored the lowest ever number of votes from its panel of expert voters. Out of a maximum possible total of 100, the song scored just 10. Nevertheless, Buddy himself loved the record and promoted it on air in the Washington and Baltimore area. George looks back on the hype with a high degree of amusement. 'I recall well how Buddy Dean appreciated "A Rose And A Baby Ruth". My recollection is that he gave the song its radio debut and he certainly kindly promoted it a lot. Even that voting slot was a form of promotion – "Is it a hit or is it a miss?" Debuting it over the air like that called attention to it and made the listeners call in if they wanted to hear the song again.'

To the radio station's amazement, following the show's broadcast hundreds of listeners jammed the switchboard with requests to hear the song. 'Sir, I'd like to hear that "Rose and Baby Ruth" again please. I'm kinda taking a liking to it!' Obviously the expert panel's decision was not mirrored in public opinion. With the help of Buddy Deane and many other DJs, the song started something of a brush fire on the airwaves. As the old saying goes, 'There ain't no such thing as bad publicity!'

Meanwhile, Fred Foster, an employee of ABC Paramount Records in Washington DC, also heard the modestly recorded song and instantly prophesied its success. It was common in the recording industry for larger companies to watch the commercial potential of smaller labels vigilantly, with a view to securing the little nuggets they could turn into hits. Foster assessed 'Rose' as one of these. Catching a plane to North Carolina, he visited the small-time Colonial set-up and asked about the possibility of ABC acquiring distribution rights. Interest at the time was mounting and Colonial was fast running out of copies. The smooth-tongued Foster secured a deal within 30 minutes. ABC agreed a 5 per cent royalty and purchased the master recording for just 2,500 dollars.

When ABC's head honcho Sam Clark heard about the deal, he chided Foster strongly as he felt the single had little or no potential. Foster, however, stuck to his guns. 'Listen Mr Clark,' he said, 'I'm convinced that those teenage kids will identify with the sentiments in the song and will fall for it. The ditty has a down-to-earth, modern plot that'll make it a hit!'

His boss was unimpressed. 'Foster, some of the backing is below standard. I remain unconvinced.'

'Sir,' retorted Foster, 'I'm gonna lay my job on the line. If that record don't get a place in the Billboard Top Ten Chart, I'll resign. But let me ask, if it's a hit, will you raise my salary by 25 dollars a week?'

Sam Clark could not resist a smile at this boldness. 'Okay Foster, you're on. If it's a hit you get a pay rise of 25 dollars a week. If it ain't, you'd better start looking at them job ads!'

Soon phone calls started coming in from listeners to radio stations from coast to coast requesting the teen love song. Step by step, enthusiasm for the single spread. It sold over a million copies and became one of America's hottest teen ballads. Initially, the company that produced and marketed the 'Baby Ruth' candy expressed strong misgivings about the use of their trade name. Their objections soon sweetened into support, however, as they saw the huge publicity opportunities unfold. Thanks to the million-selling success of 'A Rose And A Baby Ruth', Fred Foster duly received a bonus from ABC Paramount Records which he used to invest in his own new label, Monument Records. His first artiste was Billy Grammer, whose debut hit was 'Gotta Travel On'. Later Fred would sign Roy Orbison, Dolly Parton and Kris Kristofferson to his label.

George's manager was entrepreneur Connie B. Gay, the founding President of the Country Music Association. Originally from Lizard Lick, North Carolina (such a colourful name for a small town!), he was also the manager of country crooner Jimmy Dean, whose self-penned, tough-talking narrative chart topper 'Big Bad John' had shot him to international fame in 1961. Born in 1928 near Plainview, Texas, Jimmy Dean had worked as a youngster in poorly paid rural jobs to support his mother. Having taught himself guitar, accordion and harmonica and picked up the basics of piano-playing from his mother, he saw show business as his way out of poverty. Jimmy was now successfully hosting a local television show in Washington DC called *Town and Country Jamboree.*

On the strength of George's first record success, an invitation came from Connie Gay to come under his management and to join Jimmy Dean's *Town and Country Jamboree* show, which Connie produced. Initially joining the television cast as a singer, George later acted as understudy to the star. As a result of his television commitments, George transferred from the University of North Carolina to the American University in Washington in the fall of 1956.

George recalls those busy days and the people he met. 'Just across from the bus station in downtown Washington there was a club called The Famous Bar and Grill where I first met Roy Clark. He was then in Jimmy Dean's band, but later went on to achieve solo fame. Jimmy Dean, the Stoneman Family and Roy Clark all started out in that little beer joint. I believe that's where Connie B. Gay "discovered" Jimmy Dean. At the time, Jimmy was in the Coastguard but was singing at The Famous at night.

The bar was quite a platform for new talent. 'Roy Clark told me the story about how Connie B. Gay brought a new girl singer from Winchester, Virginia into The Famous one night. Connie really wanted Roy to hear her and he insisted that Roy let her up on stage to sing. It was Patsy Cline, though at that time Connie may still have been calling her Virginia Hensley (her given name). Roy said nobody had ever heard of her before but she got up, sang a song and the entire club fell into a stunned silence. Roy told me he had never heard that beer joint so quiet. He remembered looking at Connie from the stage and nodding his head, signalling, "You're right – this girl is something else!"'

So that was how the tough-talking, hard-living newcomer called Patsy Cline burst into the limelight. Born Virginia Patterson Hensley on 8 September 1932 near Winchester, Virginia, Patsy's girlhood ambition was set on Grand Ole Opry stardom. She married builder Gerald Cline, but after some record success with Bill McCall's Four Star record label in Nashville in the mid-fifties, she divorced him. A second marriage followed to Charlie Dick. Eventually she found commercial success with Decca Records producer Owen Bradley. Massive hits resulted, including 'Crazy' and 'I Fall To Pieces'. Stockily built and often attired in flashy clothes, with behaviour and language to match, she seemed a very overpowering character to the young George Hamilton IV. She was killed along with Cowboy Copas, Hawkshaw Hawkins and her manager Randy Hughes in a plane crash on 5 March 1963.

For a time during the late fifties, Patsy Cline appeared alongside George in Jimmy Dean's television show. Work over for the day, the weary cast would assemble in the foyer of the television studio to wait for their transport home. Patsy would take every opportunity to tease her shy student colleague. 'Hey, George!' she would exclaim in her deep voice. 'I just can't help believing that you're the first hillbilly singer who ever went to college! Does your Ma know you're still wet behind the ears?'

With every eye turned in his direction, George would cringe. 'Oh, come on, Patsy! Why are you giving me such a hard time?' He would search frantically for some suitable put-down to counter her mockery. He was reluctant to be insulting, however – underneath, he knew she did not mean what she said in an unfriendly way. But Patsy would give him no time for a response. 'George, you don't look at all like a hillbilly to me! You're more like the college goody-goody, the Pat Boone of country music...' Then she would add, 'But ya know that I love ya!'

George looks back nostalgically to the days when Patsy Cline, Jimmy Dean and he were on a country music 'package tour' in Canada in the dead of winter. That was a little later in his career. 'I believe it was the winter just prior to when Patsy was killed. Patsy, Jimmy and I made an interesting "package" because we'd all worked together back in the fifties in Washington DC on Jimmy's television show. We were being driven in a Cadillac limousine, as I recall, by a chauffeur who was hired by the promoter. We were in the middle of a blinding ice and snow storm. It was very difficult driving and it took us a long time to get where we were headed.

I was sitting in the back seat between Jimmy and Patsy. Somebody produced a flask of whiskey – Patsy, I think. It got passed across me to Jimmy, who took a sip and then passed it back to Patsy. We were all reminiscing about the good old days in DC…'

This went on for a while and the trio were all rocking with laughter. Between them they had a real sense of camaraderie going. Then suddenly Patsy turned to George and spoke with a really stern look on her face. 'Hey hoss, you think you're too good to drink with Dean and the Cline?'

'I can't remember what I said back to Patsy,' says George. 'I guess I was a little embarrassed to be called down by her for not being more sociable. I took a sip of the liquid refreshment and passed it back to her, and after that the three of us passed the bottle most of the way to our matinée performance that day. By the time we got to the gig, I was the only one who was out of it, of course! Jimmy Dean and Patsy Cline could hold their whiskey a whole lot better than I could, since I very seldom drank anything other than beer then. When we got to the matinée, I was in rare shape indeed! It was quite hilarious, I'm sure, judging from the reaction of Patsy and Jimmy. Mr Goody Two Shoes, as Patsy often referred to me, was clearly tipsy. I wasn't drunk, but I was very happy, and it was the subject of much mirth on the part of Jimmy, Patsy and the band that day!'

Patsy's rough, 'honky-tonk' persona coloured all her conversation and behaviour, but it belied the real, caring human being underneath the mask. She was genuinely concerned for George IV. Indeed, Patsy and Mrs Hamilton III became firm friends. Patsy felt that George's awkwardness and shyness were unsuited to the rough-and-tumble world of show business, and in her own sometimes hurtful way she was simply trying to toughen him up.

'My mother became very friendly with Patsy and her husband Charlie Dick, when they came through Winston-Salem on tours, both with me and on their own. A couple of times I remember my mother had a backyard barbecue for Patsy and the other entertainers. Tex Ritter was also on one of those package shows. On one occasion, Patsy must have mentioned to my mother that she was going to ride all night back to Nashville after that evening's show.

Patsy wasn't looking forward to that 450 mile drive! My mother had a pillow headrest with a U-shaped cushion that you could place behind your neck to cradle it, and she gave it to Patsy to use on the long trip back to Nashville. Patsy wrote my mother a really warm thank-you note and sent her an autographed photo. They became good friends and I remember they exchanged Christmas cards right up until the time of Patsy's death. Charlie Dick told me Patsy had really appreciated that pillow – he even told me recently that he'd found it in the attic amongst some of Patsy's belongings.'

In 1956, before 'A Rose And A Baby Ruth' had become a really big hit, another opportunity opened up for George, as he recalls. 'Connie B. Gay arranged for me to audition for the Arthur Godfrey Talent Scout contest. This was a major nationwide network television show from New York City, hosted by one of the most popular television personalities around. Arthur Godfrey came from Virginia, not far from where Patsy Cline was born. It's possible Mr Godfrey had seen me on the regionally networked Jimmy Dean show – it was certainly where he first became aware of Patsy Cline.

'So I went up to New York City to audition for the Talent Scout programme. "A Rose And A Baby Ruth" had already been released in the south-eastern part of America, having been picked up by ABC Paramount Records by then, so I sang the song at the audition. Mr Godfrey's people weren't at all interested in the song, though. What they liked were the little country-style novelty songs that I'd been writing, such as "I've Got A Secret", "Sam", "If You Don't Know, I Ain't Gonna Tell You" and "It Was Me". Those little songs were much influenced by the work of Tommy Collins, Little Jimmy Dickens and others.

'Tinky was at college in Greensboro at that time. She came up from Carolina to be my "talent scout" and introduce me on the show. Mr Godfrey was quite taken with her. He must have spent at least five minutes of the show talking with Tinky about her aspirations to be an airline stewardess and admiring her deep Southern accent. He was probably more impressed with her than with me!

'Anyway, I decided to sing "I've Got A Secret", a corny little country song that I'd written in the vein of Tommy Collins' "You Better Not Do That" and Little Jimmy Dickens' "Out Behind The Barn". On the recording you can hear Mr Godfrey chuckling away in the background. He really got a kick out of that sort of hillbilly, novelty-song thing! Well, good fortune had shone on me before, so why not again?'

Being on a national television show, George was naturally nervous. He had already lost count of the number of times he had performed before large crowds, but this was altogether different. 'Should I tone down my Southern accent for the Northern audience?' he wondered. 'No, sir!' came the reply. 'Just be yourself, boy – no false airs and graces!' Backstage, he apprehensively ran through his routine, sorting out in his mind where he should stand and when to look at cameras. As his spot drew closer and he listened to the other acts, he felt torn between impatience to get on stage and dread of his coming exposure in America's 'front parlour'.

At last, the stage hand ushered him into position and George looked to Mr Godfrey for his cue. As the introduction was made, George took in the glare of the lights and the stares of the audience. Then, forgetting his nerves, he launched confidently into the catchy lyrics and melody. Just as he had rehearsed it, he sang his part to perfection and moved around with precision. Before he knew it, he was singing the final note. As the sound died away he awaited the audience's response, and was euphoric when they burst into loud applause.

Reminiscing about the show now, George's thoughts are laced with amusement and satisfaction. 'Ironically, on the show that night was a group from Nashville called the La Dell Sisters. Some of them were the descendants of the Denning Sisters who were a pretty popular act in the early fifties. Delores Denning was a member of the group and their "talent scout" for the evening was the receptionist at WSM Radio, Nashville. Her name was Frances Williams. She later became Frances Williams Preston, and later still became the head of BMI (Broadcast Music International). Another contestant – now here's where the plot thickens – was an operatic tenor who had literally just got off the boat from Italy! How he stumbled into the Godfrey production office and why he was auditioned for the show, I have no idea, but he was absolutely wonderful. He couldn't speak a word of English, but he was one of the finest singers I ever heard – a Pavarotti type of guy. Mr Godfrey was his "talent scout", and that was unprecedented for him.

'So right from the start that sort of stacked the deck, you could say! But, in all fairness, the guy was sensational. I don't know what happened to him. I don't even remember his name and I never heard any more of him. He got a huge ovation from the audience and he was the winner of the show by far according to the applause meter. Mr Godfrey and most of the audience were in tears because this poor guy was an immigrant, right off the boat. He had just come to America to seek his fame and fortune. As Mr Godfrey announced that this Italian tenor fellow was the winner, he went on to speak about being seen to be fair. "This is very unusual for me to act as a talent scout," he said. "So, in fairness to all the other contestants who did a wonderful job, I'm declaring *everyone* a winner tonight! I therefore declare them all to be co-winners!" '

George's thoughts on the outcome at the time were not quite so philosophical as they became in later life. Decades later, he was able to assess the situation much more objectively. 'I had convinced myself that winning the talent contest would lead to fame and fortune. I now know that's rarely the case!'

Arthur Godfrey was personally impressed by George and considered him to be 'a rural version of Pat Boone'. On occasions he even booked the young singer as a stand-in for Pat when he was abroad. However, the big prize for a winner on the Arthur Godfrey programme was to appear the following week on network television, every morning, coast to coast. As well as the Talent Scout show, Arthur had a Wednesday-night variety show and a five-days-a-week morning show. He was the king of television in America back then. All the winning contestants were therefore invited to stay over to be on the Arthur Godfrey morning show. That was where George first met Pat Boone. He was a regular performer, as was Carmel Quinn from Ireland and the baritone Julius LaRosa.

Tinky, George and his mother (there as a chaperone) enjoyed their stay in New York City, and George made some new friends. 'I got a chance to get to know Pat Boone and found him to be a wonderful fellow. We had something in common in that we were both going to university – I was in Washington DC and Pat was attending Columbia University in New York. Of course, Pat had married Red Foley's daughter Shirley, so of course there was a Nashville connection with him!'

Arthur Godfrey invited George to stay over for a second week. 'He invited me back several times to do guest appearances on his morning show and on his Wednesday-night prime-time live network show as well. He finally let me sing "A Rose And A Baby Ruth" on one of the Wednesday night shows! I can remember how surprised I was that it didn't get the same good reaction from him as the novelty songs. He said to me that he liked my funny songs better. Still, Mr Godfrey took a liking to me and gave me a fair amount of exposure on his show.'

As the weeks went by, 'A Rose And A Baby Ruth' climbed further up the national pop music charts, until eventually it reached the Top Five. It made no dent in the country music charts at all, although George still perceived himself to be a country singer. Pressure of work soon began to encroach on his college education, and he found that recording and concert commitments prevented consistent attendance at lectures. Suddenly, exciting new doors were starting to open up for George, such as appearances on *Dick Clark's American Bandstand*, *Rhythm At The Roxy*, *The Perry Como Show* and the *Steve Allen TV Show*. These engagements gave him national publicity, followed up by 'pop-rockabilly' tours with the soon-to-be greats of rock'n'roll, Gene Vincent, Buddy Holly, the Everly Brothers, Eddie Cochran and Dion and the Belmonts.

In November of 1956, Orville Campbell arranged a ticket for Tinky to travel via Greyhound bus to attend George's next recording session at the University of North Carolina's Swain

Hall. Minted that day was Joe Tanner's 'Only One Love', together with 'If I Possessed A Printing Press'. The two songs were to complete George's brief sojourn with Colonial Records.

A month later, on a very cold December evening, came George's first major theatre booking as a headliner – set up to honour his hit song 'A Rose And A Baby Ruth'. After its initial misgivings, the chocolate bar manufacturer seized its opportunity to optimize the product's profile. In the lobby of the Brooklyn Paramount Theater in New York, amidst lavish publicity, George was invited to cut an enormous 500-pound 'Baby Ruth' candy bar.

At another booking at Christmas of 1956, back at the Brooklyn Paramount, George performed on the DJ Alan Freed's *Christmas Rock'n'Roll Show*. 'Alan used a huge package show during holiday weekends, with a cast of thousands! Alan and his rock'n'roll shows were later the subject of a very successful movie called *American Hot Wax*. I was booked to be a part of this show during the holiday season. I remember Screamin' Jay Hawkins was one of the stars and Jo Ann Campbell, with whom I later toured Australia. There was also a guy named Teddy Randazzo. All these people were very well known in the New York area and, of course, Alan Freed was the king of rock'n'roll at that time. He's the man credited with *naming* rock'n'roll.'

In April 1957, the network television debut of the new *Jimmy Dean Show* featured all the old regulars from the *Town and Country Jamboree*, including George. It was aired on CBS TV from Monday to Friday, from seven in the morning. George was an instant success. Not only could he perform and sing well in front of the cameras, but he also developed a rapport with the guests. When Jimmy holidayed in the Caribbean, George was an immediate choice as the stand-in compere. The increased television exposure fuelled the growing George Hamilton IV fan club.

At around this time, Louis Armstrong, celebrating his 40 years in the industry, hosted a week's celebration at the Roxy Theater on Broadway. He invited George onto the prestigious show as a guest star. With billboards and flyers featuring Mr Armstrong and his All Stars along with young George printed up and widely spread, the week-long run was all set to be a tremendous thrill. Then disaster struck. George caught a bad case of laryngitis and only achieved the opening night's performance.

'I was booked to play the Roxy Theater with Louis Armstrong,' he recalls. 'The Roxy Theater was on Times Square in New York City and they were booking teen singers of the day to appear with legendary folks like Louis Armstrong and his band. They hoped to draw a younger audience, I suppose. My Mom and Dad went up to New York for the special date.' George had performed on Jimmy Dean's late-night *Town and Country Jamboree* show in Washington DC the night before, so he took the overnight train and joined his parents in New York. He arrived feeling lousy and with a raging sore throat. 'I rehearsed the show with Louis Armstrong and his band, but after the opening day I had to cancel the rest of my shows there: I'd lost my voice! That was always the trouble in those days, trying to juggle my calendar to fit in as many shows as possible. Looking back on those times, I can easily see how so many of my peers developed addictions to pep pills and amphetamines, resorting to artificial means to get them through their tight touring schedules.'

From June 1957 George IV's recordings were made on the ABC Paramount label, and included 'High School Romance' and 'Everybody's Body' written by George himself. The former entered the Billboard Charts at number 80. His producer, the famous orchestra leader Don Costa, had also found the song 'Why Don't They Understand?', written by two guys from England, one being Joe 'Mr Piano' Henderson. The sleeve of George's recording of this number boasted the immortal line, 'The IV's IInd smash'! George remembers, 'I initially fell in love with the song because Tinky and I seemed to identify with the lyrics. Tinky and I were very much in love and were experiencing some of those not-so-unusual problems of getting our parents, manager, agents and friends to understand!'

George's bass-playing friend from high-school days, Henry Heitman, went with him to New York when he cut the song. It was done complete with a full orchestra and chorus, benefiting from one of Don Costa's renowned smooth arrangements. DJ Dick

Clark started to play the song every day on *American Bandstand. Billboard Magazine* commented that it was 'by far the strongest disc by the artist recently'. *Variety Magazine* said the song 'sets up an appealing country feeling that will once again win over this youngster's fan club contingent'. Pretty soon, George was once again in the nation's pop Top Ten as the single sold over half a million copies that year. In December 1957 George minted his album *On Campus* with Don Costa and his orchestra. In his estimation, however, the project 'lacked a sense of country'.

Back home in Winston-Salem, George's family and schoolfriends proudly watched from afar as their hillbilly dreamer began to make his dreams come true. The boy next door was truly achieving international fame and recognition. Yet he seemed to be moving away from his beloved country music. During those years, the pop hits just seemed to roll on and on. 'Only One Love', 'Why Don't They Understand?' and 'Now And For Always' were all teen ditties that made the pop Top 40. George Hamilton IV, a country music lover since childhood, was being sucked into an unexpected career as a teenage pop singer.

'I wasn't the only country singer being pulled into this newly evolving music phenomenon called rock'n'roll,' George explains. 'There were many of us "boys from the South" who – it if hadn't been for Elvis – would have been straight, true-blue country singers. And that list included Conway Twitty, Carl Perkins, Buddy Holly, Wanda Jackson, the Everly Brothers, Bobby Bare, Jerry Lee Lewis, Pat Boone, Roy Orbison, Brenda Lee, Don Gibson, Johnny Burnette and many others. Elvis's success simply opened the floodgates for kids from the South who played guitar!'

George was never, in his own view, a genuine rock'n'roller, yet his recordings were being featured on rock'n'roll shows, so agents started to book him with the rock acts on major concert tours throughout the world. Despite his regret at being pushed away from country music, such opportunities were certainly not something to complain about. George says he felt somewhat out of place, but he took a liking to many of the people he met. Buddy Holly and others like him, for example, were gentle guys to whom

George could relate very well. 'We all seemed to hit it off perfectly. We were willing pawns in the exciting phenomenon that was to revolutionize show business in the latter part of the fifties. All of us kids may have been green, but each had artistic, creative aptitudes. Our hearts and souls were wrapped up in the music. Screaming young girls were common at the concerts, of course, but I honestly have to admit that my ballad style, unlike that of Elvis, never generated any of that! Even way back then, I was being groomed as "Gentleman George".'

Nonetheless, George could not settle into the hype as he found himself being pushed and pulled in all kinds of directions. He was never entirely comfortable with that rock'n'roll scene. This was not the kind of direction he wanted to follow. His sights were on Nashville, not Broadway. 'What I really wanted was to be a Nashville-based country singer. But I wasn't! My records were blasting the pop charts not the country charts.' For some time, however, it seemed impossible not to go with the flow. Pop music opportunities continued to pour into his manager's office. He recorded a historic single, 'Teen Commandments', with fellow stars Paul Anka and Johnny Nash. Then, from 5 April to 1 June 1958, George embarked on a tour billed as 'The Biggest Show of Stars'. That, he felt, was a somewhat presumptuous title.

'But wow! What a package show that was! Promoted by Irvin Feld, we travelled in two Greyhound buses. Those Greyhounds were nothing like the touring coaches of today, let me tell you! Sam Cooke, Clyde McPhatter, LaVerne Baker, Frankie Avalon, Paul Anka, Bobby Darin, the Midnighters, Jackie Wilson, Buddy Holly, Jimmie Rodgers, the Everly Brothers and others – they were all there, along with little ol' me! We travelled around for two months, coast to coast across the USA and Canada.

'On the road, an interesting bond developed between the black and white performers. It seemed that whenever the Everly Brothers, Buddy Holly, Jimmie Rodgers and I returned to our dressing rooms, having been out for a hot dog or whatever, our guitars would invariably be in the hands of Sam Cooke, Clyde McPhatter and Jackie Wilson. These great black entertainers all seemed to like country music. They'd likely be strumming away on our guitars singing Hank Williams songs! We never had any problems in a racial sense – we all got along real great and the music was a common denominator. That was until we got to the South, below the Mason-Dixon Line.

'I remember very well when we first arrived in the deep South. We had to take the black entertainers to the "black side of town", to be checked into a somewhat seedy-looking motel. The white musicians and entertainers were transported to a much better class of motel on the "white side". That was really my first strong indication that something was awry in America as far as civil rights were concerned. It made a profound impression on me and is probably why I later became such a fan of John F. and Robert Kennedy. I admired them because they were such leaders in the civil rights movement of the early sixties.

'One time, Sam Cooke and I were in a taxi in Atlanta heading for our concert. We were stopped by a policeman and the taxi driver was given a ticket. When I asked the taxi driver if he'd been speeding, he said, "No I wasn't. I was driving an integrated taxi." In other words, he was given a citation for letting a black man and a white man ride together in his taxi! This may be hard to believe today, but it really did happen!'

The tour was a great success, and George was home just in time for his wedding to Tinky on 7 June. Less comfortable times were in store for George a few months later. He was admitted to hospital for surgery to correct a congenital lung disorder. In his late teens George had developed a lung condition called spontaneous pneumothorax, which meant that on occasion either of his lungs would 'spring a leak' and let air into his chest cavity. This started to occur fairly frequently and soon both lungs were springing leaks intermittently.

At Winston-Salem's Baptist Hospital in the fall of 1958, Dr Frank Johnston performed pneumothoracotomy surgery on George because both his lungs had sprung air leaks at the same time and were both partially collapsed. At that time, this type of surgery was considered to be pretty pioneering, and the operation was full of risks. George recalls his brush with near tragedy. 'I do remember people saying that they thought they'd lost me during the lung surgery. They thought I'd died on the operating table.' The *Washington Post* and *Times Herald* recorded the singer saying in jest, 'It didn't help one bit. I still sound as bad as ever!'

At the end of 1958, some great news came through which took George's mind right off his lungs. He was chosen to host the morning *Jimmy Dean Show* spot for more than a month. The following April, the *George Hamilton IV TV Show* debuted and ran for 13 weeks. Always down to earth, the now pregnant Tinky heard about the impending television show in a phone call from her excited husband, but was more concerned with the other priorities pressing upon her. 'That's fine, George,' she said calmly. 'Now, when are you coming home for supper?'

Yet still, through all the hype, hit records and fantastic tour dates, George was frustrated deep down. 'That wasn't where I wanted to be! There was no real fulfilment. Was I grateful? Yes – but not fulfilled. As far as I was concerned, it was all just a big detour on my way to the Grand Ole Opry.'

'Things are going well for you, George. Don't kick a gift horse in the mouth!' This was a strong rebuke from his manager, Connie B. Gay. He knew of George's nagging frustration and craving desire to 'go country', but as a sharp-eyed businessman he had no sympathy for such dreams. He was an opportunist who wanted to make hay while the sun shone in the fast-growing teenage music field of the late fifties. (Later he did go on to become the founding President of the Country Music Association, but in the fifties it was hard-nosed business all the way.) 'I don't wanna hear you expressing too much disdain for the pop scene,' he said firmly. 'You're plumb lucky to have Top Ten records and bookings by the score coming in.'

Looking back over the years, of course, George is thankful for the help he received. 'I must express my gratitude to Orville Campbell and John D. Loudermilk for giving me my first hit song. Also to my manager Connie B. Gay for setting my feet firmly on the show-biz stairway to success. These three gentlemen were visionaries!' Orville Campbell passed away in June 1989 while George was in England as a guest singer with Dr Billy Graham's *Mission England* tour. He was deeply upset not to be able to attend the funeral service.

Those early, heady years could have provided great moral pitfalls for George. Indeed, he could have followed the same tragic path to ruin trodden by many of his peers. 'I praise the Lord for his providential care,' says George now. 'The temptations of women, booze and pills for the most part passed me by. Sure, there were female fans, but they always wanted to mother me rather than anything else! I did drink a lot of beer in those days and occasionally took some 'keep awake' pills on those long, exhausting, all-night drives to concerts. The drug culture hadn't really developed in the music scene at that stage, however. Mercifully, I was never hooked – and I never liked hard liquor. When I tried it in college it just made me violently sick. The nearest I got was Bristol Cream Sherry during my early touring days in Britain! Sadly, many of my colleagues didn't make it, but I'm so grateful that I can look back now as a *survivor* of those crazy days.'

CHAPTER 5

CLOSE ENCOUNTERS OF THE EGO KIND

> I've seen them come and go and I've seen a lot of great ones, but I've never seen a greater guy all the way around than George Hamilton IV.
>
> Billy Byrd (guitarist, Nashville, Tennessee)

DURING THOSE 'CRAZY DAYS', George's busy touring schedule and increasing success brought him into daily contact with the pop and rock stars most fans could only dream of meeting. Many of them stopped by at the Hamilton home if they were passing through the town. One of the highlights of George's brother Cabot's teenage years was a visit from his hero Gene Krupa, the famous solo drummer. No doubt the neighbours kept an eager eye out for the latest celebrity to pay a visit to the Hamilton household, and autograph hunters would be sure to try to catch Buddy Holly popping in for some home comforts while out on his travels.

Soon the mailman became all too familiar with Winston-Salem's home-grown hero, as 'A Rose And A Baby Ruth' began to scale the dizzy heights of the Billboard Charts. Fan mail began to flood in. Letters, photos, teddy bears, flowers and Baby Ruth candy bars seemed to come by the truck-load. The first chapters of the official George Hamilton IV Fan Club opened in Winston-Salem and Chapel Hill, and produced newsletters, photographs and press releases, telling the tales behind the songs and concerts.

George was just one star among many, however, and he has vivid recollections of the great personalities he worked with over the years. Good and bad, funny and sad, here are just some of his best memories.

Small in stature but big on talent, Brenda Lee, 'Little Miss Dynamite', was a child prodigy. Musically, Brenda cut her professional teeth on country songs like 'Jambalaya', but it was not long before she found success in the pop charts with songs such as 'Sweet Nothin's' and 'Jingle Bell Rock'. Then came rock concert bookings – most notably with a teen balladeer from North Carolina called George Hamilton IV. Their shared Nashville roots brought the two young stars into a natural kinship.

Brenda and George were scheduled to appear at the State Theater in Hertford, Connecticut, with perhaps the most colourful character of the early rock'n'roll years, Little Richard. Brenda and George looked forward to meeting and working with this cult hero. As they chatted backstage before the show, their attention was caught by the sight of a super-sleek limousine that drifted smoothly up to the stage door. Everyone backstage watched open-mouthed as a smartly dressed chauffeur stepped out of the car and proceeded to unroll a luxurious red carpet from the vehicle to the door. As he straightened up the carpet with a white-gloved hand, the chauffeur picked off the loose threads with meticulous care.

Brenda and George looked at each other in disbelief. The chauffeur ceremoniously opened the door of the Cadillac and Little Richard emerged, wearing an ermine cape around his shoulders and a crown on his head. 'You know, Brenda,' murmured George in amazement, 'I do believe that our friend Little Richard *sincerely* considers himself to be the "King of Rock'n'Roll"!' Brenda stifled a giggle as the star swept regally through the stage door like some visiting potentate and disappeared into his dressing room without a backward glance.

'George, do you think we should introduce ourselves to him?' asked Brenda once she had straightened her face. George was lost for words. He had never seen anything quite like this. He stepped forward and knocked gently on the dressing room door. Immediately a high-pitched voice responded, 'Come on in baby! I got what you need!'

Not knowing what to expect, George cautiously opened the door – and there in front of the mirror sat the King of Rock'n'Roll, having his hair dressed in curlers. The smell of hair lacquer hung thickly in the confined space. Back in the fifties, this was outrageous. Men just did *not* curl their hair, not even in show business. They went to the barber; hairdressers were for the women. George remained lost for words!

Looking back today, George considers that Little Richard was a one-off model to whom appropriate credit should be given for his contribution to popular music history. Before Elvis, the Beatles or the Rolling Stones, there was Little Richard! His outstanding repertoire was borrowed by many of the greats who followed him, including Elvis Presley and Pat Boone – songs like 'Tutti Frutti' and 'Rip It Up', for instance, were standard songs for Elvis in his formative years. In George's opinion, Little Richard was a great pioneer of rock'n'roll music – and a larger-than-life character into the bargain.

George's first encounter with Buddy Holly was in Norfolk, Virginia, at a rockabilly show about a year before Buddy died. He discovered that Buddy was another shy, gentle person – like Eddie Cochran and Roy Orbison, both of whom he had already met.

'Hi, Buddy!' George spoke politely as a busy Buddy Holly paused in his guitar-tuning routine and raised his bespectacled face to the visitor. 'I'm George IV and they've put me in the dressing room next door to you.' George did not want to be a pest; he was simply anxious to be sociable with his new colleague.

'Oh hi, George! It's good to meet you … I sure enjoy your music!' Buddy's reply was delivered with a friendly grin and a Texas drawl.

As they chatted on, it dawned on George that the customary abrasive rock-rebel image was grossly misplaced with reference to Mr Holly. 'Far from being rebellious,' George recalls, 'Buddy Holly was a sensitive, caring young gentleman who was easy to get along with.'

Buddy Holly was an 'all-action' show-biz extrovert onstage, but offstage he was warm towards others and also quite introverted, with no evidence of an ego problem whatsoever. Chuck Berry, on the other hand, was something else!

On a journey to Australia in 1959, when George was to participate in a rock'n'roll tour of Melbourne and Sydney, the exhausting and bumpy flight from Los Angeles seemed to take forever. Sitting back in the main section of the plane, George was woken from a doze by the sound of bluegrass music drifting out from the first-class seats.

George caught the eye of an air stewardess. 'Miss, could I slip up from here to first class to see where that country music's coming from, please?' He had his suspicions about the source of the disturbance.

'Why, of course sir,' the stewardess replied, smiling soothingly at George's fellow passengers, who were showing signs of irritation at having their peace disturbed.

Opening the dividing curtain, George stepped gingerly through into the plush first-class compartment. There before him was Chuck Berry, his seat almost horizontal, his long legs stretched out as far as space would allow. The flight was not very full, but the blaring music was creating quite a stir nonetheless. Perched precariously on the stomach of the apparently slumbering Chuck Berry was a small portable record player, the source of the commotion. It was a cheap make, typical of the machines teenagers carried around in the fifties. It was just a little box with a handle on it, but it was making a big noise!

Blaring out from this modest contraption were the sounds of a bluegrass album by the Louvin Brothers entitled *Tragic Songs Of Life*. The Alabama duo's high nasal sound and the colourful White House emblem on the Capitol record label spinning round on the turntable were both familiar to George. Anyone who knew the Louvins knew that their hillbilly sound was about as 'earthy' as it gets. It was a far cry from rock'n'roll, or even rockabilly music. It was certainly out of place in first class, and entirely unwelcome on an aeroplane so late at night!

George chuckled to himself as he walked up the narrow aisle. Chuck opened one eye, apparently oblivious to all the fuss he was creating, disdainful of the irritated stares from his fellow passengers. Introducing himself to this famous personality, George said with a smile, 'I'm sure surprised to hear you playing bluegrass music, Chuck!'

Chuck's eyes flashed as he responded sharply, 'Why's that? Why assume I don't like country music, boy?'

George was surprised at the retort and recognized that he had inadvertently touched a raw nerve. 'Well,' he said carefully, 'I guess, Chuck, I'd always thought of you in a different way, musically speaking.'

George's conciliatory tone obviously did the trick and the stern expression left Chuck's face. Relaxing back into his comfortably horizontal position, he responded, 'George, I love country music! Have you ever listened to ma song "Johnny B. Good"? All it is, boy, is country music with a *beat*! Just 'cause I'm a black person don't mean I can't sing country music! Besides, George, didn't ya know Hank Williams learned to play guitar from a guy called Tee Tot, a black street-singer?'

'Sure, I'd heard that story!' George smiled again, more confident now. He seemed to be making a new friend.

Chuck grinned back. 'Well, listen again to my voice – I got as much country soul as any of you white boys!' Then he stopped smiling. 'Let me tell you the difference between you and me, white boy: I've been to the Grand Ole Opry too, but when I went, I stood out in a side alley and listened. I tried to buy a ticket and was refused!'

Chuck's words cut through George like a knife. This was a true indictment against his white-dominated culture. He had often seen discrimination against black people in his home state of North Carolina, and he was appalled to think that the talented Chuck Berry had been refused entrance to the Grand Ole Opry simply because of the colour of his skin. Returning to his own seat, George's feelings were decidedly mixed. He was still amused by the scene he had just witnessed – well-heeled business travellers subjected to bluegrass music by a laid-back singer with a record player on his stomach! – but he had also been challenged morally. One thought went round and round in his head. 'Why should I deserve better treatment merely because I was born white?'

Chuck and George struck up a close friendship during their tour down under and George was sure it all originated from that plane-ride encounter. It was during the tour that news came through of the deaths of their mutual friends Buddy Holly, Ritchie Valens and the Big Bopper, all killed in a tragic plane crash.

The friendship caused great consternation back home, however. George's old-fashioned mother-in-law was apparently shocked when George wrote about his new friend in a letter home. And when George later passed round photos of the tour, some shameful comments were made by George's Southern relatives and friends. 'It just doesn't appear fitting for a white guy to be rooming with a black guy!' was a typical comment. George was immensely saddened. Old Confederacy attitudes were taking a long time to die out in the 'land of the brave and the free'.

On their Australian tour George discovered that Chuck Berry could never be described as a humble individual. A great talent, he would allow no one to push him around and – quite rightly, George thought – he expected to be treated as the equal of anyone else. He refused to be treated as a second-class citizen.

At a press conference in Melbourne, Chuck and George shared exposure with Bobby Darin, Jo Anne Campbell and Johnny O'Keefe, the Australian teenage sensation of the day. To George's great surprise, Chuck Berry responded to one question with a quotation from Shakespeare. He was an English Literature Major, after all. Over those two weeks in Australia, Chuck surprised his new friend several times with his intellect and knowledge. A very bright human being, he challenged George about his inherited white prejudices. The Australian adventure was a brand-new experience for the previously closeted product of the South.

Years later, George was pleased when someone sent him a page out of Chuck's autobiography, in which he recalled the Australian tour and in particular the incident on the flight out. Chuck's remarks were made with typically dry humour, as George recalls. 'Chuck wrote that Bobby Darin and Jo Anne Campbell were always cuddled together in a passionate embrace, so he was left to converse with George Hamilton IV – who proceeded to give him the full history of Georges I, II and III! I think it's funny he should remember that. I like Chuck Berry, but I must admit that I'm in awe of him. I perceive that he holds in a great, pent-up anger beneath his intelligence and creativity. A powerful personality, he isn't the kind of individual you'd want to get on the wrong side of!'

Bobby 'Dream Lover' Darin, George's colleague on that Australian tour, always wanted to be another Frank Sinatra. Motivated by a somewhat inflated ego, he used to bore George and the others with his continual boasts. 'I'll be a legend before I'm 25!' he would say. George sincerely believed that Bobby Darin had the talent to back up such claims, but sadly, he did not live long enough to fulfil his grandiose plans.

On the return flight from Australia George sat next to Bobby. Bobby was peering out of the window while George was dozing off in an aisle seat. Suddenly Bobby poked George painfully in the ribs and said abruptly, 'Hey, Hamilton, d'you wanna know somethin'?'

George stirred slowly, raised his eyebrows and mumbled, 'What's that, Bob?'

'I'm great! Yeah, I'm great, man!' Bobby blurted out this boast in all seriousness and without further qualification.

George's Southern culture had always majored on modesty. He was therefore dumbstruck, as he emerged fully from his doze, to catch the wholly serious expression on Bobby's face. Bobby was not joking.

George smiled and settled down again. 'Sure, Bobby! I know you may think you're great, but I've been touring with you for two weeks and I've seen how human you really are! Even *you've* got feet of clay – but I ain't gonna be arguing with ya. What the heck, anyway...'

Bobby, however, was suddenly angry at George's offhand tone. '*What* is so funny, Hamilton?' he snapped.

Seeing how furious he was and not wanting to become too deeply entrenched in a pointless argument, George replied placidly, 'Yea, sure, Bobby. Yea, I agree, you're great, man! Yea, you're great!'

George was astonished when Bobby nodded and replied without any trace of irony, 'Trouble is, Hamilton, the dumb, stupid *public* just don't recognize how great I am!' Bobby Darin was aware that his days were numbered. He suffered from a heart problem, and was keen to achieve stardom as quickly as possible, fearing the onset of middle age.

Soon after the tour of Australia, Bobby Darin's 'Mack The Knife' became a major hit and Bobby was suddenly elevated to playing the big supper clubs and night clubs. He was booked to perform at the Casino Royale in Washington DC. George knew Bobby was in town, but had not got round to going to see his show. One day the phone rang at the Hamilton apartment in Arlington, Virginia and George heard a very strange voice on the other end of the line. Speaking in a 'Mafia godfather' type of accent, the caller started making threats.

'I just wanted you to know that we know where you live and we know about that little kid you just had.' Their first son Peyton was only a month or so old at that time. The intimidating voice went on. 'We're coming after you! We're gonna get you, man!'

George turned as pale as a sheet. Tinky said he looked as if he was having a heart attack. Panicked questions raced through his mind. 'Why are they coming after me? Why are they after my kid?'

A few moments after George had hung up the phone, it rang again. He picked it up in trembling hands, only to find a laughing Bobby Darin on the line. 'Well, I got you!'

Looking back with some displeasure, George sees the joke as being a very sour one. 'He sure did get me! Bobby had scared me as bad as I've ever been scared.'

Bobby Darin lost his battle for life not long after those heady days of touring with Chuck Berry and George IV. Although he had designs on a star-studded career that would outshine even Sinatra, in the end he just ran out of time.

It was a dull, damp February day and George Hamilton IV had decided to use a rare patch of spare time to catch up with a few purchases. A busy Nashville shopping mall was not the first place he expected to bump into old friends, but he was in for a surprise that day when he bumped into his long-lost pal Doyle Wilburn, one half of the vocal duo known as the Wilburn Brothers.

When the two friends had caught up with each other's news over a coffee, they fell to reminiscing about times past. In their heyday the Wilburn Brothers were the unchallenged best of the 'brother duos', with the exception perhaps of the Louvin Brothers, Charlie and Ira. Mulling over old memories, George laughed. 'I remember when the Louvin boys came to play the radio show back home in Winston-Salem when I was a kid. I ran out to the highway and waited till I saw their limo with the Tennessee licence plate. Then I jumped in front of that ol' limo and waved Charlie and Ira down! You should have seen Ira's face – he was so mad, he was 'bout ready to spit!'

'Why did you flag 'em down?'

'I just *had* to tell them – as you do – that I was a country singer!'

'No way, man!' Doyle laughed out loud in the coffee shop and many customers turned round to see what the commotion was all about. George continued the tale.

'I can't believe I did such a stupid thing! The rest of the guys in that limo thought it was real funny. Charlie said he would look forward to seeing me on stage sometime, but Ira grumbled, "Yea, I guess ... *if* you ever make it!" Apparently Ira cussed me all the way to the hotel.'

'And I thought George Hamilton IV was a quiet, shy kid!' joked Doyle.

The Wilburn Brothers' biggest challenge came in the fifties from two young teenagers named Don and Phil Everly who took the pop charts by storm. 'You know, George, it seems funny to recount now,' mused Doyle, 'but those young Everly Brothers would follow us Wilburns around Nashville like puppy dogs, especially when we had our own television show. Yes sir, they sure idolized me and my brother Teddy!'

'I remember folks used to say that,' George told him. 'When they were young, they'd often wait outside the backstage door of the Grand Ole Opry for you and your brother. It's as if you cast a spell over those Everly boys...'

All too soon, George and Doyle had to say goodbye. George

was still in nostalgia mode as he pulled out of the parking lot and headed for home. He let his mind drift back over the years, to his own special memories of the Everly Brothers.

George's hit 'A Rose And A Baby Ruth' was high in the Top Ten in the cool autumn of 1956 when he found himself in Nashville for a Grand Ole Opry guest spot. He felt good as he sauntered into the comfortable Clarkston Hotel, conveniently located next to the old National Life building where WSM Radio used to broadcast. To George, it was always a joy to join the other artistes for coffee and sandwiches at the hotel.

That day, as he sipped his coffee and tucked into his hamburger, a young, rather poor-looking couple sat down at the next table. George was busy wondering to himself what they were doing in this plush Nashville hotel when suddenly the jukebox burst into action with his own song, 'A Rose And A Baby Ruth'. George was more than a little proud to hear it played in such a prestigious public place, right in the middle of Nashville. Now he had really arrived! He decided he must thank the couple accordingly.

He leaned over. 'Excuse me, did you folks play that record?' When the couple responded with smiles and friendly nods, George continued, 'Well, thank you very much. My name's George Hamilton IV. You've just selected my record!'

Their mouths dropped open in genuine surprise, then the young man spoke in a shy Southern mumble. 'We sure are privileged to meet you, Mr Hamilton. That record's our favourite! We had no idea you were in this hotel when we started the jukebox.'

About a year later, George found himself on a plane with Don and Phil Everly, heading for New Orleans where he had a date to play at the Lake Ponchetrain Park with Dick Clark. George's disc 'Why Don't They Understand?' was climbing the national pop charts at the time. This was George's first meeting with the brothers, and he soon found himself deep in conversation with Phil Everly, the more talkative of the two. He was distracted by the knowing smile on Don Everly's face, however, and soon broke off to ask, 'Don, why do you keep staring at me with that funny look?'

'You don't remember me, do you, George?' Don laughed.

'What d'you mean, Don?' asked George, bewildered. 'We've never met before, have we?'

'Oh yes we have, George! Do you remember introducing yourself to a couple in the Clarkston Hotel in Nashville about a year ago? You thanked them for playing your record on the jukebox.'

'Sure, I recall that! The couple played 'A Rose And A Baby Ruth.'

'Well George, believe it or not, I was that guy!'

Don and George both burst into laughter. 'Man, Don, you never know!' exclaimed George. 'Be careful how you treat people on the way up – 'cause you might meet them on the way down...'

The Everly Brothers became major stars following 'Bye Bye Love' and 'Wake Up Little Susie' about 12 months after that first encounter. Along with Buddy Holly, they were original inductees into the Rock and Roll Hall of Fame. 'Phil and Don Everly had a cutting edge to their winsome personalities,' George comments. 'Good looking, very talented, they knew what they wanted and where they were going, but they were never aggressive or anti-establishment.'

George's first recollection of another rock'n'roll great, Eddie Cochran, was in connection with John D. Loudermilk. By the late fifties John and George had become good friends. John had written and recorded a song called 'Sitting In The Balcony' on the Colonial label, and it had done very well. Then it was covered by a new young singer called Eddie Cochran on the Liberty label – and in George's eyes, that song put Eddie on the map.

At about the same time that Jimmy Dean's television show was being networked early in the morning by CBS, George received an Easter weekend booking at the Mastbaum Theater, Philadelphia. It was to be an out-and-out rock'n'roll show with Eddie Cochran, Gene Vincent and some other great acts. George's young brother Cabot joined him in Philadelphia for the weekend and was most impressed by the friendly way he was treated by Eddie and Gene.

Also on the show was the television producer Gene Nash from Nashville, who was also a highly creative singer and choreographer. The country stage shows that he produced always had a plush, sophisticated Las Vegas touch to them. In casual conversation over the weekend, Gene Nash related at length how interested he was in animals. This caught Eddie's ear and, once out of Gene's earshot, he made an announcement to the cast. 'Say, guys,' he said. 'You've noticed how much Gene likes animals, haven't you? He's always mouthing off about his pet cat and dog! Why don't we buy Gene an Easter bunny?'

Everyone laughed and voiced their approval, but they were only thinking of a furry toy bunny. Eddie, on the other hand, was serious about getting Gene a real *live* rabbit. The next day they all went shopping, and onstage that evening a live baby rabbit was presented to Gene. The whole cast got a kick out of the surprise, George remembers, but none more so than the kind-hearted Eddie. 'What a practical demonstration that was of the other side of the "wild man of rock'n'roll"! Eddie Cochran had a powerful onstage persona as the angry young man, yet offstage he had quiet, polite, Southern gentleman ways.'

The black-leather-clad Gene Vincent was another onstage 'wild man'. He had broken his leg in a serious motorcycle accident and in a very real sense epitomized the James Dean lifestyle of 'a rebel without a cause'. Doctors advised him to quit 'shaking' onstage while his leg healed, but, as he explained to George, he just could not help himself. 'Man, when I'm singing rock'n'roll, I've just gotta move!'

Standing in the stage wings night after night, often grimacing in sympathy, George would watch Gene perform with his Blue Caps band. Time after time, for emphasis at a particular point in his performance, Gene would smash his plaster-cast leg violently on the stage floor. 'Oh, brother! That must do real damage to your bones!' George would think to himself. 'You're pressing down on a self-destruct button, man!'

Later, George heard that the problem was serious enough to warrant steel supports to hold the leg bones together. Gene had rebroken the leg so many times that artificial support was essential. 'Gene, it seems, just couldn't contain his extrovert behaviour when it came to his performances. Looking back, it's so sad to recount that many of my peers, including Gene Vincent and Eddie Cochran, are not around today. Who knows what kind of exciting music they'd be performing if they were still alive?'

Although George Hamilton IV was a faithful country music devotee, the smooth crooner Perry Como was also among his musical heroes. Born in Canonsburg, Pennsylvania in 1912, Como started work as a self-employed barber, but had a driving ambition to sing his way to the top of the show-business ladder. A deep thinker, he once commented on his fame and fortune, 'I now have what money can buy. But what money can't buy, I've always had.' What George admired most about the great song-stylist was this kind of simple wisdom and his laid-back personality. Perry communicated in a warm and modest style, and was a significant influence on George's life back in the fifties.

In 1958, when George's version of the British song 'Why Don't They Understand?' was in the Top Ten, he was thrilled to receive an invitation to be a special guest on Como's prime-time network television show on NBC. Tinky was also a big fan of Perry Como, so she decided to join her husband on the day of the show. It was, without doubt, the most prestigious booking that George had received so far.

While George was in the rehearsal hall, Perry surprised both him and Tinky by sauntering over, dressed casually and without any kind of fanfare introduction. It was not what they had been expecting of such a huge star. Right hand extended to greet them, he said simply, 'Hi, I'm Perry Como.' As if they didn't know!

Friendly small talk ensued, and George was taken aback when Perry told him, 'I sure have enjoyed your records, George – thanks for coming this far north to do our little ol' television show!' Judging from the look in his eyes, he really meant what he said.

'Why, I'm the one who has the pleasure, Mr Como,' stammered George. 'Tink, my wife here, watches your show every week without fail!'

'I've always been a fan of yours, Mr Como,' Tinky chipped in. 'My favourite song is "Hot Diggity, Dog Diggity, Boom, What You Do To Me"! Me and the other girls at high school, we'd sing along to that song every night on the jukebox...' All three of them laughed.

'That sure was a dumb ol' title for a song!' exclaimed Perry. 'But it was popular and kind to me, so I can't complain ... and now, Mrs Hamilton, kids are singing your husband's songs on the jukebox!'

Of all the rock'n'roll greats, Jerry Lee Lewis stands out very sharply in George's memory. He certainly lived up to his reputation. Born in Farriday, Louisiana in 1935, Jerry Lee was cousin to two other famous singer-pianists, Jimmy Swaggart and Mickey Gilley. Theirs was a talented family indeed!

Jerry Lee and George were booked simultaneously on the Patti Page television show *The Great Record.* 'We had never met,' recalls George, 'but I had heard many stories about this "wild man"!' In the stressful afternoon dress rehearsal, Jerry Lee was pumping out 'Great Balls Of Fire' on the piano. Looking on was a whole phalanx of media people, making the most of their preview rights. Everyone's attention was transfixed by the contraption inside the open grand piano which puffed out bursts of flame at regular intervals – a forerunner of the smoke effects commonly used many years later.

Oklahoma-born Patti Page (whose biggest hits were 'Tennessee Waltz' and 'How Much Is That Doggie In The Window?') could not have been sweeter to George, brimful of charm and politeness. She was a dignified professional in every way. Breezing up to the rumpled Jerry Lee, when he came to the end of 'Great Balls Of Fire', Patti was intending to rehearse her hostess chat with him. While the final bursts of flame were still diminishing, she spoke in her enthusiastic hostess voice: 'My goodness, Jerry, that was marvellous! Thank you so much! It was great!'

Jerry's energetic performance had left him breathless and sweaty. His floppy hair dangled all over his face like a mop. He wasn't in the mood for sweet talk. With a wild look in his eye, he spoke sharply back at Patti. 'I hope that damn thing don't burn ma hair!'

Everyone in the room stood stock still, aghast. No one addressed the prim and proper Miss Patti Page in that language or in that tone! Patti, however, was the first to recover. She smiled sweetly and continued with her lines, like the true professional she was.

Jerry Lee Lewis was undeniably unique. George found him to be unlike anyone else he had ever met. On or offstage, he was always the same – outrageous! A born entertainer if ever there was one, he upset many on his way up. 'Yet I couldn't help but take a liking to Jerry Lee Lewis,' smiles George.

In the early eighties, when George was compering the International Country Music Festival in Wembley, England, Jerry Lee was the show's headliner. That year, the show's producer Mervyn Conn also took the Festival from London to Stockholm, Frankfurt, Zurich and Rotterdam. At five thirty one morning, the star-studded cast were all assembled at the airport for the charter flight to the next booking. Shortage of sleep and perhaps an excess of liquid refreshment the night before had taken its toll. Many eyes were red and blurry, and yawns were plentiful. George himself sat with eyes closed, only half aware of what was going on around him, waiting for the call to board the plane.

Tom Perryman, Cajun artiste Jimmy C. Newman's manager, had been very impressed with Jerry Lee's performance the previous night and started to tell him so. Jerry was stretched over his seat, apparently asleep, head resting on the back of the chair, his hair still wet from a very brief, very early shower.

'Jerry,' said Tom, 'your concert was great last night!'

Barely raising his head, Jerry Lee responded through tight lips. 'Thank you kindly, man!'

The curt answer did not seem to satisfy Tom. 'Yes, really, Jerry Lee ... you don't realize how great you were on stage!' George opened his eyes, curious to see how Jerry would react to this persistent disturbance. Tom continued to burble. 'Let me tell ya, Jerry, watching you from the wings I'm now convinced you are the greatest entertainer I have *ever* seen! You were brilliant, buddy!'

'Yea, yea, thank you, man!' Jerry said, impatience creeping into his tone. He turned his back on Tom and shut his eyes again.

Tom, oblivious to the vibes, just carried on. 'Yea, Jerry, I've seen 'em all come and go – Hank Williams, Jim Reeves – but you're the finest entertainer I have *ever* seen onstage. I've never seen anyone thrill me more!'

Stimulated at last, Jerry Lee had heard enough. He spun round to Tom. Peering over his dark glasses, Jerry Lee exclaimed in a loud voice for everyone to hear, 'Yeah, man! Just show me the piano, give me the money, and kiss my ****!' And thus another conversation was ended in typical Jerry Lee Lewis fashion.

Singers and rock stars are not the only famous figures to stand out in George's memory. He first remembers hearing about his namesake George Hamilton, the Hollywood actor, in the late fifties. A show-business columnist in a New York newspaper wrote an article about how George Hamilton was 'romancing Wendy Vanderbilt'. Somebody sent a copy of the article to Tinky, who was still in university at that time. Tinky immediately called George and asked the obvious question. 'What's this about you romancing Wendy Vanderbilt?'

George reassured his alarmed girlfriend and then did some hurried checking around. He found out that there was a wealthy young actor named George Hamilton who had just arrived on the Hollywood scene. Soon after that, George (the actor) appeared in a movie with Robert Mitchum called *Home from the Hills*.

In 1959, George's tour of Australia with Chuck Berry and Bobby Darin took place at the same time as Anthony Perkins (star of *Psycho*) was down under filming a movie called *On the Beach* with Fred Astaire and other famous names. George admired Anthony Perkins. 'I heard that he was in the same town as us working on the movie, so I called the hotel and asked for his room. The desk clerk said she would pass a message on to Mr Perkins and he called me back, said hello and invited me over. I was surprised he'd heard of me. When I got to his room, he answered the door and looked a little startled when he saw me. Of course, it was the actor George Hamilton he'd heard of, and I certainly wasn't what he'd expected! But he was very cordial and invited me in. He had a guitar on the bed and he mentioned to me that he played guitar, but had never learned to play with a guitar pick. I think I gave him a few tips...

'I had a feeling he was sizing me up, checking me out. He was very quiet, but friendly. During the course of our conversation, he asked me if it was true that I'd auditioned for the role of Hank Williams in the movie *Your Cheatin' Heart*. I hadn't. Apparently he'd heard that I'd been invited to play the part of Hank – and he'd also been up for the same role! This was all news to me. We had a great time talking together, though, and I was very impressed by Tony Perkins.'

In fact, when Audrey Williams (Hank's former wife) eventually put together the film *Your Cheatin' Heart* in the sixties, she chose the actor George Hamilton to play the lead role of Hank. He came to Nashville at a time when George IV was out of town. George remembers that the actor was asked to appear on the Ralph Emery morning television show on WSM-TV. 'He met some of the Nashville folks and, of course, my name came up and that caused a little bit of a stir because of the confusion between us!'

The first time George IV actually met George the actor was in Boston, Massachusetts sometime in the sixties. George was there for a country music package show and he was checking into the Boston Hilton. The man at the hotel desk expressed some surprise. 'Well, this is interesting! We've got two George Hamiltons here today – the movie actor's in the coffee shop over there.'

The country singer sauntered off to the coffee shop and spied his namesake sitting at a table with a young singer named Jimmy Boyd. Jimmy gained fame with the song 'I Saw Mama Kissing Santa Claus' and later also became an actor. George the actor was in Boston performing in a 'summer stock' production at one of the theatres there.

'As I entered the room and started across to his table,' George recalls, 'I'll never forget how he looked up and started shaking his head. I could just hear him saying, "Oh no! Here he comes!" I went over and introduced myself. He was very friendly and gracious. I don't know if he was just trying to make me feel good, but he said he often got confused with me in Hollywood and many people had asked him to sing "Abilene" at parties. He said he did play the guitar and had learned "Abilene", and now, when people asked him to sing it, he just sang it rather than try to explain the confusion again! We had a good time talking.'

Some years later, the movie star was invited to guest on the *Arthur Smith Television Show* in Charlotte. While they were taping the show, George IV asked him if there was a number after his name too. He clearly remembers the actor's reply. It was a pretty good line: 'No, George – my father told me to go out into the world and make a name for myself, not a number!'

'At the time,' George remembers, 'the actor George was "squiring around" Lynda Bird Johnson, President Lyndon B. Johnson's daughter, and later the actress Elizabeth Taylor. It seemed as if George was always in the newspapers and, more often than not, the numeral IV appeared at the end of his name in the headlines! I guess people assumed we were one and the same, especially in British newspapers. Often, when any reports were printed about George romancing Elizabeth Taylor, the journalists would sort of leap to the conclusion that it was me...

'Actually. George the actor is also a singer and a very good one. He recorded for a while for ABC Paramount, and that caused even more confusion. On one of my greatest hits compilations, *George Hamilton IV – The ABC Collection*, they even included three or four tracks by George the actor! When I told him about that he said to me, "Get me a copy of that album. My lawyers would like to hear that!" I really like George. He's the ultimate leading man, and I guess he's almost as famous for all the ladies he's romanced as he is for all his movies.'

The confusion between the two men was naturally enhanced by the fact that George the actor was chosen to play the part of country singer Hank Williams in the film *Your Cheatin' Heart*. It really set the seal on the mix-up! Purporting to be Hank's life story, the film caused a certain amount of controversy. Hank's son, and others who knew the singer very well, maintained that at best the film was 'partly truth and partly fiction'. Hank's former wife Audrey was closely involved with the film, and George comments, 'I guess Audrey sort of "tailored" that to suit her own designs and wishes, because it put her in a very favourable light and in some ways made Hank the villain of the piece. I never knew Hank Williams in person, although I knew and liked Audrey, and I have no special information about their married life. It sounded like one of those situations where they couldn't live together but they couldn't live apart. They were two strong-willed people and I guess that led to tension between them.'

George believes that it was John D. Loudermilk who first introduced him to Audrey Williams. John was by then a hit-writer for Acuff-Rose Publishing, which also published all Hank Williams' songs. 'Soon after we moved to Nashville,' he remembers, 'John invited me to go with him over to "Miss Audrey's" house for a little social gathering. I found Audrey to be very gracious, friendly, warm and a very open person. She didn't come across as putting on airs; instead she seemed very earthy. I remember Audrey referred to everyone as "honey" and "darling". She was a very outgoing, vivacious lady.

'I always had the feeling that she wanted to be a singer like her husband Hank. She had been part of his radio show for a long time and, I think, had joined in on some personal appearances. Unfortunately, in the view of many people, singing wasn't her gift, but I don't think she was content to be in the wings, to be just "Mrs Hank Williams". She tried very hard to be a star. I remember one time, I happened to be hosting the Grand Ole Opry down at the Ryman Auditorium on one of the show evenings. Audrey performed that night with her All Girl Band, featuring some very talented young women musicians, although Audrey was the leader. I think that was the first time I'd seen an all-girl band!

'The next time I remember being around Audrey was when I was on the Louisiana Hayride in the early 1960s. Hank Junior was still a teenager then, but he was also on the show. Audrey was there with him and I remember Hank Junior was all dressed up just like his daddy used to be, in a white suit decorated with black musical notes and a white stetson. Audrey was resplendent in a cowgirl outfit with fringes and rhinestones and, of course, her silver hair. She was quite a striking-looking woman and she looked more like one of the performers than simply Hank Junior's mom! Audrey always carried herself well.

'As I recall, Hank Junior sang some of his daddy's songs that night, complete with some of Hank Senior's voice inflections. I've never seen a more miserable young man. You could tell that he didn't enjoy being the "heir to the legend" or the "keeper of the flame"! That's what Audrey had in mind, I believe. She wanted Hank Junior to carry the torch and look and sing as much like Hank Williams Senior as possible. You could see that Hank Junior just didn't want to do that, though. He wanted to be his own man.

'To his credit, as soon as he got a little older and was able to untie the apron strings, Hank Junior got out on the road with his own band and his own bus, away from his mom. He certainly blossomed into quite a different person and certainly enjoyed his onstage performances then. He seemed to get a big kick out of playing as many instruments as possible onstage. You could tell he was heavily influenced by "Southern rock". He was more interested in that than in trying to be a rerun of his father. I know he respects and loves his dad and his legacy, but he was determined to be his own man.'

Audrey Williams and her business partner Vic Lewis were also involved in a couple of 'stand up and sing' movies that were filmed in Nashville with country music singers taking part. Some critics, none too impressed with the films, called them 'cartoons'! George remembers the movies with a wry smile. 'Audrey and Vic Lewis produced one called *Country Music on Broadway*. I don't recall if I was in that one or not, but I was certainly in the movie called *Second Fiddle to a Steel Guitar*. It was financed and produced in Nashville, and was mostly just an excuse to get country stars of the day to sing their latest hit within a very thin sort of storyline. None of us actually did any *acting* in it – we just sang our songs. For many of us the experience was like a precursor to what became "country music television".

'I also appeared in a film called *Hootenanny Hoot* which was shot in California. Tinky went out there with me to film that. We were only there for a day or two and I sang "Abilene" in that film. It was a bit more of a real musical production. There were some fairly well-known actors and actresses too, or at least they were up-and-coming performers. Johnny Cash and Sheb Wooley were also involved, along with other music people from the "folk revival" days of the early sixties. It was kind of exciting to be on the Hollywood soundstage. When I went into "make-up" on the first morning, Debbie Reynolds was in the chair beside me! In those days they were filming two or three different movies at the same time, so it was possible to run across famous movie actors and actresses in the make-up room or the cafeteria. Tinky and I were quite thrilled to be spending a couple of days in "Movieland".'

Through the years, the paths of Hollywood and Nashville have often crossed. George clearly remembers his encounter with the tough-guy movie star Robert Mitchum. The Hollywood legend came to Nashville to do some recording for Fred Foster, the man who had 'discovered' George IV during the days of 'A Rose And A Baby Ruth'. By the time the celebrated movie star came to Music City, Fred Foster was flying high with his own record label, Monument Records. Robert Mitchum was his latest signing, and came to record for Fred's label sometime after the film *Thunder Road* had appeared. Robert Mitchum had sung the theme song for the film.

'Robert was a pretty good country singer,' George comments. 'He was interested in a song by John D. Loudermilk called "Bad News", which I later recorded myself. The song seemed to fit Robert's image and personality. John D. Loudermilk was out of town, so he asked me to drop by the studio and take Robert Mitchum the demo tape and lyrics. I got a chance to meet Robert and we had our picture taken together. He later autographed the photo for me, with the words, "Dear George, if I didn't please you baby, goodness only knows I tried. Warmest regards, Bob"! Robert Mitchum surprised me. He was very gentlemanly, warm, friendly and more of an intellectual than I'd thought from his films. Apparently he was a very well-read, very serious man and not at all like the "heavies" he often played.'

Moving away from the distractions of Hollywood, no collection of memories from those heady musical days would be complete without some picture of Elvis. George personally found Elvis Presley to be likeable and friendly, and not at all eccentric, abrasive or rebellious. He speaks with great affection for the huge star who shared the same record label.

'The sensation-seeking media, and some of the "establishment", displayed undue paranoia about his so-called outrageous charisma. They considered him and his music to be a threat to the morals of young America. True, he had a wild, sensual, almost animal magnetism in his stage act, yet he revered his parents, he was respectful of women, and he always called older people "Sir" or "Ma'am". Elvis even served his time in the army for Uncle Sam without attempting to shirk his responsibilities. Musically, however, he revolutionized his generation. He represented a monumental watershed in the history of popular music. Elvis dramatically cracked through the musically banal wall which had been built by the show-business establishment of the day. He unleashed a torrent of fresh new talent from a host of young Southerners who picked guitar and sang – and I was one of them!'

George does not pretend to have been a great friend and confidant of Elvis Presley but, like many, he says he was deeply influenced by him, and will carry that impression with him for ever. The 'Elvis influence' all started during George's freshman year at college, when he had the opportunity to attend a country music show at the Memorial Auditorium in Raleigh, North Carolina. He managed to talk a couple of his classmates into going, and fortunately one of them had wheels! The auditorium was a 30-minute drive from the college. 'It's worth noting,' he says, 'that it was Hank Snow "the Singing Ranger" who spotted Elvis Presley's great talent early on, and in fact he went to Memphis to convince Gladys and Vernon Presley to let their son sign with RCA. Elvis and his parents were massive Hank Snow fans and in Elvis's early onstage photos, he's often pictured playing a guitar covered with a hand-tooled leather case, exactly like the Singing Ranger's.'

Scheduled to appear that night in the Raleigh Auditorium were Hank Snow himself, the Louvin Brothers, Justin Tubb and Benny Martin. It was a typical country music package. As they stood outside the Auditorium, George's gang gazed at the billboard sign advertising the show. At the bottom they noticed, in tiny letters, the words, 'Introducing from Tupelo, Mississippi, "The Hillbilly Cat", Elvis Presley!'

George and his adolescent friends were tickled by this. 'Elvis Presley – what a name!' they laughed. 'Sounds like a girl's name!' Unknown to young George and his friends, the newcomer Elvis had just recorded a couple of modestly successful 78 records for the Sun label, operating out of Memphis. The new phenomenon of rockabilly music was already threatening to break out worldwide, and to rock the security of the well-established country music scene into the bargain.

That night at the Raleigh country concert the audience were in for a shock. Backing up the unknown 'Hillbilly Cat' were Bill Black on bass fiddle and Scotty Moore on guitar. After Elvis was announced, with a good deal of ceremony, the stage curtains were pulled towards each other until they were almost touching. Suddenly through the narrow gap jumped an outrageous-looking figure with greased-back hair and long sideburns, dressed in a pink and black suit. The stunned audience of country music fans gasped. They had not been expecting this! In the mid-fifties, this kind of flashy attire was only associated with rhythm and blues performers such as Jimmy Reed, Sam Cooke and Little Richard. Elvis was a violent contrast to Messrs Snow and Tubb, that was for sure.

'My goodness ... he's *real* different!' George could not drag his eyes from the brightly lit stage. The Elvis charisma was already charming the audience, despite their initial shock at his appearance. 'Elvis Presley just don't look like any country performer that I've ever seen, by any stretch of the imagination!' George's friends shared his feelings.

George describes the ensuing performance: 'The "Hillbilly Cat" started to shake from head to toe as he energetically strummed on his guitar. He soon snapped the strings that night as he pounded through punchy songs more associated with Little Richard than a country music show. The auditorium exploded as the audience became captivated and mesmerized by this guy's antics. Some people were standing on their seats, others screamed and hollered. Many others jived in the aisles. The conservative town of Raleigh had never seen the like!

'From personal experience, I can totally reject the claim that Colonel Parker [Elvis's manager] conspired with the media in creating the "Elvis myth". Single-handedly, solely through talent and charisma, and without hype or gimmicks, Elvis took over the show that night ... he took over the whole building! I had never seen grown people acting with such abandonment. It must have been so difficult for Hank Snow to follow such an uproar. Apparently, by the end of that tour, Hank wasn't even trying! Instead, he closed the first half and allowed Elvis to finish the show. Never again was Elvis Presley to be billed as a supporting act to *anyone*!'

After the powerful show, George ventured backstage to congratulate this new phenomenon. Elvis was leaning lazily against a wall next to his modest dressing room, combing his slick black hair. 'Elvis,' he said enthusiastically, 'that show was magnificent – I thought you were tremendous!'

'Thank ya, man ... appreciate it!' As Elvis responded with modesty, George noticed hair oil dripping from the back of his neck, staining the back of his colourful shirt. His flashy appearance was by no means neat and tidy!

It was hard to imagine back then what a superstar the young Elvis was destined to become in hardly any time at all. Within a year of that introductory encounter, Elvis Presley returned to Raleigh, but this time he was the undisputed star of the show. This time, at the Carolina Theater, he was again surrounded by Grand Ole Opry stars, including Mother Maybelle and the Carter Sisters. The difference was that it was now 'The Elvis Presley Show'.

Elvis assimilated country, rhythm and blues and gospel traditions into his special sound. George is convinced that single-handedly, Elvis created a whole new musical art form. 'The singer Webb Pierce was standing in the wings at the Ryman Auditorium, apparently, when Elvis Presley first performed at the Grand Ole Opry. I think that must have been 1954. Elvis was dressed very much like a typical black entertainer of that time, and neither his appearance nor his sound went over too well with the folks in the Opry house. As I understand it, some of the other entertainers were giggling and putting Elvis down as they watched from the wings. Webb Pierce, who at that time had more number one country hits than any other man in history, was watching Elvis very carefully. Webb was quite a businessman. He turned to the others who were laughing at Elvis and said firmly, "Hey boys, I wouldn't be laughing. That kid just might put us all out of business!"

'That was prophetic, of course, because Elvis would later turn the whole music world upside down and for a while country music would struggle to survive. A lot of the Opry folks who had been in the wings laughing at Elvis would soon begin discarding their rhinestone-studded outfits. They were soon to grow side-burns and longer hair, just like Elvis, and use back-up vocals which sounded like his. Soon, too, they'd be using lots of echo and drums on their recordings, just like Elvis. In my view, Webb Pierce was a visionary!'

George adds thoughtfully, 'Elvis is now part of show-business history and legend. I cherish his memory, and I'm somewhat tired by the "tell it all" stories of his human weaknesses. There but for the grace of God go any of us! Who could say that they would be able to handle all that fame any better?'

A decade or so after those heady Raleigh concerts, Tinky and George were in neon-lit Las Vegas where George was appearing at The Mint with cowboy movie star Tex Ritter. By then Elvis was a very major movie star himself. Hollywood and Vegas had become his playgrounds. 'Honey,' said George one morning, 'let's go see Connie Francis perform at the Stardust Hotel. I ain't working tonight.' Arriving at the hotel that evening, Tinky and George found the foyer was crowded, and they had to be content with seats towards the back of the theatre. Suddenly a commotion arose at the front door. A flashy gold Cadillac had arrived. 'I wonder if that's Elvis's car,' whispered George as they found their seats. 'Perhaps he's staying here.' Tinky looked sceptical.

The lights dimmed and the attractive Connie Francis emerged into the spotlight and launched into a selection of her top-selling hits, including 'Who's Sorry Now?' and 'Carolina Moon'. The Hamiltons settled back to enjoy the show. Then some shadowy figures, obviously latecomers, made their way to a vacant table at the front of the room. George turned and whispered jokingly to

Tinky, 'I wonder if that's Elvis and the Memphis Mafia up there!' ('Memphis Mafia' was the nickname given to Elvis's buddies and bodyguards.) Tinky raised her eyebrows, gave her spouse a cynical smile and shook her head.

The first hit song over, Connie Francis leaned down over the footlights and spoke off-mike but still audibly. 'Is it all right if I tell them you're here?'

The answer must have been in the affirmative, because as she stood up she pointed proudly to the front table and declared, 'Ladies and gentlemen, I must tell you, it's such a thrill to announce that the greatest entertainer of the century is with us tonight!'

The room exploded into loud applause as the audience gave Elvis a standing ovation. Through the din, George muttered to Tinky, 'Ain't it amazing – nearly all this crowd's middle aged. We're about the youngest here!' Elvis waved royally from his seat as the excited audience took time to settle down again. George continued murmuring to his wife. 'You watch, honey. He won't hang around after the show. He's sure to slip away during the last song.'

How little he knew! When Connie's show ended, Elvis and his gang were still sitting at the front, making no effort to slip away. That was the signal for every single person in the room to line up and shake hands with Elvis Presley, including Tinky and George. George was not to know that this would be his last chance to chat to Elvis, although he saw him several times later in his concerts. Standing patiently in line, the Hamiltons listened to his polite comments, laced with that distinctive Southern drawl. 'Thank you, ma'am ... Thank you, sir...' Elvis's words were routine and repetitive, but the wide-eyed fans were more than happy.

When it came to the Hamiltons' turn, however, Elvis showed obvious surprise and pleasure at seeing George. Rising from his chair, he smiled broadly and asked question after question. 'Hi, George, how are you? How's Chet? Say, is this your beautiful wife? Hi, honey! How are you?' Elvis smiled down at Tinky. She was thrilled to think that the great Elvis Presley should know her husband, a fellow stablemate at the most renowned record label in the world.

George admitted years later that the experience had given him great pleasure too. 'It sure made me feel kinda good too, if I'm honest! I get real upset when I hear people put Elvis down and say mean things about him and his problems. Hank Williams once put it so succinctly when he said, "Unless you've made no mistakes in your life, be careful of stones that you throw!"'

CHAPTER 6

MOVING OVER TO NASHVILLE

> George IV has negotiated the subtle shifts in musical terrain, but there has been a thread of consistency in his work, a singular ability that stands out over time. His greatest gift is his ability to pick good songs, songs that reflect his knowledge of music, but also his best qualities as a person.
>
> **Frye Gaillard** (author)

There was no doubt that the young George Hamilton IV relished his encounters with so many talented rock and pop stars, as he worked alongside them at concerts and on tours. But what was happening with his own career? Was he content? Was success coming in the way he wanted? The hit songs were there, the fact that he was making a name for himself was undeniable, but the picture was not all rosy – especially at home with his new wife Tinky, upset and struggling with George's many absences. Underneath, too, George remained uncertain about his position on the rock/pop scene. He was a long way from his roots. Yet, if this was where the success was, he could hardly walk away, could he? So many people were eager to help him on his way.

Radio and television music presenter Dick Clark was just one of George IV's supporters. George remembers him with affection. 'Today he's often referred to as "America's oldest teenager"! Dick Clark was really kind to me. I appeared on his long-running television show *American Bandstand* many times in the fifties. That's where I met Frankie Avalon, Bobby Rydell, Fabian, Dion and the Belmonts, Bobby Darin and lots of other characters from those days. The thing that looms large in my memory was the way Mr Clark took a liking to my song "Why Don't They Understand?". He really took that song to his heart, much like Buddy Deane had done for "A Rose And A Baby Ruth".

'In 1958, two years after "A Rose" had appeared, a lot of people were wondering if I'd been a one-hit wonder. Then Dick Clark started playing "Why Don't They Understand?" and it made it into the Top Ten – largely due to the constant airplay on *American Bandstand*, which was on network television on weekday afternoons after everyone came home from school. I did guest appearances on his television show and I also did "record hop" live personal appearances for him. I especially remember one time in 1959 when he invited me to Miami, Florida to do a prime-time evening teen music television show. Bobby Darin was also there, singing his hit "Splish Splash". Dick Clark was a gentleman, and I'll always respect him.'

Professional success, therefore, was coming thick and fast as the fifties drew to a close. Life at home was rather less glittering. Married in the summer of 1958, George and Tinky had to work through a whole new set of difficulties presented by his developing career. Looking back, George expresses guilt and regret for his long periods of absenteeism. It was a time of constant pressure and busyness. 'One of my favourite lines from Tinky about our life together was her quote from Dickens, "It was the best of times, it was the worst of times." There were many upheavals, heartaches and separations from each other due to my touring. To all intents and purposes, for example, I deserted Tinky to tour Australia in 1959 with Chuck Berry and Bobby Darin. Poor Tink was left at home in our little one-bedroom apartment in the Presidential Gardens, Alexandria, Virginia.'

The grand address sounded impressive, but that was merely the result of it being in a suburb of Washington DC, once the home of George Washington! In truth, it was a modest, rather uninspiring dwelling place. Tinky could not drive in those days, so at best she became neighbourhood-bound, if not housebound. It was a traumatic experience for a young mother-to-be, stuck in an alien environment away from family and friends.

George was torn two ways, between his wife and home and his now thriving career. His lonely spouse was pulling him homeward, while his mercenary management was pulling him outward. George seriously attempted to be all things to all people. He struggled to finish his education in order to please his parents. He tried to hang in with his fledgling 'teen balladeer' career. He tried to be a good husband and, soon, a good father too. But it was simply not possible to be all things to all people all of the time. 'I left Tinky at home, expecting her to try and hold down the fort at the tender age of 19. On reflection, that was wrong and I'm sorry!' Painful separations became common for the young married couple as George hit the road time and time again. If he was serious about his career, he had to tour – and after all, he loved performing.

Their eldest son Peyton was born on 24 May 1959, 11 months after the wedding. George discovered later that the date had a religious significance. 'Ironically, that's John Wesley Day, the day when the founder of the Methodist Church was converted in a Moravian Meeting House fellowship on Aldersgate Street in London.' Peyton's full name is Edwin Peyton Hamilton and he was named after Tinky's father, Edwin Peyton. Originally the couple did not plan to carry on the 'George Hamilton number' tradition. It is interesting, therefore, that their second son, who was named George Hege Hamilton V, was the one who became the singer!

Suddenly the pressing responsibilities of parenthood were thrust upon the couple, and Tinky inevitably bore the greater burden. Most of the time, George was simply not at home. There was not enough time for everything, and personal tensions between the couple often threatened to build up to something explosive. Neither of them wanted that, however, and they both worked diligently to hold everything together. 'I praise God,' says George, 'that there was no disillusionment over our marriage. We both had a commitment to make it work! Our problem, common to many "entertainment" marriages, was to make it work in a positive way.'

Expensive, long-distance phone calls helped to bridge the hundreds of miles that often separated them. Tinky took every chance to tell George how she felt. She was particularly unhappy with their apartment. 'George, we do need to move,' she would tell him. 'I've never liked this neighbourhood!'

'But honey, we haven't been there very long!' George would protest.

And Tinky would retort firmly, 'But George, *you* don't have to stay here every hour, every day and every month! And the baby's getting more and more fussy…' Eventually George saw that he would have to capitulate and agree to a relocation. 'Anything for an easy life!' he laughs now. The family duly moved from Presidential Gardens to the Dominion Arms apartments in Arlington, Virginia. It was still only a one-bedroom flat in a high-rise development, but it was more upmarket, and it did have a swimming pool at the back!

George's career continued to progress, and it was not long before the Hamiltons could afford to move once again. This time it was to a duplex, a semidetached house, in Maryland. Their new neighbours were Dick and Sandy Flood. An excellent songwriter, Dick had written 'Trouble's Back In Town' which was recorded by the Wilburn Brothers, and he was one of George's colleagues on the *Jimmy Dean TV Show*. Dick and George became lifelong friends and so did their wives. Sadly, some years later Dick and Sandy were divorced. The Hamiltons nonetheless remained good friends with them both, and their respective new partners.

Meanwhile, George was still purporting to be a 'teen balladeer', having been marketed on these lines from the start. His pop concerts were now with the likes of Brenda Lee and Little Richard. Yet he was managing to keep one foot on the territory of his first love, country music, thanks to his Jimmy Dean and Connie B. Gay connections. 'I was being miscast as a pop singer and therefore, begrudgingly, I had to live up to it. The show-biz industry kept telling me that country music was just not cool as far as teenagers were concerned – but my eyes were still set on the Grand Ole Opry.'

Sing Me A Sad Song, George's Hank Williams tribute album for the ABC Paramount label, was the result of his struggle to remain at least partly 'country'. The album producer was the late Don Costa, originally a great guitarist. By then he had also become an excellent orchestra leader and went on to become a skilled record producer and arranger. He signed George up from the Colonial label to ABC Paramount, where he joined Paul Anka, Frankie Avalon, Fabian, Edie Gorme, Steve Lawrence and others. Don understood country music. He particularly loved the heart-tugging songs of Hank Williams and recognized their universal appeal, reaching way beyond the limits of farmers, hillbillies and rednecks.

The classy string arrangements for George's Hank Williams album were worked on together by Don and George at Don's home in Nyack, New York. The slick backing was to be provided by a New York orchestra. George's mellow vocals had a plaintive appeal that capitalized on his 'teen balladeer' image. As well as the old favourites 'Jambalaya' and 'Your Cheatin' Heart', George also took the chance to record his first gospel songs among the Hank Williams fare, including 'House Of Gold' and the emotive 'How Can You Refuse Him Now?' For George, these thought-provoking songs were rich with spiritual meaning, on which he was to ponder at length in later life.

'"House Of Gold" spoke to me about life's priorities. Christ asked, "What shall it profit a man if he gains the whole world and loses his own soul?" He also said, "Seek ye first the Kingdom of Heaven and all these things shall be added unto you." Unfortunately, for me the business of living offered little time to think much about such priorities in the early days of my career. Then "How Can You Refuse Him Now?" spoke firstly of seeing the crucified Christ as a living sacrifice for each individual. Secondly it spoke of coming to terms with what his claims on every individual should be. Yet I gave these thoughts little head-room then. I was too busy chasing the rainbow's end of my career!'

By mid-1959, however, George felt he was at the end of his tether. He had just about had enough of his teenage balladeering act, and he and Tinky were faced with a momentous decision. 'I refused to consider myself as some kind of teenage heart-throb!' he explains. 'After all, I was a married man with a wife and a baby that I loved and wanted to care for. My three years of being miscast had been exciting, and of course I'd enjoyed being treated to celebrity status, yet in my heart I felt a phoney.'

In the autumn of 1959, George went with his manager Connie B. Gay to the Country Music DJ Convention back down south in Nashville, Tennessee. Connie, of course, became the founding President of the Country Music Association and George was one of its first charter members. He used that visit to try to promote himself to the country DJs. He received a disappointingly cool reception, however, because in their minds he was pigeonholed in the 'pop' category.

Sitting with Connie amongst the audience in the Grand Ole Opry House, George watched the performances of Patsy Cline, Ernest Tubb, Porter Wagoner, Marty Robbins, Faron Young and other heroes of his, and fell into deep thought. 'George, this is home!' he said to himself. 'What's wrong with you? Where have you been? Why have you been wasting your time on the pop scene?'

Cross with himself rather than anyone else, he felt the same sense of outrage as he had done several years earlier when his father had suggested he should not marry Tinky. 'I was never overly forceful and I hated controversy or confrontation, but I *knew* what I wanted! I felt so strongly about the Grand Ole Opry and Nashville that as I watched the show that night I actually started to weep. Sure, I was successful – but I wasn't fulfilled.' The show over, singer and manager returned to Washington DC in Connie's sleek limousine, but small talk between them was sparse. It gave George time to think.

Two weeks later, he asked Connie to lunch with him at a little restaurant on the Potomac River in Washington DC. George had some startling news for his manager, and he was dreading the confrontation. 'Connie,' he told the other man, 'it's all over for me! I've had enough. I just don't want to act out this part any more. You've been real good to me and I appreciate all you've done, but I've made up my mind. I want to move to Nashville and try to get on the Grand Ole Opry!'

What would his manager say? Connie B. Gay was by this time a highly successful millionaire. Businessmen of his ilk do not usually take kindly to losses of income at any time. Yet that day he acted out of character. He smiled and then, sighing, replied to George in an unexpectedly measured tone. 'I ain't gonna hold on to you while you're trying to change career,' he said. 'I'm gonna release you. My advice is to look up Jim Denny's Artist Bureau in Nashville and tell him I sent you. He's already booking Mel Tillis, Webb Pierce, Carl Smith and other country acts. Tell you what, I'll call him up and see if he'll book some dates and help get you settled.'

This was more than George had expected, and he was delighted and grateful. As soon as Connie realized how sincere and committed George was to making this change, he tore up their contract. True to his word, he made some phone calls for George to try to get him some connections in Nashville, including the promised call to Jim Denny, the booking agent. 'This was quite a moving thing for me,' George recalls, 'because Connie had a pretty good contract with me. I think it was 25 per cent of the gross of everything I earned, before expenses, for probably another five years. But he tore that up and gave me my "freedom", as they say. That was quite something in those days. It was very kind of him and very helpful.'

A month later, at the beginning of January 1960, George left Washington DC with his wife and baby, their Siamese cat and a puppy. They headed south in a crammed two-seater MG roadster, towards the country music capital of the world. As he sped south through the night while Tinky slept, George had plenty of time to mull over his decision, and the situation he faced in the immediate future. He knew there would be no one there in Nashville waiting to greet them with open arms. They would have to start all over again in every respect. It was not going to be easy.

He was sure of one thing, however: as young parents, his and Tinky's first responsibility was to their child. 'We clearly saw that our responsibility was to teach our children well,' he explains. 'Then in due time, when they got older, they would have the same responsibility to *their* children. Trends and fashions sometimes cloud issues, but basic truths never change and it's those truths that children need to grasp!' Without doubt, Tinky and George struggled in those early Nashville years. They soon learned that their children were vulnerable and did not live in a vacuum as far as unwholesome influences were concerned. However carefully the young parents tried to teach and uphold Christian values, they realized that all children are subject to strong counter-influences from the 'secular' world. All the more important therefore, maintains George, that parents should try as hard as they can to outbalance the bad with the good.

The late Conway Twitty was often referred to as the first established pop singer who went country, but George Hamilton IV strongly disputes that assertion: 'I want to be presumptuous and arrogant, and suggest that I preceded Conway Twitty on the path from pop music to country music by a couple of years at least! I was the first established pop act with a strong record of Top 40 hits to go country. Conway Twitty was the next, followed by Jerry Lee Lewis.' George is absolutely right. When Tinky and George arrived in Nashville, 'Music City USA', Conway was still doing rock'n'roll alongside Carl Perkins and Jerry Lee Lewis. They all followed George into country music stardom.

Looking back now, those early days in Nashville stand out very clearly in George's memory. It seemed that the same question was on everyone's lips: 'Why are you here in Nashville?' The question was usually followed – without allowing George space to answer – by the same light-hearted but pointed comment: 'You must be crazy!' When George made his shift from pop to country, such a move was almost unprecedented. There were certainly no shortages of those who wanted to shift in the opposite direction. It seemed as if every young country singer was trying to cross over from country to pop. They all wanted a bit of the success Elvis was achieving, of course. George, always contrary, had moved against the tide.

Tinky and George rented a little apartment in Chesterfield Avenue, off West End on the west side of Nashville. They initially felt very alone and isolated – ironically, it was not until much later that the Hamiltons discovered that Ernest Tubb's guitarist Billy Byrd actually lived across the street! George had worked hard at redecorating the new family home in advance of the arrival of his wife and baby, but much to his disappointment, Tinky just could not settle down and feel at home in Music City. 'Bless her heart, but I don't think Tinky was too impressed by Nashville. This great, "got-it-all-together" gal had married a guitar-picking country music freak! It was an obsession that never passed with time, and I guess my one-track mind bordered on selfishness...'

Tinky had always hoped against hope that George's college education would lead eventually to a sober, sensible teaching career or something similar. She continued to hold on to her secret hopes, despite her husband's continued record successes. George maintains that it is to her everlasting credit that eventually she 'bit the bullet' and accepted that her husband's love affair with country music was not going to fade away. In retrospect, he deeply regrets that he never truly considered his wife's wishes when he set off to pursue his own goals.

The move to Nashville was an enormous, not very clearly calculated risk. Perhaps later in life, George muses, he would not have been so foolhardy. 'Today's decisions are much more carefully analysed, scrutinized, criticized and pulverized before I take action! Top of today's agenda must be my family's desires and needs. I confess that the arrogance of youth is mellowing into the wisdom that comes with age.' He freely admits now that he was wrong to expect Tinky to follow him just because she was his wife. 'Yet she stood by me through thick and thin. Because of this, not only do I still love her dearly today, but I sincerely appreciate her long-suffering support. It must have been painful at times!'

The Hamiltons arrived in Nashville in the middle of a New Year snowstorm. Coincidentally, it was the same month that singer-songwriter Bill Anderson and his wife Bette moved to Nashville from Georgia. In time, the two singers and their spouses became close friends. Born a few months later than George in Columbia, South Carolina, Bill Anderson gained experience as a sports journalist and radio DJ. A skilled songwriter, he gave Ray Price 'City Lights', Eddy Arnold 'The Tips Of My Fingers' and, rather surprisingly, England's Ken Dodd the songs 'Still' and 'Happiness'. His sentimental narrative 'Mama Sang A Song' was a number one hit, covered years later by George Hamilton IV on a Wes Davis production.

To begin with, however, there were no close friends to offer support, and circumstances would severely test the young

Hamilton couple. Nashville proved to be a tough nut to crack, and matters proceeded from bad to worse. There were no country bookings coming in and George stubbornly turned down any pop bookings he was offered, as well as the chance to record 'Roses Are Red', which became a smash hit for Bobby Vinton instead. Tinky was concerned that George was hurting himself badly by being so single-minded, and she took every opportunity to tell him so! It only served to increase the pressures on George, but looking back, he does not blame her for voicing her worries.

Mealtimes offered the best chances for Tinky to start a discussion with her husband. 'George, honey,' she would begin, 'I was listening to the radio earlier today and DJ after DJ played Bobby Vinton's "Roses Are Red". It's a great song and even *I'm* getting to like it!'

'Please, honey,' George would reply rather desperately, 'please don't ask me *again* why I turned that song down! I made that decision and I've gotta live with it!' He was worried himself, and was finding it increasingly difficult to maintain an impression of calm composure in front of his concerned partner.

Tinky understood, but said what she thought nevertheless. 'George, I don't want to criticize, but I can't help but think sometimes you're too stubborn for your own good! I know you want to be country, I know that George, but we've got to *eat* too!' More than once, George found himself having to console his tearful wife, but he knew he had no real comfort to offer, no progress to report.

Economically, the stark truth was that his radical career move to Nashville meant that he was starting all over again from the bottom of the show-business ladder. Every booking, no matter how far away, was a prize to be grasped with both hands. George had been trying to complete his education, but with the pressures of building a whole new career, his aspirations on that front sank lower and lower down the priority list. Road dates were not all that frequent at first, but when they did come, they necessitated his absence from home and family for weeks at a time in order to make the whole thing viable. He would go to California, for instance, to play a string of 'honky-tonk' dates at 100 dollars a night. Such engagements would not work out profitably if he only went for a couple of days, because the travelling costs had to be met first. Well, he had known all along that it was not going to be easy.

The pressures were certainly mounting, yet amid the gloom there were some carefree moments and good times too. During the early part of 1960, under the guiding genius of John D. Loudermilk as producer, George recorded eight songs in the Bradley Film and Recording Studio on Nashville's Sixteenth Avenue South. Three of the songs gained moderate chart success. Stonewall Jackson's 'Why I'm Walkin'' reached number 21, Wayne Walker's 'A Walk On The Wild Side Of Life' reached number 18, and 'Before This Day Ends' by McAlpin, Drusky and Wilson reached number four.

By then George had discovered that he had a near neighbour in Billy Byrd, and the two men had become friends. Billy, indeed, became George's first Nashville musician. He could not afford a full band, but Billy doubled up magnificently and made the most of his many skills. George counted himself immensely lucky to obtain the ex-Texas Troubadour's generous support.

In May 1960 Billy, George and his brother Cabot took a trip to Kansas, where George was booked to play the Chestnut Inn in the town of Independence. Having discovered that ex-President Harry S. Truman was going to be at the impressive library named after him in Independence, the trio waited outside the building to catch a passing glimpse of the famous figure. Cabot was excited. 'I've always wanted to meet President Truman!' he told his companions. Billy and George assured him, rather pessimistically, that such an honour was definitely not in the offing. Cabot, however, took the bull by the horns and went to enquire. He talked to a security guard, who told him that President Truman was going home early that day because Senator John F. Kennedy was due to visit the next day, seeking Truman's support in his bid for the US Presidency. George recalled the scene vividly. 'The security guard told Cabot that Mr Truman would be leaving shortly by the back door if we wanted to go around and see him. So we went around to the back of the library, and waited and waited.'

Eventually the three sat down under a tree nearby. Was all this waiting really worth it? Suddenly the door opened and out came Mr Truman. Spying the small group under the tree, he wandered over and to their amazement shook their hands warmly. The thing that struck George the most about the scene was that there was no security, no guards and no secret service personnel. 'In those days, I guess Presidents and former Presidents could go their own way without worrying so much about assassinations. Billy, Cabot and I just stood up and brushed off the grass to make ourselves presentable, and Mr Truman left the sidewalk and casually walked across the lawn right up to us!'

Truman sounded very friendly as he approached. 'Hey,' he said, 'where are you fellows from?' As soon as the trio replied, 'Nashville,' he beamed at them. 'Nashville, Tennessee ... the Grand Ole Opry ... yes!' he said with enthusiasm. 'How's Minnie Pearl doing these days? You know, boys, I used to listen to a little country radio station, WARL, from Arlington, Virginia. I used to listen to their country show in the White House!' George recognized the station as the one where his former manager Connie B. Gay had been a country DJ at the same time as Mr Truman had been President. What a connection! Mr Truman went on to mention Ernest Tubb and Roy Acuff. George and his companions were thrilled that he actually knew these people. Then, of course, Billy Byrd introduced himself. Mr Truman smiled again and began to chuckle. 'Oh yeah!' he said. 'I've heard Ernest Tubb say those famous words many times: "Play it, Billy Byrd!"'

The three men and their ex-President remained deep in conversation for a good few minutes, talking animatedly about the Nashville scene. Having waited so patiently for a glimpse of the former President, the trio were now so absorbed that they completely forgot to make use of the camera they had brought with them. Fortunately, the keen-eyed ex-resident of the Oval Office was aware of the oversight. As the conversation started to draw to a close, Mr Truman looked quizzically at them. 'Well?' he said.

'I beg your pardon sir?' George asked, puzzled.

Mr Truman chuckled again. 'Well, aren't you going to take my picture? Come on, guys, I see you've brought your camera – didn't you want to take my picture?'

'Oh, yes sir! We surely do!' Photos were duly taken amid much laughter, and the three visitors made their way home, impressed by the down-to-earth friendliness of such a great world figure.

Back in Nashville, the Hamiltons' isolation was easing as George sought out some of the people he knew from previous touring engagements. Don and Sue Everly, for instance, had bought a home not far away. The Everly Brothers were big stars by this time. Also nearby were Roy and Claudette Orbison. Roy's career was currently riding high on 'Only The Lonely'. All three couples became close friends during the years that followed.

One day, while George was visiting Don Everly's house, Don's brother Phil telephoned from California. Don and Phil chatted for a while, then Don turned round to George. 'George,' he said, 'Phil wants to say hi to you!'

Don dutifully passed the phone over to his visitor. 'Hi, George!' said a voice. 'Are you living down in Nashville now? Why'd ya move? I thought you had more sense, man!'

'Well, Phil,' said George, not sure how to explain his decision to someone who clearly thought it was irrational, 'I've decided I'm gonna switch over to country!'

The caller interrupted him, clearly baffled, and spoke quite brusquely in his consternation: 'Why, George? That's *weird*, man!'

George was startled. He hadn't expected his erstwhile colleague to put him under this kind of pressure, but clearly he needed to try to give him some kind of rational answer. All he could offer, however, was a very simple statement: 'I love country music, Phil, and so that's what I wanna do from now on!'

One person to whom George did not need to explain himself was John D. Loudermilk. He and his first wife, Gwen, moved to Nashville at about the same time as George and Tinky. The two couples became firm friends, and John and Gwen made every effort to be encouraging and hospitable to the Hamiltons, helping them settle into their new home while George found his feet in his chosen arena.

When friends of either couple came to visit them in Nashville, they used to take them around to see the 'homes of the stars'. Since people seemed to get such a kick out of this sightseeing, it soon occurred to the two couples that it might be interesting to start a little business, a 'Tour of the Homes of the Stars'. 'John and I hired a Nashville bus on Saturdays,' George remembers. 'Tinky and Gwen sold tickets for the tour on the front stairs of the Ryman Auditorium, and John and I would take turns being the tour guide on the bus. We had a megaphone and would ride along, pointing out where all the stars lived. It became so successful that in the end we had to run several buses and hire extra tour guides to help us out.

'At some point, it became very obvious to people at WSM Radio and the Grand Ole Opry that this was a flourishing business. We were reminded, quite rightly I suppose, that we were parking our buses in front of the Ryman Auditorium and taking advantage of our associations with the Opry to promote our tours. It was suggested to us that maybe WSM should go into partnership with us on the venture. So we went into partnership and it became quite a successful business – of course it helped, being promoted by WSM on the radio! It became the 'George Hamilton IV and John D. Loudermilk Tour of the Homes of the Stars'.

'At the time, John was a very busy hit songwriter and he became a little disenchanted with the distractions of being a businessman too. And then, at about the same time, "Abilene" became a number one country hit for me and I was getting a lot of bookings on the road, so I was seldom in town. These facts were subsequently put to us by our partner WSM in a very businesslike way, with the suggestion that maybe it was time for us to step back from our share. I have no regrets with the choice I made – I could have decided otherwise, but if I was going to stay in partnership with WSM I would have had to come off the road and get more involved in the sightseeing business. I didn't want to do that, so I made the decision to give up my involvement there and then. John had previously kind of turned the enterprise mainly over to me anyway, because of his own pressing schedule. He needed the time to promote his songs to producers and so on. The bus tour became "The Grand Ole Opry Homes of the Stars Tour" and today in Nashville there must be about 25 sightseeing companies! I'll leave it for history to decide whether I missed my calling and should have stayed in the sightseeing tour business...'

One of the first bookings that the impresario Jim Denny managed to secure for George was at the State Fairground in Louisville, Kentucky. George was booked to appear with Pee Wee King (co-writer with Redd Stewart of the hit 'Tennessee Waltz'). Pee Wee, one of the friendly father figures of country music at that time, was chatting with George behind the outdoor stage. It had been a busy day, but Pee Wee always found time to talk.

'I hear you moved to Nashville, George,' he said, looking curiously at his fellow performer. 'Is that right?'

George shyly nodded agreement. 'Yes, sir!' he said cautiously, rather tired by this time of defending his position.

Not satisfied with such a brief reply, Pee Wee persisted. 'Why?'

'Well, Pee Wee, I'm trying to get a foothold in country music 'cause it's been my first love since as far back as I can remember!' This time George responded with all the conviction he could muster, but his voice caught on the words. The pressures of Nashville had left him feeling tense and strung out, struggling with a wavering confidence.

Pee Wee's next comment was no comfort at all. With a concerned expression on his face, the older man placed his hand in a kindly way on George's shoulder. 'Get off the ship, son!' he said, shaking his head. 'It's sinking, George – it'll never survive all this rock'n'roll revolution!' Pee Wee's pessimistic attitude was all too common on the Nashville scene of 1959/60. Elvis had almost single-handedly blown away country music's popularity and appeal. Just about everyone, it seemed, was trying to jump on the rock'n'roll bandwagon, discarding their ornate cowboy suits along the way.

Examples were not hard to find. Faron Young, doing his best to live down his 'Young Sheriff' persona, was growing long side-burns, wearing tuxedos and singing with a hand mike. Marty Robbins was wearing a white sports jacket and a pink carnation. He was even performing covers of some of Elvis's songs, doing whatever he could to ditch his western background. Jim Reeves had also suddenly abandoned his western suit and stetson in favour of more 'uptown' attire. He was no longer using such 'corny' material as 'Pickin' A Chicken With You' – instead he was delving into a repertoire of songs more associated with Sinatra, Como and Bennett. The uptown, country-boy crooning image had been pioneered by Eddy Arnold, and with it came drums, echo chambers and velvet-smooth vocal quartet backings. Musically speaking, the so-called 'Nashville Sound' had moved from rural to city environs. Yet here was George, uncool as ever, swimming against the tide!

George's decision puzzled many in the country music community, and he had to contend with endless challenges to his thinking, to say nothing of a certain amount of cynicism from some quarters. En route to a country concert in Canada one day, a tricky conversation on the subject developed between George, the Wilburn Brothers and Ray Price. A tough native American born in 1926, Ray had 'paid his dues' and was by then a unique talent in the country genre. Some of his biggest hits became honky-tonk classics, including 'Crazy Arms', 'City Lights' and 'Heartaches By The Number'. Ray was a contemporary of Hank Williams, whom George naturally held in awe.

When the subject of the Hamiltons' Nashville move came up, George was not pleased. The last thing he wanted just then was to go through several rounds of verbal boxing, defending himself in such articulate and experienced company. There was no avoiding it, however. Ray, who had downed a couple of drinks, commented abruptly, 'Hamilton, are you gonna live in Nashville permanently?'

'Yes, Ray, I've joined the Grand Ole Opry,' George replied with a determined smile. 'Ott Devine has invited me, and I'm real thrilled about it. I'm gonna be a country singer from now on – it's all I ever wanted to do, Ray!'

'Well, George, by God you better live it, son ... you gotta be real 'bout it! It ain't gonna work if you're gonna just play "pretend" with us country boys!' Ray's uncompromising words cut deep. He was right, of course. Why should people automatically believe that George was serious about the venture? Reluctant to face further questioning, George closed his eyes, settled his head back and did his best to feign sleep. To his relief, the conversation switched to a different subject.

There was another side to this sceptical coin: George was welcomed with open arms by some country artistes. As well as the visit to Canada, in the autumn of that year he toured extensively with Hank Snow, Carl Perkins, Norma Jean and Alec Houston across Texas, Kansas, Washington, Idaho, New Mexico, Oregon and Colorado. Nonetheless, the excitement of the tour was dampened to a certain extent by the knowledge that once again George was absent from home while Tinky awaited the birth of their second baby.

George remembers the tours from those early days very vividly. 'In the early sixties, during the time I was having hits like "Abilene", "Truck Drivin' Man", "Early Mornin' Rain" and "Break My Mind", we travelled on tour in station wagons [estate cars]. Most country entertainers did back then. Porter Wagoner, Johnny Cash and a lot of other folks just toured in Cadillacs and station wagons with custom-built trailers on the back for their musical instruments. I can remember clearly touring across Canada in the winter one year. Billy Byrd was playing lead guitar with me in those days and Mother Maybelle and the Carter Sisters were touring with us. They were riding with me and Billy, sharing the fuel expenses. At one time on this winter tour, it got so cold that the heat wasn't reaching the back of the car where Mother Maybelle and the Carter Sisters were seated. Billy Byrd and I were up in the front seat, stripped down to our undershirts so the heat could be turned up high enough to keep the ladies warm in the back! That was the way we toured in those days – none of your glamorous touring coaches with state rooms, showers, bunks and so on!

'While we were touring with Mother Maybelle and the Carter Sisters, I got a chance to hear some firsthand stories about my Grandfather Hamilton's favourite singer, Jimmie Rodgers "The Singing Brakeman". Mother Maybelle was a part of the legendary Carter Family, often called "the First Family of country music". One of the stories she told me was about the historic first recording sessions that the Carter Family did with Jimmie

Rodgers in Bristol, Tennessee. Jimmie Rodgers' doctor had recommended the high mountain air of Asheville, North Carolina for his lungs (Jimmie suffered from severe tuberculosis) and while he was there he worked for the fire company and also did some radio work in the area with a group of string musicians.

'Apparently the string band heard about Ralph Peer's recording sessions in Bristol, Tennessee and they set off for an audition – but somehow left Jimmie behind in Asheville! Jimmie drove over to Bristol himself the following day, and it just happened to be the same day that the Carter Family arrived for a recording session. The recordings that Jimmie and the Carters subsequently made there in Bristol are often referred to as a groundbreaking event in the birth of what we now know as country music, and it all happened quite by chance.

'The Grand Ole Opry announcer Grant Turner once told me he was a DJ in San Antonio, Texas when Jimmie Rodgers came to sing at the radio station. Grant said there was a lot of excitement around the station in anticipation of the event. Jimmie had already released some recordings and had been kicking up a little dust. Jimmie finally turned up, accompanied by his wife. Mrs Rodgers was very quiet and shy and stayed out in the lobby while Jimmie went into the studio. Jimmie then took out a guitar and sang some songs. Grant said that what he remembered most about Jimmie Rodgers was not the music, but his yellow fingers! Apparently the whole time Jimmie was there in the studio, he wasn't without a cigarette in his mouth or in his hand. Jimmie's fingers were stained yellow from being such a chain smoker. He eventually died of the tuberculosis. I can't imagine the chain-smoking helped much!'

One person above all others in Nashville was to have a decisive, galvanizing effect on George's country career. Guitarist Chet Atkins had befriended George as a gawky 12-year-old on his first visit to Nashville, and the friendship they had formed was to last a lifetime. Through the early years of George's singing career, they had stayed in touch via occasional letters and phone conversations. Chet had monitored his friend's career with a shrewd eye right from the start. Indeed, when George recorded his North Carolina hit 'A Rose And A Baby Ruth', Chet cheekily covered it with a group called the Country Gentlemen. (Incidentally, two of that group were the Crutchfield Brothers, Jerry and Jan, and in an odd link across the years Jerry's wife Patsy was to become one of Tinky's best friends in Nashville, teaching the Bible Study Fellowship at the local church. Jerry himself went on to produce the talented Tanya Tucker, Lee Greenwood and many others, and was a good friend to George.)

Once he had made the move to Nashville, George shared his career dreams and ambitions with Chet, now a hugely influential figure on the country scene. George was a great admirer of Chet's guitar skills, to say nothing of his record production work with RCA Victor. How the Nashville newcomer wished he could become part of Chet Atkins' so-called 'RCA clan'!

Every so often, dreams do come true. One eventful morning Chet invited George to a breakfast meeting in Shoney's Restaurant in downtown Nashville. To George's surprise, once they had finished their eggs and bacon and sat back with cups of hot, black coffee, Chet offered him a contract, together with a piece of hopeful advice. 'George, you've had a lotta luck in pop music,' he said, 'but I don't know whether it'll work for you as a country singer. Still, let's see. Let's see whether you can get any country hits – we'll give you a shot!'

ABC Paramount agreed to George's contract transfer to RCA Victor on the condition that George gave them a couple more recording sessions as a 'goodbye' payment. John D. Loudermilk produced these Nashville recordings for Paramount, which included the songs 'Trouble' and 'Before This Day Ends', at Owen Bradley's Quonset Hut studio. As another landmark, this was the first recording session in Nashville at which the legendary Pete Drake played steel guitar. Leading country DJ Ralph Emery gave the songs good airplay time and helped turn them into hits in the country charts by the spring of 1960.

As the months progressed, Nashville society gradually seemed to come to terms with George Hamilton IV. Before long, the industry also came to accept his talents as a country man, especially when Chet Atkins started to produce hits for him such as 'Truck Drivin' Man', 'Steel Rail Blues', 'Early Mornin' Rain', 'Break My Mind' and 'Three Steps To The Phone'. For George, however, there was still one special step to take before he could begin to believe that his dream was coming true. He longed to join the elite membership of the Grand Ole Opry. This privilege had eluded him so far, although he was invited to do occasional guest spots.

After one such set, George made his bows and sauntered offstage into the dimly lit wings. Strolling over to him with a broad smile was the Opry Manager himself, Ott Devine. 'George,' he said directly, 'how'd you like to become part of the family? I'd like you to join the greatest country music family on earth!'

George knew immediately what he meant, of course, and he confesses that his heart skipped a beat. His beaming face said it all. 'Sir,' he managed to croak eventually, 'you don't know *what* that invitation means to me!' It was an emotional moment. Ott Devine silently embraced the latest member of the Grand Ole Opry, who was quite lost for words.

That was on Saturday 6 February 1960. The following Monday George signed the paperwork which officially made him an Opry member. On 5 March that year he made his first appearance on stage at the Ryman Auditorium as a fully fledged member of the Grand Ole Opry. At last he felt certified as a country performer, supported as he was by the Opry management's endorsement as well as membership of Chet Atkins' exclusive 'RCA clan'.

George was on his way to realizing his dream. That much was clear. It was not all plain sailing from then on, however, and there were many difficulties still to face and hard choices to make. The bare economics of country music dictated that for anyone to make a reasonable living they would have to hit the road and tour. No matter how prestigious the show, Grand Ole Opry membership by itself would not house, feed and clothe a family very effectively. The Hamiltons' eldest son Peyton was joined by the new baby George V in 1960, then came a daughter, Mary Dabney, in 1965. Money was short in the early days in Nashville, and Tinky was left once again to cope during George's absences without the benefit of any family members close by.

George's original intention had been to return to college to complete his long-postponed degree, as he had just one year of grace left before completion became impossible. He had been in and out of college studies for the previous five years, but had only amassed three years' worth of credits to go towards his degree. However, quite apart from the obvious problems of squeezing any study into a busy performance schedule, this last-ditch attempt to complete his education was to be foiled in a rather extraordinary way.

George applied to the David Lipscomb College, the Church of Christ school that Pat and Shirley Boone had also attended, and was interviewed by the Dean of Admissions. The Dean quizzed George very carefully, apparently concerned about his willingness to adhere to the strict college rules and conventions. 'Aren't you with the Grand Ole Opry, Mr Hamilton?' he asked with frown. 'And don't you play in night clubs?'

'Yes, sir,' George replied, not sure why this might constitute a problem.

'Well, this is a Church of Christ school and we don't condone dancing or alcohol here. We don't think a night club is the right kind of atmosphere for *anyone* to be in, Mr Hamilton!'

Although a fair percentage of George's income as a country singer involved work in night clubs and honky-tonk bars, he was willing to give up this part of his livelihood if it meant that he could finish his degree, and therefore his initial reply was conciliatory. 'Well, sir, that's okay. I'm willing to give up those dates if you'll let me into your College.'

'Yes, Mr Hamilton, but ... but that doesn't deal with the Grand Ole Opry – and they have dancing there, do they not?'

'But sir, the only dancing they do at the Grand Ole Opry is square dancing,' George retorted in desperation. What was this man getting at?

The Dean's reply was decidedly testy. 'Yes that's right ... but it's still *dancing*!'

Now George was annoyed. 'Sir, I'd never thought of square dancing as being sinful!' There was, surely, nothing objectionable about square dancing. George could see, however, that to his stony-faced interviewer it was a major issue. After that, it was hardly a surprise when George was refused entry to the College.

Remembering the dispute now, George shakes his head. 'That sad decision was an extreme example of the type of religious legalism that discredits the Christian Church and does untold damage to its witness. And it was so inconsistent, never mind the other issues. When I went for my interview, Pat Boone had recently donated a large sum of money to the school from his show-biz earnings, to go towards the cost of a new building. Some of that income, I'm sure, was earned from rock'n'roll and night club performances, some of them in Las Vegas! There was nothing wrong in that – and I'd like to say that I respect Pat as a sincere and articulate Christian diplomat!'

George may have lost the chance to complete his degree, but there were compensations. Nashville was full of fantastic characters and talented musicians, and to work with these people was an education in itself. Some individuals stand out particularly strongly in George's mind. Roy Orbison was one such towering figure, and George shared a manager with him in the form of Wesley Rose of Acuff-Rose Publishing and the Acuff-Rose Artist Corporation.

'Roy and I did quite a few shows and concert tours together,' he remembers. 'We got to know each other quite well through Wesley Rose and Fred Foster. Roy recorded for Fred's label Monument Records. I liked Roy a lot. He was very shy and very much a quiet individual. One time he told me the story behind his trademark dark sunglasses. Apparently he'd boarded a plane for a concert tour and realized that he'd left his normal prescription glasses at home. Luckily, his sunglasses were also prescription lenses, so when he arrived at his destination that night, he simply wore the dark glasses. At the airport and the concert that evening, those glasses caused such a stir that Roy decided to make them a permanent part of his image!'

Marty Robbins was a different prospect altogether. With a Polish family background, he was a forthright person and far from shy. He rose to massive fame with such songs as 'The Story Of My Life', 'El Paso' and 'Devil Woman'. George remembers getting into hot water with him during an argument about politics.

'Marty was from Arizona, so I guess you'd say he was a "Goldwater Republican". They used to refer to Barry Goldwater, the Republican Senator from Arizona, as "Mr Conservative". He was pitched very much against President Lyndon B. Johnson. One night in the sixties, Marty came up to me backstage during the Opry at the Ryman Auditorium. We got into this great, heated discussion regarding the Kennedys. Now, Marty was way to the right of centrefield politically! He said that he'd heard I was a supporter of those "left-wing, liberal Kennedys". He was pretty insistent that I explain myself and say why I was so fond of them. Our conversation quickly deteriorated into an intense argument – Marty didn't think much of the Kennedys. In fact, there weren't so many "Kennedy Democrats" around in Nashville then, and I guess I was considered something of a political oddball at the Opry!

'Later, I was on tour with Marty Robbins in November 1963 when President John F. Kennedy was killed. When the news came that the President was dead, the whole country pretty much shut down. We were supposed to do a concert that night and, as I recall, Marty wanted to go ahead and do the show, even though the promoter had already decided to cancel it. Marty was most upset that the concert didn't go on, and there were a few strong words batted back and forth between us about that as well. Despite those disagreements, I still consider that Marty Robbins was a wonderful man. I found him very friendly and a great talent. I don't think anyone ever got a warmer response at the Wembley Festivals in England than Marty did. I always got along very well with Marty at the Opry and on tour – just as long as we avoided the subject of politics!'

Of course, George maintains firmly, 'My number one hero remains Chet Atkins. He's the greatest man I ever met in the music business. I often refer to Chet as being "Lincolnesque" because he reminds me of the kind of man I think Abraham Lincoln probably was – warm, witty, a dry sense of humour, quiet, private, very humble and gentle. I have immense respect and love for that man.

'I'll never forget the story Chet told me about how he got to Nashville. He had gone out to Springfield, Missouri with the Carter Family to perform on the radio there. Jim Denny, who was then manager of the Opry, called Mother Maybelle and wanted to hire the Carter Family for the Grand Ole Opry. Mother Maybelle told Jim about their guitar player, Chester Burton Atkins, and said she wanted to bring him with them to the Opry. Jim's reply was something like, "Well, we don't need any more guitar-pickers around here – we're covered up with them! They're a dime a dozen in Nashville." Chet said Mother Maybelle's told Mr Denny very firmly, "Well, if Chet doesn't come, we don't come!" And so Chet came to Nashville, and forever after took every opportunity to speak warmly of Mother Maybelle and the Carter Family!'

Chet Atkins was born in 1924 in Luttrell, Tennessee and rose to be one of the true myth-makers of Music City USA. Starting out as a backing guitarist, he went on to find international success as a guitar virtuoso. His greatest legacy, however, is the 'Nashville Sound' itself. Promoted by RCA to their top job, he headed up the greatest stable of popular and country music recording artistes ever assembled. Chet Atkins' RCA Victor clan, of which George was an integral part, was an elite group of fine country performers. They were destined to set the pace and establish the musical phenomenon that became known simply as the 'Nashville Sound'.

The years spent in the inspiring company of those great artistes, under the guidance of Chet Atkins, were glorious and creative times for George, a unique period of his life. 'Under Chet,' he says, 'it was just a great, big happy family. We not only respected our boss, we loved him! It was no wonder that, in addition to us country boys, there was a whole host of international stars such as Perry Como, Roger Whittaker and even Paul McCartney of the Beatles queuing to record under Chet Atkins' guiding genius.'

CHAPTER 7

THE NASHVILLE SOUND

> Only optimists make history. No monument was ever built to a pessimist! Pessimism is an investment in nothing, optimism is an investment in hope.
>
> (Author unknown)

THE FIFTIES HAD CLOSED with George Hamilton IV's career riding on the crest of a wave, yet he had turned his back on blossoming pop success in order to pursue his first love, country music. What he urgently needed now were a few solid hits to establish him in his chosen field. Whenever he was off the road and back home in Nashville, George was always scouting for quality songs. There was plenty of material to choose from, but guessing which ones might catch the ear of the public and become chart-topping triumphs was not at all easy.

Not long after moving to Nashville, while his prospects were still looking uncertain and George himself was struggling to find some confidence, he heard the song 'Before This Day Ends', written by Roy Drusky, Vic McAlpine and Marie Wilson. He really thought it was something special and set his heart on recording it. By contrast, however, Tinky was not impressed with it at all and neither was John D. Loudermilk. Swayed by their negative comments, George decided not to record it.

On the morning of 3 May 1960, George was well into an ABC recording session when Roy Drusky and Vic McAlpine dropped unannounced into the Bradley Studio on Nashville's Sixteenth Avenue, mistakenly believing that he was recording their song. George was so embarrassed about the mix-up that he decided at the last minute to record 'Before This Day Ends' after all. With producer John D. Loudermilk at the helm, the song was hurriedly rushed through in the last 15 minutes of the session. Musicians Ray Edenton and Hank Garland (guitars), Pete Drake (steel), Buddy Harmon (drums) and Lightning Chance (bass), backed up by the Anita Kerr Singers, tackled the unexpected project with some enthusiasm. Much to everyone's astonishment, 'Before This Day Ends' went on to become a number three song in the charts that year. The song they had spent the most time perfecting during that session was 'Loneliness All Around Me'. Ironically, it was put on the flip side and, in retrospect, George concluded that it was the flop side too!

Once George had signed with Chet Atkins to join RCA Victor, his search for winning songs came under the guidance of a genius. Thanks to Chet's creative vision, George enjoyed country hit after country hit, including 'Three Steps To The Phone', 'Truck Drivin' Man' and 'Steel Rail Blues'. 'Three Steps', however, was one that nearly got away. One warm Nashville morning, George was lounging about in Chet's office listening to some demos and deciding on new material to record. Propped up against a wastepaper basket was an unwanted-looking tape. Curiosity piqued, George asked Chet what it was.

'Oh, it's something that Jim Reeves discarded, George,' Chet told him. 'He was just in the office before you. I guess he's becoming tired of people sending him rewrites of "He'll Have To Go"!'

George was reluctant to leave any stone unturned, however, and persuaded Chet to give the demo tape a spin. Chet unpacked the tape and set it to play, clearly with no expectation of finding anything out of the ordinary. But as soon as they heard 'Three Steps To The Phone' they were convinced it was a winner – and it was! Recorded on 15 March 1961 at the Hawkins Street RCA Studio in Nashville, the musicians were once again Ray Edenton and Hank Garland (guitars), Pete Drake (steel), Buddy Harmon (drums) and Lightning Chance (bass), plus the Anita Kerr Singers. By the end of 1961 George IV's first RCA single was a Top Ten country record.

George with his parents, Hege and Sis, and his brother Cabot in 1958. © *George Hamilton IV Library*

With Perry Como. © *George Hamilton IV Library*

Left With President Harry Truman.
© *George Hamilton IV Library*

Below On the beach in Hawaii with Chuck Berry.
© *George Hamilton IV Library*

Right With Gene Vincent and Eddie Cochran.
© *George Hamilton IV Library*

Below right With Jim Reeves.
© *George Hamilton IV Library*

With John D. Loudermilk,
Chet Atkins and
Jimmy Moore.
© Jimmy Moore

Charlie Dick, Sis,
Hege, Patsy Cline
and Joe Haymore.
© Joe Haymore

Boarding a plane for the 1969 European tour with Connie Smith, Skeeter Davis, Nat Stuckey and Bobby Bare.
© George Hamilton IV Library

At the Kremlin with Mervyn Conn and Soviet soldiers.
© George Hamilton IV Library

With Robert Mitchum and Fred Foster.
© *George Hamilton IV Library*

Taking Ted Kennedy on a tour of the Country Music Hall of Fame.
©*Nancy Warnecke*

Introducing Carl Perkins at Wembley.
© *George Hamilton IV Library*

With Billy Graham and Tinky at Mission '89 in the UK.
© Billy Graham Evangelistic Association

At John Newton's church in the UK with Cliff Barrows and George Beverly Shea.
© Billy Graham Evangelistic Association

With the Duke and Duchess of Hamilton, the Mayor of Nashville and George V.
© City of Nashville, Davidson County

George's three children, Mary Dabney, Peyton and George V.
© Robert N. Nance

In the spring of 1963, during one of his sessions recording folk-style songs, George heard a familiar voice coming through his headphones. 'Hey, George! Do you know any cowboy or western ballads? We need somethin' compatible with the Carter Family's "Jimmie Brown The Newsboy", the Bailes Brothers' "Oh So Many Years" and Jimmie Davis's "You Are My Sunshine" ... got any good ideas?' It was the familiar drawl of the producer, Chet Atkins.

George racked his brains for a few seconds and then replied, 'Well, I know a few, and I've got one tucked away in my dresser drawer back home, Chet! It ain't much – just a simple little thing called "Abilene". I've been holding onto it for a couple of years.'

'Well, let's hear it, George!'

Glancing up as he tentatively brought the song's lyrics and melody back to mind with the help of his guitar, George saw that Chet was gaining in enthusiasm. 'Yes,' said the producer with assurance, 'let's cut it for this album. I kinda have a gut feeling, George, that this little ol' song's gonna be a winner!'

If anyone could spot a winner, it was Chet Atkins. George swallowed his surprise and assembled the musicians – Ray Edenton, Wayne Moss, Joseph Tanner and Billy Byrd (guitars), Pete Drake (steel), Henry Strzelecki (bass), James Isbell (drums), Pig Robbins (organ) and Floyd Cramer (piano), along with the Anita Kerr Singers once more. Bob Gibson the folk singer and his then manager Les Brown had put together the first version of 'Abilene', and John D. Loudermilk arranged and updated the song for George's RCA version. The song was recorded on 20 March 1963. In all honesty, George himself never thought the ditty was very commercial, and no one else in the studio seemed unduly impressed either. Chet, however, went to play the song to the RCA top brass. Astutely, they decided to release 'Abilene' as a single.

The catchy song went all the way to number one in the Country Chart and even rocketed into the USA's Top Twenty Pop Chart. George is still surprised and amused by the astonishing success of that 'lightweight' song. 'I've been searching through my dresser drawers ever since, looking for another "Abilene"!' he laughs. To cap it all, 'Abilene' eventually made it into the Trivial

Pursuit quiz game, with the question, 'What is the prettiest town George Hamilton IV has ever seen?' The simple ballad became a country classic, and something of a 'signature song' for George IV. In 1993 it was featured in the film soundtrack for Clint Eastwood's and Kevin Costner's *A Perfect World*. A large part of the original success of 'Abilene' was due to the folk song revival which was gathering pace at that time. The revival carried groups such as the Kingston Trio, the New Christy Minstrels and Peter, Paul and Mary to international fame. In their wake came Bob Dylan, Barry McGuire, Joan Baez, Judy Collins and a host of others.

As a follow-up to 'Abilene', John D. Loudermilk custom-wrote the song 'Fort Worth, Dallas or Houston' for George. Then, just before its scheduled release date, came the terrible news of the Dallas assassination of President Kennedy in November 1963. The whole world was in a state of shock after the President was killed. Certainly nobody wanted to hear a song about Dallas. RCA postponed its release for over a year, and it was a wise decision. When the song did come out, George was delighted – and perhaps a little relieved – that it sold surprisingly well.

When it comes to likes and dislikes, George makes no apologies for being very opinionated about 'his' kind of country music. One thing is for sure: he likes what he likes and dislikes what he doesn't like, and no one is going to change his mind! He is never backward about voicing his opinions.

Musically, he has always been a bit of a revolutionary and during his lifetime there have been what he describes as a few 'quiet, beautiful revolutions' in the world of country music of which he strongly approves. He likes to think that he was on the front lines when those revolutions were happening, and without doubt he was. More than once he has been the catalyst for change. 'I got kinda tired of people telling me what was country and what wasn't,' he says. 'Country music was and is a state of mind! It's a big state – even bigger than Texas! – because it embraces everything from the wonderful, old, traditional sounds of Bill Monroe, Jimmie Rodgers and Gene Autry through the smooth country sounds of Eddy Arnold, Jim Reeves and Glen Campbell, to the modern sounds of Ricky Skaggs, Garth Brooks, Alan Jackson and Marty Stuart.' The genre is certainly no longer limited to rednecks in rhinestones and stetsons – George himself is proof of this!

George's lengthy career has seen a wonderful parade of diverse and poetic songwriters, all willing to use their imaginations and try new things. Their names make an impressively long list, ranging from Hank Williams to John D. Loudermilk and including Harlan Howard, Gordon Lightfoot, Tom T. Hall and Paul Overstreet along the way – to mention just a few. 'I'm so glad that many of these great writers progressed beyond the "honky-tonk trauma" and the "slipping-around lifestyle" in their material,' George comments with appreciation. 'Thank heaven for our thinking poets!'

George also believes that he witnessed a revolution in the growth of a new generation of energetic and enthusiastic DJs. Along with some modern creative artistes, they have refused to accept that country music should be necessarily static, stagnant and unchanging. Listeners have played a vital part too. 'The new generation of country music fans are constantly looking for fresh and innovative performers to join the ranks of the great artistes of the past,' he says. Since George first moved to Nashville in the sixties, hundreds of country music radio stations have seeded themselves across the USA and he is delighted to have witnessed their growing maturity. 'Many present their country music with taste, class and intelligence. They've avoided that corny "howdy friends out in radioland" approach. That served its purpose once, but it's had its day now!'

To George's mind, the country music revolutionaries of today have been well schooled and well trained by the 'master sergeants' who grace the Country Music Hall of Fame. Theirs is a living, breathing legacy as far as he is concerned. 'I love the past – but I recognize that country music, like an army, continually needs fresh, new recruits to fill its ranks. Unless a river receives fresh supplies, its waters soon turn stagnant.' George himself learned a huge amount from great figures such as Hank Williams, Ernest

Tubb and Hank Snow, but he was schooled by an amazingly wide range of teachers. After all, he was building his career through the so-called 'golden rock'n'roll years'. Cross-fertilization was inevitable. George puts it this way: 'Those mean rockers spied on us country folk and purloined some of our best songs and talent! Yet we in turn stole some of *their* new sounds, like echo, voices and drums. We used them to win over new recruits to our side. Country music in the twenty-first century will be a rich, diverse tapestry of colour and sound that embraces both past and present generations.'

Historically, one of the greatest trend-setting styles to have affected the world's recent popular music culture is the genre known as 'the Nashville Sound'. In the thick of it all, of course, was George Hamilton IV. As a member of Chet Atkins' clan, he revelled in the excitement and creativity of those years, as the RCA Victor label became the flagship of the Nashville Sound.

George recalls those heady days with great affection. 'Much hype has been produced about the Nashville Sound, but in my mind, just two guys should take the first bows – Chet Atkins and Owen Bradley. Between them these two gentlemen, both father figures, both music-lovers above all else, created the Nashville Sound. Nashville wasn't built by accountants, lawyers, salespeople or computer programmers. There's too much talk nowadays about units, merchandising, products, markets and such. Too little is said about the arts of music and songwriting! Owen Bradley started early in Nashville as the piano player with the WSM Orchestra, and he went on to become the producer for Patsy Cline, Loretta Lynn, Conway Twitty, the Wilburn Brothers, Webb Pierce, Burl Ives, Bill Anderson, Kitty Wells, Brenda Lee, Bobby Helms, Jimmie Davis, Ernest Tubb and many more. He could produce the masterly touch because he was at heart a *musician* not a businessman.'

With Chet Atkins' clan, George really was at the centre of things, working with the most glittering array of talented musicians he could ever hope for. Nothing before or since has been quite like it, and he treasures many vivid memories from those days, some now tinged with sadness as he recalls long-lost friends. Jim Reeves was one of these. Before George ever moved to Music City USA, he and Texas-born Jim Reeves had crossed paths on several occasions, mainly in pop music venues. Jim's deep, velvet voice was still to mature at that time, and he was struggling to gain pop recognition while George was desperate for country success.

It was under the auspices of Chet Atkins, however, that Jim Reeves enjoyed his greatest success, with the smooth sounds of 'He'll Have To Go'. George remembers his colleague and friend with respect and affection. Life had been hard for Jim, whose father had died when he was just a baby, leaving Jim's mother to fend for nine children on the family farm. There were no easy breaks, but eventually, via radio announcing work, Jim made it to stardom as a vocalist, initially finding success with novelty songs such as 'Bimbo' and 'Mexican Joe'. George describes Jim as a gentleman, but his early struggles had clearly toughened him up and he was not someone to be trifled with. 'Undoubtedly, he commanded respect! I'd seen him get into some pretty serious arguments with agents and promoters whom he considered were trying to abuse him and his band. He knew exactly what he wanted, which made him professional and meticulous in everything, and in turn produced great artistry.'

When the Hamiltons first moved to Nashville, Jim and Mary Reeves were most friendly and welcoming to them, inviting them over for meals and doing whatever they could to help the newcomers. George was therefore astonished one day to find himself at loggerheads with his 'gentleman' friend. He had a booking for a show, but was without a band to back him. In the hope that his pal would be able to help him out, George called on Jim Reeves. 'Jim, can I ask a favour of you? Can I ask you to kindly loan me your band for a few songs?'

Jim just flatly refused. His blunt dismissal of the request shook George to the core. He certainly had not expected such a change of mood. Camaraderie, it seemed, was not allowed to interfere with business. To Jim it was irrelevant that he and George were friends, or that they were both with RCA Victor, members of the Chet Atkins clan. 'My boys work only with me!' he told George in no uncertain terms. 'You need to understand, George, my band doesn't work with anybody but me!' Jim was never one to mince his words, and George was not the only one to find himself on the wrong end of a verbal bashing from Jim Reeves.

They remained friends, however, and when Jim died near Nashville in an appalling plane crash on 31 July 1964, George mourned his premature passing and for years afterwards missed Jim's colourful personality. The whole of Chet's clan were knocked sideways by the fatal accident. 'The day that Jim Reeves' plane went missing,' he recalls, 'there had been eyewitness reports from folks who said they'd heard the sound of a low-flying plane, obviously in trouble, during a heavy rainstorm. It was said to have been moving west from Franklin Road, so much of the searching was done in that direction. Chet, myself and many other RCA artistes all helped with the search, but we found nothing in the first couple of days. No wreckage, nothing.

'Then someone at the Emergency Rescue Service found a transcript of a call from Marty Robbins, who lived on a street just west of Franklin Road. He had contacted the search team to report that he had been taking a shower when the rainstorm hit that day. He decided to go out into the yard to rinse his hair! But as he was doing that, he said he heard a loud explosion to the east of his house, on the *east* side of Franklin Road. Another search party started out, and sure enough, they walked right up on the crash site. There were several houses in the area but all the people had been away on the day of the crash. Nobody had heard or seen the plane go down in the woods, and the trees completely hid the crash site.

'Jim Reeves was most likely confused by vertigo at the time of the plane crash. He probably lost his bearing in the storm and thought he was pulling his plane up and out, but in fact he probably did a loop, much like Randy Hughes, the pilot on Patsy Cline's fatal plane trip, apparently did. As I understand it, neither Jim Reeves nor Randy Hughes had an instrument licence. They weren't really authorized to fly in bad weather or at night. It was an awful tragedy, and a real loss for the Nashville scene.'

Another bright star in the Nashville galaxy was Kentucky-born Skeeter Davis. A bubbly and genuine personality, invariably talkative and outgoing, George says she was always a special lady for him. He and Skeeter recorded two duets for RCA, 'Everything Is Beautiful' and the folkish 'Let's Get Together', both produced by Ronnie Light. In those days the duo were affectionately referred to as the Opry's 'Flower Children'!

'In the early sixties,' George reminisces, 'Skeeter and I were having pop hits at about the same time. Skeeter's "The End Of The World" was a dual pop and country hit at around the same time as "Abilene", so we were kinda like soul mates in Nashville. We did pop shows together as well as country shows, because of the crossover success of our songs. We hit it off really well and became dear friends. When I first moved to Nashville, of course, I remembered Skeeter as part of the Davis Sisters before her sister Betty Jack's death. Their duet song, "I Forgot More Than You'll Ever Know" was always a favourite of mine.'

Unlike many of the female country singers who had to fight for their success, Skeeter never came across as tough or hard. In many ways, her warm and open character reminded George of his mother, Sis. He remains very fond of the RCA recordings he made with Skeeter Davis, as they hold such happy memories.

One female country star with a completely different personality from Skeeter was, of course, Patsy Cline. George had known her for several years before making his move to Nashville and, he says, she may have had a heart of gold, but she was undeniably a tough lady! Like Jim Reeves, she knew what she wanted and was not prepared to make concessions to anyone. 'She was capable of cussing like a sailor and holding her liquor with the best of them, but she was by no means an alcoholic or a crude person. I don't ever remember her letting the bottle get the best of her! Nobody dared cross Patsy, but I got on well with her despite her bluntness and abrasive exterior. She was probably bemused by me. I recall her once slapping me on the back and laughing, "George, you're just too nice for your own good. You need to get some backbone, or you're gonna be taken for a sucker!" Patsy didn't spend much time teasing or making fun of people she didn't like, so I always took her playful picking on me as a seal of approval.

'Patsy had paid her dues via rough honky-tonk venues and she'd had to learn to take care of herself in a world dominated by men. She was a good person to have on your side in a fight; she could sure hold her own with the guys! Up until then, the female artistes were just sort of window-dressing on the men's shows, to brighten the proceedings between the male acts. Patsy was determined to be centre-stage, a star in her own right, and she did exactly that! She was a very strong, independent woman, but she was a real lady with a big heart.'

News of her premature death rocked the whole of Nashville. As with the day Jim Reeves died, George recalls very vividly how he heard about Patsy's death. 'Along with the whole of the industry, I was shocked and saddened by her plane-crash death on 5 March 1963. It happened just at a time when she was becoming world famous. I was at home in Nashville on that spring day and a DJ from my home town of Winston-Salem telephoned me before dawn to ask for my reaction to "the news". He told me we were live on air, but I'm sure my tone was initially less than friendly. I was pretty upset about his phone call waking me up so early!

'I asked rather tersely what "news" he was talking about and the DJ went on to tell me that Patsy Cline, Hawkshaw Hawkins, Cowboy Copas and Randy Hughes had all been killed in a plane crash in the town of Camden in West Tennessee. That's all I really remember about that phone call. It was a shocking blow, to say the least, and very difficult being asked to do a live radio interview with immediate reactions to the news, especially having only just been awakened from a deep sleep. Of course, when I went to bed the night before, none of us had even heard that Patsy's plane was in trouble or missing. It must have happened after the local television newscast.' Nashville was once again in mourning for a lost star.

A rather less abrasive character was Bobby Bare from Ohio, who enjoyed early pop success with his song 'The All American Boy' – the story of a Southern boy who became a rock'n'roller in Nashville.

Bobby and George were signed up by Chet Atkins at about the same time. Both easy going, they made the most of their common bond as part of the Atkins clan and discovered a mutual affinity in their liking for the Canadian folk-country music performed by the likes of Gordon Lightfoot and Ian Tyson. Both Bobby and George recorded several of those artistes' songs in the early sixties, along with other folk-orientated pieces. Later Bobby also tried his hand at some movie acting as Hollywood beckoned. George was surprised and delighted to spy his old buddy up on the silver screen, chasing the proverbial Indians across a painted desert, dressed in US cavalry uniform! He readily expresses great appreciation for Bobby Bare, and reckons that his story-telling balladeering was second to none. 'A real, charming, likeable guy, Bobby Bare and I have remained buddies down the years. He is aptly named when I describe him as a "Teddy Bare"!'

There were other equally endearing individuals in the clan too. Instrumentally, apart from Chet Atkins, Louisiana-born Floyd Cramer was the pride of the Nashville sessioners with his world-famous keyboard skills. A quiet Southern gentleman, Floyd was very well liked and his RCA Victor recordings outsold those of all his peers, a fact which impressed George enormously. 'With his slip-note style, he had a sensitive touch on the piano on great hit tunes like "Last Date" and "On The Rebound". His innovative style was mimicked and utilized around the world. Without doubt, Floyd was instrumental in helping to mould the art form that became known as the "Nashville Sound". You seldom hear a *truly* innovative musical style, but Floyd Cramer did produce one, and RCA marketed it so very successfully.' His death in the late nineties was a sad moment for George. The Chet Atkins clan members were more than mere work colleagues – in George's view, they were like family.

Eddy Arnold was one of the most senior members of the RCA team, along with Hank Snow. Another Atkins family member, the Tennessee-born Eddy Arnold, was one of George's biggest boyhood heroes. At a time when Hank Williams' gutsy honky-tonk style (the forerunner of rock'n'roll) ruled the roost, Eddy, wearing suits and ties, was determined to upgrade the image of country music. He evolved into a crooner of great class and was a worthy inductee into the Country Music Hall of Fame.

His costumes and easy-going attitude greatly influenced George in his own stage presentation, and he too favoured smart suits, ties and blazers rather than the 'rhinestone cowboy' look. 'No one could cynically say, "Yee, haa!" to Eddy Arnold's classy crooning,' he says. 'It certainly matched the "Yankee" crooners such as Perry Como, Frank Sinatra, Tony Bennett and Bing Crosby. In that easy-listening sphere of the business, Eddy proudly waved the country music flag for a long lifetime!' George consequently held the superstar in high esteem, and when Eddy covered George's recording of 'Before This Day Ends', the newcomer from North Carolina took it in good spirit as a backhanded compliment. In any case, fortunately for George, his version won the battle for sales!

George's memories of Eddy Arnold go right back to his early visits to Nashville as a schoolboy. 'On one of my Greyhound bus trips to Nashville, I went to the WSM studio rehearsals for the 'Prince Albert' Opry show. I went over to the Clarkston Hotel, which was the gathering place where all the hillbillies went to eat and get coffee before rehearsals. It was a Saturday morning and the Willis Brothers, who were also known as the Oklahoma Wranglers, were there. They had played on Hank Williams' first recording in Nashville and had toured quite a bit as Eddy Arnold's early country road band. Little Roy Wiggins, Eddy's steel guitar player, was there too. I recognized Little Roy, so I went over and told him how Eddy Arnold was one of my heroes and favourite singers. He and the Willis Brothers told me that if I wanted to meet Eddy, he was out at his office in Brentwood that morning. They said they were *sure* he'd be thrilled to meet me.'

Young George failed to twig that this was a practical joke they were trying to play both on him and on their friend Eddy – sending this teenage 'spook' out to bug him! Unaware, George duly hailed a taxi and went to Brentwood. He steadfastly went up to the front door of Eddy's office. Being a Saturday morning, most business offices were closed, so Eddy was not expecting company that day. George knocked on the door. Eddy opened it, looked a little surprised to see his visitor, yet spoke politely and patiently.

'Yes, can I help you?'

Pleased as punch to meet his hero, George replied confidently, 'Good morning Mr Arnold. Roy Wiggins and the Willis Brothers sent me out here. They said you'd be here this morning and maybe I might get a chance to meet you.'

A knowing smile crept over the star's face. 'I'm sure he knew right off the bat that this was their way of playing a practical joke, but he was most cordial. He invited me in and never let on that he was in the least bothered by me dropping in on him. He offered me a seat and let me have my say about what a great guy I thought he was. He then said, "Excuse me a moment." He went back into his office and returned with an autographed picture which I still treasure to this day.

'I could hear somebody singing down the hallway. It was the voice of Marty Robbins singing a western song in one of the offices. Marty and Eddy were really good friends and they both lived in Brentwood. Marty had come by to see Eddy and sing him a few of the new songs he'd written. Eddy really had more important things to do than listen to me prattling on! I didn't get to meet Marty, but I left Eddy's office that morning firmly believing that he had been thrilled to see me on his doorstep! I'm sure Little Roy Wiggins and the Willis Brothers heard a rather different opinion about their practical joke...' When George finally made it to Nashville as an adult, the earlier escapade was forgotten and Eddy made him welcome all over again. 'I came to value most highly Eddy's counsel as a wise business person,' George comments with a smile.

Many of George's colleagues in the Chet Atkins brigade could be described as big personalities. Perhaps one of the most charismatic was Missouri-born Porter Wagoner, whose earthy ballad style was always a hit with George IV. 'My first demo as a teenager for the Colonial Records label,' he recalls, 'was Porter's hit "A Satisfied Mind". Tall and lanky, Porter's loud Nudie Cohen western suits and cowboy boots were to remain his trademark, despite the changing styles around him.

Porter Wagoner rightly takes credit for first introducing Dolly Parton to the world, initially as his show's featured female soloist and duettist. 'Although his partnership with Dolly Parton ended in some acrimony, Porter is a real charmer! I don't think Porter's got a mean bone in his body. This so-called "Thin Man from the Missouri Plains" has done more than is sometimes appreciated to keep things country, especially during the days of the rock'n'roll onslaught. Porter nailed his country colours to the mast. Refusing to budge, he defended them against tremendous odds. Although he's quite renowned for his glitzy, rhinestone-suited stage persona, Porter has recorded quite a few spiritual songs too, especially with the Blackwood Brothers – "Trouble In The Amen Corner", "Green, Green Grass of Home", and "Men With Broken Hearts". He developed quite a forte for recitations and recordings with a spiritual flavour. Of course, his very first hit, "A Satisfied Mind", was a very spiritual song.'

Hank Snow, 'The Singing Ranger', was another vocalist of outstanding quality and added something unique to the country genre. Highly respected for his professionalism, he enjoyed a very lengthy career. With his high-heeled western boots and sequinned cowboy suits, Hank Snow was an imposing personality. He was a major star in country music since before World War II and was another of George's boyhood idols.

Born Clarence Eugene Snow on 9 May 1914 in Brooklyn, Nova Scotia, his parents divorced when he was only eight years old. Hank went to live with his elderly grandmother, but he ran away from home at the age of 12. The sea beckoned, and he spent four years on the Atlantic doing exhausting, dirty work with the fishing fleet. During these years, however, he managed to develop a love of and a talent for country music. During the tough days of economic depression, he somehow managed to scrape a living out of his fledgling musical career. As a boyhood fan, George enjoyed hearing Hank's ballad 'My Nova Scotia Home', which painted an evocative musical picture of the life of the Nova Scotia fishermen. Later George chose to record a version himself. It was so popular that it was often requested on George's performing trips to Toronto's Horseshoe venue.

Hank joined the Opry on 7 January 1950 and recorded more than 80 albums comprising more than 2,000 songs and instrumentals. His wonderfully rich voice, gaudy rhinestone suits and million-selling hit songs such as 'I'm Movin' On' made him a country music legend for more than 50 years. Country music was not his only concern, however, and in 1978 he started the Hank Snow Child Abuse Foundation.

A committed professional, Hank was a founding member of the Chet Atkins clan and left an enduring, monumental audio legacy. He died just 10 days before the dawn of the new millennium. He was a pivotal figure on the Nashville scene, yet he was not without his enemies, as George explains. 'Hank Snow was one of the most misunderstood guys in country music, I guess. Sometimes he was called the "little general" behind his back. Without doubt, he was a most proud individual, yet when one fully appreciated all he had been through, it should have been enough to soften one's attitude to him. Life's experiences leave their scars on us all. Originally from a broken home, I believe he suffered abuse as a child before running away to sea to join Canada's fishing fleet. That was the toughest kind of life.

'Despite his outstanding talents, as a Canadian making his way in American show business, Hank was too often treated as a foreigner, even when he settled in the USA! He was often misjudged as being remote, arrogant and aloof, but he wasn't like that at all. I deeply respected him. At heart, he was very shy and private. I think he may have compensated for those things by being very serious about what he did. I have been proud to tour with Hank Snow. When he relaxed, let down his guard and felt at home with someone, he would display a warm and jovial spirit. You had to have respect for his skilful artistry in performance and musical terms. A musical legend in his own lifetime, he spent almost half a century with RCA Victor, and his Grand Ole Opry membership nearly exceeded 50 years too – a phenomenal achievement!

'On one of my boyhood trips to Nashville I had the joy of meeting him backstage at the Ryman. It was quite a thrill for me, as his songs were among the first I learned to play on my guitar. Also, even at that age, I was much impressed by all things Canadian! I told Hank I was a singer and guitar-player myself and that someday I hoped to be a full-time professional like him. Then I asked if I could have his guitar pick as a souvenir. I think it kinda caught him off guard for a moment, as he looked at me rather quizzically. Then he spoke kindly in his clear voice: "Well son," he said, "I need it for my next spot on the Opry, but if you'll write down your address for me, I'll send it to you first thing next week." You can imagine how thrilled I was when an envelope arrived a few days later with the return address 'Rainbow Ranch', Madison, Tennessee! Inside was not only the pick, but also an autographed colour photo of The Singing Ranger himself. I still have the photo and the guitar pick, framed and hanging on my wall at home.

'In the early sixties Hank had a music store, the Hank Snow Music Center, in downtown Nashville. It was managed by the songwriter Ted Daffan. I went in there one morning and they had a little three-quarter-size, cherry-red Sunburst Gibson guitar hanging on the wall. Ted sold it to me for 125 dollars. That's the little guitar I used on every BBC TV series of the *George Hamilton IV Show*. Most folks still associate that guitar with me, and I still use it to this day on the Opry.

'All in all, I found Hank to be a very reserved but also a warm and gracious man who really cared about people. It always impressed me that although he came from the "traditional school" of country music, he was always most kind and supportive to my son George V at the Opry. That meant a great deal.'

Another veteran figure who surprised George by encouraging his son was Roy Acuff. Not one of 'Chet's boys', but often dubbed as one of the kings of country music, the late Roy Acuff gave his life to the cause. Born in Tennessee in 1903, he was often accused of narrow-mindedness on matters such as changing hair fashions (he strongly objected to long-haired men!) and attempts to add new dimensions to country music. 'Keep it country, boys!' was his repeated message. He sometimes had blunt and unkind words to say about 'country rock' and people who tended to dress down. George was therefore delighted to see how Roy joined Hank Snow in encouraging his son, George V, as he pursued his own musical style, pushing out the boundaries of country music. 'Whenever

George V joined me on the Grand Ole Opry, Roy would introduce him with great encouragement and enthusiasm, *despite* the long hair and faded jeans! Hank Snow took quite a shine to my boy too. It made me realize that both he and Roy weren't half as narrow-minded as they were accused of being!'

Hank Snow's own son, Jimmy Rodgers Snow, pastored the Evangel Temple Church in Nashville for many years, helped by his wife Dottie, hosting the 'Grand Ole Gospel Time' radio show that followed the Grand Ole Opry broadcast each week. The Evangel Temple Choir provided the back-up vocals to the million-selling Johnny Cash hit, 'A Thing Called Love'.

During the twentieth century, the Christian name Hank was very popular amongst the country music fraternity. Williams, Snow, Thompson, Cochran and Locklin, all famous Hanks, became household country music names in George Hamilton IV's lifetime. Born in Florida at the close of World War I, Hank Locklin was another singer who enjoyed his greatest hits under the auspices of Chet Atkins, including 'Please Help Me I'm Falling' and 'Send Me The Pillow You Dream On'.

As a young farm boy, Hank worked in the cotton fields and later on the roads during the Depression of the thirties. He learned to 'pick'n'sing' and gained local success at dances and on the radio. He made his professional debut in 1938, but then military service interrupted things for a while. He was later elected mayor of his home town, McLellan in Florida, while still working as a top country star. Hank is a colourful personality with his own unique contribution to the Atkins clan's art form and the Nashville Sound. George believes his music should have found greater success worldwide. 'I've always considered that like Slim Whitman, Hank Locklin could have enjoyed a great career in the British Isles. Both have an appeal to folks who enjoy easy-on-the-ear, tenor voice music, as often performed by singers from the Emerald Isle.'

Another man with a marvellous voice – this time a baritone – is the Canadian-born George Beverly Shea, whom George considers the finest gospel singer of the twentieth century. He is also the writer of great songs such as 'I'd Rather Have Jesus', 'I Will Praise Him' and 'The Wonder Of It All'. His rich voice is known around the world as a result of his 50-plus years of work with evangelist Dr Billy Graham. Together with the song-leader Cliff Barrows, George believes they were a unique team.

'I remember George Beverly Shea often visited Nashville to record. A member of the Chet Atkins clan, his numerous spiritual albums were also on RCA Victor in those days. He was usually produced by Darol Rice or Danny Davis, with arrangers like Anita Kerr and Billy Walker in attendance. Bob Ferguson, one of my producers who was also a songwriter, gave Bev "The Wings Of A Dove" to record, and it's wonderful. Previously, the song was a hit for Ferlin Husky. Incidentally, Bob also wrote Porter Wagoner's "The Carroll Country Accident" and my Christmas favourite with a Mexican flavour, "Natividad".'

The Nashville/gospel connection does not stop with George Beverley Shea. Connie Smith of Elkhart, Indiana was discovered by songwriter Bill Anderson and moved to Music City USA. She achieved great fame, but did not find the fulfilment she had been expecting. Then, with the help of Nashville pastor Jimmy Rodgers Snow, Connie experienced a profound conversion to the Christian faith and found her life transformed. From that time on, she became a very vocal, articulate advocate of the faith in Nashville.

'We Opry members think of Connie Smith as the unofficial chaplain of the Grand Ole Opry,' George comments. 'Roy Acuff used to introduce her as the "Sweetheart of the Opry". She became an active Christian much earlier than many of the rest of us did, certainly before me. She has always been a real witness and inspiration backstage at the Opry. Skeeter Davis too. Connie and Skeeter stood out because they didn't play beer joints and honky-tonk bars. Neither of them are preachy about their faith, but their values and sincerity make a strong impression on many people. Connie often sang gospel songs on the Opry when not many other artistes were doing that. For me, the way she sings "How Great Thou Art" is absolutely wonderful! She sang on Dr Billy Graham's Nashville Crusade quite a few years ago.'

New talent was always welcome, of course, particularly in terms of fresh material. Chet's clan were forever on the lookout for imaginative songwriting. In the early sixties George was getting ready to record his first album for RCA, which became *To You and Yours (From Me and Mine)*. Songwriter Hank Cochran, who was then a 'song-plugger' for Pamper Music, invited him out to Goodlettsville, Tennessee, to hear some material by a new young writer named Willie Nelson.

'I remember Willie drove up in an old, beat-up pick-up truck. At that time he had a little farm in Goodlettsville. This was before Willie went down to Texas and started to become part of the country music legend! He was a struggling, starving songwriter when we first met. Hank Cochran played me a tape of a couple of Willie's songs. I was quite impressed with one of them, called "I Want A Girl", and we recorded it for my first RCA album.

'Years later, after Willie became world famous, we were doing a Grand Ole Opry special for television together. I walked up behind him backstage and started singing a line or two from the song. Before I could get to the next line, Willie turned round and started singing, "Just like the girl who married dear old dad..." He didn't even know what I was referring to – he'd started singing the old pop standard rather than his own song! "No Willie," I told him. "That's a song of *yours* that I recorded back in the sixties!" Willie looked genuinely surprised and said, "Did *I* write that, George?" He'd completely forgotten it!'

Willie had the kind of musical talent that was meat and drink to the enthusiastic artistes working with Chet at RCA Victor. They were all music-lovers together, and George is sure that love affair was at the heart of their huge success. Everyone just revelled in what they were doing, and that surely came across to their public. The biggest problem with Nashville today, George believes, is that it has largely been taken over by accountants, lawyers, computer programmers and pen-pushers! It is not an opinion he voices with any pleasure, and he hopes it is a state of affairs that can be reversed. 'Modern Nashville folks may be good with computer printouts,' he says, 'but they really don't have a love for the ability to create music!'

Fortunately, there are a few notable exceptions to this. George cites Jimmy Bowen as an example. 'He may not have been really popular in all parts of Nashville in the nineties, as he replaced many people in their jobs. Hugely successful as a record man, I believe the prime factor in that success was his own musicianship. He and Buddy Knox were making progressive rockabilly records way back in the fifties! Jerry Crutchfield, Allen Reynolds and Billy Strange (guitarist to the late Tennessee Ernie Ford) are also good examples of the better breed of successful producers whose starting points are as musicians.'

Some appalling decisions have been made by the pen-pushers, there is no doubt about that. Even the great Hank Snow was one of the victims. George tells the story. 'If Chet Atkins had his way, Hank would have been retained by RCA in the same way as Bill Monroe remained with MCA throughout all the business changes there – since the year dot, or so it seemed! MCA sensibly recognized that Bill was a patriarch of country music and RCA should have recognized that Hank Snow was no less a central figure. Hank and Bill, and others like them, are innovators who gave birth to original American art forms. They should surely be in a category beyond the reach of the "business henchmen" of modern Nashville! Hank Snow was very close to being with RCA Victor for half a century. At the threshold of that achievement, he was cruelly given the chop by some office-bound accountant from New York or wherever. No wonder it broke Hank's heart. I can't imagine how he must have felt. If only Chet Atkins had been in the seat of power, history might have been different.'

In the light of developments over the past decade, George has a serious warning to deliver. ' "Muzak City USA" is the possibility I see emerging in place of "Music City". I know some will say I'm just bitter because I haven't been in the charts lately. That's not true. Nevertheless, I do think the industry needs to be aware of the dangers and take appropriate action before the heart and soul departs entirely from Music City USA!'

He is keen, however, that people do not misunderstand his words. The prognosis is not entirely black. George cannot say enough good about such artistes as Randy Travis, Paul Overstreet,

George Strait and others like them. These individuals, he says, are all true originals. 'They are real artistes in the tradition of Chet Atkins. I have plenty of time for the "New Country" breed when it means the likes of Nanci Griffith, Lyle Lovett, Steve Earle, Dwight Yoakam and so on. I do get a little tired and bored with the "hat acts" of Nashville, however. Every label is trying to create its own clone, it seems. Acts who sing like Merle Haggard and dress like George Strait seem to be proliferating! Let's have more individuality, and some real creativity.'

Times do change, of course, and George appreciates that it is impossible to live in the past. Country music has had a great history, but it is not over yet. There may be worries in the present, but the future surely has more greatness in store. This was all brought home to George on a recent visit to Oak Hill, West Virginia, where that innovative genius Hank Williams died. On his way through the area, George made a point of stopping at the Sky Line Drive-In, the truck stop where Hank Williams was found dead on the back seat of his car after a lengthy journey.

In the few years before that fatal day, Hank had blasted into the country charts with a succession of 'heart' songs that eventually crossed over into pop territory. Some, like 'Your Cheatin' Heart', 'Cold, Cold Heart' and 'Jambalaya', have become timeless classics in the half-century since Hank first gave them prominence. Hank was not yet 30 when, on New Year's Eve 1953, his 17-year-old chauffeur Charles Carr drove into the Sky Line Drive-In for a break. He was taking Hank to a concert booking in Canton, Ohio. Charles was not aware that anything was wrong until he offered his passenger some coffee and Hank failed to reply. Hank had died, very quietly, very suddenly, at a time when his singing success was heading for unknown heights.

Always an admirer of Hank Williams, George Hamilton IV wanted to visit the place where he had died. As he walked into the truck stop restaurant, several decades after the tragedy of 1953, he was enormously touched to find the sounds of 'There's A Tear In My Beer' blasting out of the jukebox. It was a duet between Hank Williams and his son. Thanks to the wonders of modern technology, Hank Williams Junior had been able to record his voice with that of his father's, even though he had been far too young to sing with his father while he was alive.

Moved by the coincidence of hearing that song in that place, George spoke to the waitress behind the bar. 'Honey, did anyone ever say anything to you about the night Hank Williams stopped here?'

The waitress looked blank. 'Sorry, no, I don't know anything about that.' Then she smiled and added something she did know: 'But Randy Travis passed through here a couple of weeks ago, sir!'

George was suddenly struck by a truth. That waitress was really too young to have heard of Hank Williams, and if she did recognize the name, she would probably picture Hank Junior rather than Senior! Time moved on, change happened. It was inevitable. Behind him, a soft voice spoke. The cook, an older lady, stood at the door of the steaming kitchen, and told George that she clearly recalled the New Year's Eve tragedy so many years before. Well, that was a crumb of comfort!

The point about the new generation was not lost on George, however. Fame was fleeting. That young waitress had no idea of the connection between her place of employment and the great Hank Williams. Why should she? Young stars like Randy Travis were all the rage now, and older figures such as Hank, however influential they had been, were steadily fading in memory and importance. And yet, the fact that Randy Travis and his band had visited the truck stop was telling. That West Virginia drive-in was not the kind of place you would expect to see a superstar like Randy – unless he had a highly developed sense of country music history and an appreciation of his place in the continuing and developing tradition. George found the thought immensely encouraging. 'Such sensitivity to the past gives me a great sense of hope and faith in the continuing integrity of the country music industry!'

CHAPTER 8

CHANGING PRIORITIES

Watch against lip religion. Above all, abide in Christ and He will abide in you.

Robert Murray McCheyne (church minister, Scotland)

THROUGHOUT THE SIXTIES, George continued to work hard at building his Nashville-based career. He was much in evidence at the Opry, of course, and busy working on new songs and sounds with members of Chet Atkins' clan at RCA. In between all that, he did a tremendous amount of live shows around the country, in all sorts of venues, promoting new recordings, making the most of hit singles, or simply earning the necessary income between those chart-topping times. It was a hectic period of George's life, and he was much away from home. He was grateful for the company of fellow stars, some of whom offered sterling support, acting as fine professional role models, and some of whom gave George pause for thought now and then.

George was thrilled sometimes to find himself in the company of celebrities who had been his own heroes from boyhood. Cowboy movies had been a passion since he was young, and he grew up thinking that Gene Autry, Roy Rogers and Tex Ritter were all at least 12 feet tall. George first met his matinee hero Tex Ritter in California on a hurried, frenetic concert trip. The two were scheduled to appear in several shows together, and even the thought of it gave George goosebumps!

In real life, he found his movie hero to be an impressive character. Slow-talking Tex had a law degree from the University of

Texas and was intelligent and well read – not the first thing you would expect from a matinee idol. Early on, however, Tex had opted for a life in show business rather than a career as a lawyer. Success on Broadway in the show *Green Grow the Lilacs* was the deciding factor. (The stage show is better known today as the basis for the musical *Oklahoma.*) After Broadway, Tex graduated to Hollywood to become a distinguished singing cowboy star with hits like 'High Noon' from the Gary Cooper and Grace Kelly movie. From Hollywood he received the call to Nashville and the Grand Ole Opry.

In Nashville Tex and George shared the same booking agency, Acuff-Rose. It was fronted initially by Jim McConnell and then by Howdy Forrester, Roy Acuff's ex-fiddler. Joint bookings with Tex were always seen as a privilege by George. On the road, he would often share the transport with Big Tex and they spent many long hours chatting as their car sped through the night along endless, two-lane rural highways. The usual pattern was to do an evening show, drive all night to the next destination, sleep all day and then repeat the process, time and time again. Night-time driving meant less heat, less traffic, less time, but the cumulative effect was exhausting. As they travelled, Tex would reminisce in his deep, gravelly drawl about his days on the silver screen with John Wayne, Gene Autry and the other 'heroes'. George loved the stories. 'Boy, was I enthralled by his exciting tales! They made the travel so much easier.'

George's memories of the late Tex are all of warm encounters and wise advice, and he expresses a deep respect for the man who became a true statesman of the country and western genre. 'I found Tex to be a human being of high moral integrity and dignity,' he says. At one time Tex even ran for a seat in the Senate. Capable of projecting the gravitas of a judge with his dignified bearing and measured speech, Tex personally considered that he would have made a great politician. George agreed, but it was not to be. 'Poor Tex was outvoted at the polls and defeated at the last post by Bill Brock, the heir to the Brock Candy fortune. I guess Tex was outgunned financially!' When Tex died in 1974, George felt he had lost more than a colleague or a friend. 'Tex was a fatherly figure, and I looked up to him. Country music lost one of its most articulate advocates when it lost Big Tex.'

Another legendary figure who made a great impression on George during this time was Johnny Cash. The thing that awed him the most was Johnny's strong Christian faith, set against the story of his traumatic life. In George's eyes, if anyone could be described as 'a diamond in the rough', Johnny Cash would surely fit the bill. Billy Graham once said of him, 'I have never met a man who combined spiritual depth, musical ability and international fame with such grace, charm and humility as Johnny.'

Born in February 1932 in Kingsland, Arkansas, Johnny Cash knew severe hardship from the start. His family struggled badly in the Great Depression, and Johnny spent most of his time picking cotton and making extra money by hauling five-gallon water jugs to the prisoners in the work gangs deployed along the banks of the Tyronza River. From an early age he was drawn to country and gospel music and in the fifties launched his own singing career, securing a record contract on the now legendary Sun Records label, along with other greats from the same era – Elvis Presley, Roy Orbison, Jerry Lee Lewis, Charlie Rich, Conway Twitty and Carl Perkins. George remembers it all very clearly. 'His stage attire was predominantly black. He said his dark clothing was indicative of the sad, social causes that his songs would be crusading for.'

His first single, the plaintive 'Cry, Cry, Cry', initially sold 100,000 copies and set the Man in Black on his way. International recognition followed soon after. 'The public loved his songs because there was realism in them. His ballads mirrored true human emotions. Johnny's road in life was far from easy, and his songs reflected his own personal battles – he sang about blood, sweat, tears, booze, prison, the hard life. Then his faith in God led him to pen many great gospel songs, many of them also autobiographical. I loved to hear his song "When He Comes" performed by our mutual friend George Beverly Shea at Billy Graham's mission meetings. Another of his songs I find very meaningful is "Over The Next Hill We'll Be Home".

'Johnny Cash is a folk-singer of the highest order. When he wraps that voice around the lyrics of any song, you know that every last syllable is steeped in sincerity. He once said that he didn't hold any strong political views and was never called to be a preacher – but I can testify that the Man in Black did the job he was cut out to do!'

George finds it impossible to explain adequately the deep pleasure he felt at being so warmly welcomed by his boyhood heroes in Nashville. Now he too was part of their scene, part of the country music 'party'. His ambitions as an artiste and his boyhood dreams were all becoming a reality. At home, however, the reality was not so rosy. The difficulties of being an absentee husband and absentee father were mounting in perfect parallel with his increasing professional success. It seemed unavoidable. At first George accepted the situation as just something that came with the territory, but it was upsetting for all concerned.

An entertainer's life is summed up so well by the late John Denver's song about some days being diamonds and other days being stones. It was a lifestyle without any real consistency, meandering frustratingly between feast and famine. George's biggest problems were the inconsistency of his income and his frequent absences from home. Some of his star colleagues suffered more severely from the temptations of drink, drugs and women. George is grateful that he was never sucked down into such dangers, which proved to be the ruin of many of his peers. 'I'm as human as anyone, of course, but I thank the good Lord that somehow I was spared from being overcome or overtaken by any of those evils.'

It was a weird, unsettling life, there was no doubt about that, and some on the music scene reacted better than others to such an unbalanced existence. Stardom affects people in different ways. Perhaps surprisingly, George's considerable experience of musical celebrity through five decades has shown him that, in fact, the nicest people in country music are generally the biggest stars. The most insufferable have often been those who had nothing to shout about as far as talent was concerned – 'one record wonders' who suddenly had a hit out of the blue and then went on to act as if the world owed them a living.

Inappropriate behaviour is not the monopoly of show people, of course, and George is keen to get all this in perspective. 'As a travelling entertainer who has spent a whole lot of time in restaurants and hotels, I've met many more waiters, waitresses and desk clerks with ego problems than I've found in show business! And I've been amazed at how some pompous people in service professions (after all, I'm in one too) behave so unbecomingly in their roles. Not everyone needs to know that you're feeling off-colour or tired! In any case, within show business or not, personality peacocks are such monumental bores, full of their own importance. How refreshing it is to meet those who exude genuine, sincere humility. Dr Billy Graham is a case in point. He's a major world figure, and he has probably spoken to more people than anyone else in history, yet he's so humble. His whole attitude speaks of servanthood, and that's just what he's about: he's a true disciple of the Christ he teaches about, an example to us all.'

George himself did not really have a problem with an excess of show-biz pride – he is not a 'personality peacock' – but he did have a problem with an excess of work away from home and family. It seemed to be necessary; it was what everyone did; and it was not just for his own benefit. George needed to support his own family, but in due course he also became responsible for others. In the late sixties he put together a band called The Numbers. Depending what the engagement was, they were sometimes placed on a salary and at other times simply on a retainer fee. This put more pressure than ever on George to come up with bookings, as the whole band was relying on him for their families' livelihoods.

Any entertainer's bookings tend to go up and down, in a series of peaks and troughs. When the troughs arrived and cash flow pressures mounted, George would do the sensible thing and keep some money coming in by accepting one-week club engagements in venues such as the Holiday Inn in Kearney, Nebraska, the Guest House in Watertown, South Dakota, the Flame Club in Minneapolis, or the Horseshoe Tavern in Toronto. It was hard work, and some venues were none too salubrious. Eventually

George came to the conclusion that the honky-tonk club lifestyle was not a healthy one for a country performer, especially a married one. 'The main purpose behind the honky-tonks was the provision of alcohol and women. Often the music was pretty incidental. The performer, no matter who it was, frequently found him- or herself ignored by the noisy drunks and so on. It was a thankless task. By the early seventies, I got real tired of that lifestyle. I guess you could call it "honky-tonk burnout"!'

George began to feel the need to address the problem, to reassess his priorities, but he was so busy that it was impossible to think clearly, and in any case he could not see a good solution to his difficulties. He needed to talk to someone older and wiser, but not anyone too closely involved in the Nashville scene. His chance came when he went back home to North Carolina to do a guest spot on the *Arthur Smith TV Show*.

One of George's most valued friends, Arthur is known professionally as Arthur 'Guitar Boogie' Smith after his famous hit which was probably country music's first million-selling instrumental. In Europe, the piece was popularized by the English guitarist Bert Weedon. South Carolina-born Arthur is a multi-instrumentalist and album producer. Many key country and Christian artistes came under his skilled studio direction. He owned a quality studio in Charlotte, North Carolina which gave George the authentic bluegrass backing featured on a couple of albums released on the RCA and Lamb and Lion labels. Avoiding the magnetic pull of Nashville, Arthur became a hugely successful businessman in North Carolina, with interests in television and radio. He also fronted his Crossroads Quartet and Crackerjack Band for many years.

He was a quality songwriter, too, and many country and gospel artistes have dipped repeatedly into the Smith repertoire. For many years Arthur shared top billing on the prestigious MGM record label along with Hank Williams. Among his best known songs were 'Acres Of Diamonds', 'The Shadow Of A Cross', 'You Are The Finger Of God', 'The Fourth Man' and 'I Saw A Man'. Many big-time artistes recorded Arthur's tunes, including the Statler Brothers, Pat Boone, Johnny Cash, Connie Smith, Paul

Wheater, the Blackwood Brothers and George Beverly Shea. By 1999, Bev Shea had recorded no less than 22 Arthur Smith songs. George himself recorded an entire Arthur Smith album entitled *Heavenly Spirituals* for the Homeland label.

A close friend of Billy Graham and George Beverly Shea, Arthur is also a good friend of Johnny Cash. Most people would not immediately associate those two men as likely friends, as they seem to have such different personalities, but the Smith and Cash families often went on holiday together. For years, Arthur was a Sunday School teacher in his home-town Baptist church, and his songs were often based directly on the Bible. A conservative churchman who took his Bible very seriously, he frequently told George that 'God worked out his plans through *ordinary* people and not through the likes of angels and so on'.

The 'Guitar Boogie' man was always one of George's heroes. As a boy he knew Arthur as a household name from his television appearances on the local station WBTV, aired from Charlotte, and he developed a high regard both for Arthur and for Tommy Faile, Arthur's vocalist in the Crackerjack Band. In time, George came to respect Arthur not only as a fine entertainer but also as an outstanding Christian gentleman.

Now, visiting him in North Carolina before appearing on the television show, George took the opportunity to confide in the fatherly Arthur. He told him how unhappy he was playing the honky-tonk bars and eking out a living in beer joints between hit records. Everything was fine and dandy, he explained, while the hits were flavour of the month, as bookings tended to be more classy and uptown during those times. Between the hits, however, there did not seem to be anything but the depressing honky-tonk circuit. Moreoever, he and Tinky were both unhappy about the amount of time he had to spend away from home. George was surprised how attentively Arthur listened to him, and he appreciated his obviously genuine sympathy and concern. Being able to share his problem had already made him feel better, even if there still seemed to be no immediate solution.

After the show, George headed back home to Nashville, back to the same old problems and pressures. Once back at home, he felt a bit down, if he was honest. It had been good to talk, but there had been no reason to expect that Arthur could come up with anything concrete to lighten his burden. He was in for a surprise. Sitting at home some time later, deep in thought and rather gloomy, George was startled by the ring of the telephone. It was Arthur Smith calling from Charlotte. 'Hi, George,' he said cheerfully. 'I enjoyed having you on my show in that guest spot you did. How would you feel about joining me on my new television series as a regular? I'm in the market for a new celebrity singer to replace Tommy Faile, and I think you'll meet the bill!'

Arthur went on to explain how he intended moving to WSOC, and his hopes of having the show syndicated coast to coast across the USA. He and his brother Ralph would put George on a percentage deal. It would, however, mean that the Hamiltons would need to relocate back to North Carolina. The deal sounded great to George. He could hardly wait to share the idea with Tinky. He knew what it would mean. 'Honey, I could give up the honky-tonks and relinquish responsibility for the band,' he told her. 'It's a golden opportunity to concentrate on television work. But more importantly, I'd be at home with you and the family!' Put like that, it was not difficult to gain support for the proposal from his nearest and dearest.

Others were not so convinced. George recalled telling Greg Galbraith, his band's lead guitarist, about his new plans. Greg retorted, somewhat disbelievingly, 'It sounds like you're retiring 15 years early, George!' No matter how it was perceived by his fellow artistes, it was a great opportunity that George did not want to miss. The new prospect of North Carolina sounded much better than the status quo of Nashville. Anyway, in the past George had taken decisions against the advice of others which had subsequently turned out to be right – he had been right to marry Tinky, and he had been right to make the move from pop to country. Once again, he would go his own way.

Soon, Tinky and the family were laying plans for the move, selling their Nashville house and returning to their home state, where they rented a cosy townhouse on the east side of Charlotte.

George was fully convinced that it would be the end of his extensive travels. How little he knew!

At first everything seemed to fall out as they had expected. The family concentrated on settling into their new surroundings, and both George and Tinky felt a profound satisfaction in being back in North Carolina. It was quite different from the hot-house atmosphere of Nashville. Things had changed over the years, of course, but it still had that familiar feel of home. They had not lived there in over a decade, however, and a new environment meant new friends and new activities as they involved themselves in the local community. Connections made in Charlotte were to have far-reaching consequences. George discovered in Arthur Smith not only a welcoming friend, but also a solid, mature Christian influence. Arthur was the first major force George encountered – and became close to – in the country music arena who clearly had a deep love for God and practised what he preached.

Arthur persuaded both George and Tinky to join the membership of Providence Baptist Church (George, although raised in the Moravian tradition, had been baptized in a Baptist church during his time in Nashville, which had no Moravian church). Arthur's wife Dorothy befriended Tinky, inviting her to become actively involved in the Christian Women's Club. Church life became a great source of inspiration and new friends. Later Tinky also joined the Charity League, a ladies' Christian organization which sponsored a day nursery for underprivileged children and working mothers. Little by little, Tinky started to put down new roots in Charlotte.

George, meanwhile, concentrated on a busy schedule as the featured male singer on the *Arthur Smith TV Show*. Now mostly at home during the week, on weekend dates he travelled further afield with the cast of the show. These were happy times for the Hamiltons, as the summer and autumn of 1972 turned into the winter of 1973. They had turned their back on Music City USA, and to all intents and purposes it felt as if they had come home to stay.

It was perhaps a little too idyllic to last. George's sincere plans to come off the road were interrupted by a surprising invitation from England. He was already acquainted with the English promoter Mervyn Conn as a result of his attendance at the very first International Festival of Country Music at Wembley during Easter 1969. Now the BBC's Phil Lewis was offering George the chance to host the first country music television series in the United Kingdom. To be broadcast from London's Nashville Rooms in West Kensington, the shows would give George an unmissable opportunity to increase his visibility in the UK market place and beyond. George jumped at the chance and spent several weeks in Britain filming the shows. Not long afterwards, concert tour invitations from both home and abroad were being mailed to him in profusion at his North Carolina home.

George was quite surprised to discover that it felt good to be out on tour once in a while. He somehow felt it got him back in circulation. He was very happy in North Carolina. It was something of a relief, for one thing, to be in a place devoid of the plastic show-biz trappings associated with centres like Nashville and Hollywood. 'Despite the undoubted professionalism of Arthur Smith and his colleagues,' says George with appreciation, 'they were thankfully not eaten up with show biz and false airs!' It was a refreshing change, but George had to admit – if only to himself – that he was starting to feel some nagging misgivings. 'I enjoyed the lifestyle, but I came to feel fearful about the possibilities of being out of sight and therefore out of mind.'

This was brought home to him one day when the late Dottie West and her band visited the Carolinas to participate in a charity telethon. Dottie shocked George with a direct question: 'George, where have you been?' she demanded. 'It's good to see you again!'

'Likewise, Dottie. I live in Charlotte now,' George replied cheerily.

Her sober response disturbed him far more than she perhaps knew. 'George, come back to Nashville with us where you belong. You belong in Music City, boy!'

George tossed and turned that night, too upset to go to sleep, and wondering seriously for the first time whether the move to Charlotte had been wise in career terms after all. Had it been a serious error to leave Nashville? Dottie had crystallized his hovering doubts, and it was not a welcome experience. That niggling worry permeated the rest of George's time in Charlotte. He was glad to be there in many ways, and was wholly grateful for the chance to spend unrushed time with his family, but somehow he could never feel thoroughly relaxed. Such ambivalence seriously affected his whole-hearted commitment to life in Charlotte, and his concerns provided a breeding ground for discontent. It seemed, after all, that the North Carolina utopia was not quite so wonderful as they had envisaged. 'When you're away from something, it's easy to fantasize and romanticize it! Life had not become perfect overnight with our move back to North Carolina. I could not stop myself wondering what I might be missing, what opportunities might be passing me by.'

Life still had to go on, nonetheless, and George was hardly without opportunities in his present situation. The Hamiltons had made their choice, and now they had to make the most of it. Neither Tinky nor George really believed in hankering after the past. It was important to look forward, and to treat the present, whatever the situation, with determination and appreciation.

Despite his career doubts and developing uneasiness about life in North Carolina, George found his time there valuable in other ways. He discovered that his views and life priorities were undergoing a gradual change, and he began to think more seriously about spiritual questions as he came under the edifying influence of two neighbourly evangelists associated with Dr Billy Graham. Looking back, George realizes how grateful he is for their subtle, unpressing Christian influence on him during that time.

North Carolina, an area with strong religious traditions, is Billy Graham country. Dr Graham lives in a beautiful mountaintop home in the Smokey Mountains, and George Beverly Shea and other associates live not too far away. The preacher Leighton Ford was one of these, and he was married to Jean, Dr Graham's sister. George would often find himself chatting to Leighton when they met at the local car-wash. Later on, Grady Wilson, a longtime friend and confidant of Dr Graham, invited George to participate in an evangelistic meeting in Danville, Virginia, the first such invitation he had ever received. Grady and his wife Wilma, good friends of Arthur Smith, were also members of Providence Baptist Church.

In truth, George felt somewhat embarrassed by the special invitation to join that evangelism team. He had strong misgivings about being on a platform with such 'saints'. His lifestyle was rather different from theirs, for a start (and he still remembered the scathing remarks about the music scene made by the Principal at the Church of Christ college where he had tried to finish his education). He also knew, deep down, that he was not totally committed to Christ – not in the way these serious evangelists meant, anyway. They continued to encourage and include George, however. Leighton Ford later asked George to join him in his meetings to sing and share in Moncton, New Brunswick. George accepted, but remained very much in awe of the committed Christians on the Billy Graham team. Who was *he* to become associated with them? His self-criticism continued to grow.

In fact, Christian influences were strong in Charlotte from many sources, including the television talk show *PTL* (Praise the Lord) with Jim and Tammy Bakker. Having become friends with them, George observed the later misfortunes of the Bakkers with great sadness. He could never have imagined that they would suffer divorce, public disgrace and even prison, in Jim's case. It left George very thoughtful. It was not his place to pass judgement. All he could say was, 'I don't condone the errors and lack of wisdom, but I would point out how easy it is to fall into Satan's carefully laid traps. We should all take heed lest we fall.'

As well as individual friends, George found himself more or less surrounded by indicators of long-standing Christian belief. Firmly positioned in America's Bible Belt, the Carolinas boasted a church on almost every street corner, most of them well supported. Gospel music radio stations were plentiful too. Then, of course, there was his own family background in the Moravian tradition. The original Moravians had been followers of John Huss, with a legitimate claim to being the first organized Protestant denomination. They preceded Martin Luther by about

60 years and helped fan the flame of the Protestant Reformation into the New World. With a strong ecumenical emphasis in their Church, the Moravian motto is, 'In essentials unity, in nonessentials liberty, in all things love.' John Wesley referred to the Moravian approach to faith as a 'heart religion'.

One annual highlight in the Carolinas' religious calendar was the event known as 'Singin' on the Mountain'. This huge get-together was held on North Carolina's Grandfather Mountain and was attended by thousands, attracted by a varied and colourful programme with leeway for spontaneity. At 6,000 feet above sea level, Grandfather Mountain boasts the highest peak of the Blue Ridge Mountains and provides a majestic backdrop to the great singing and worship event. Down the years, many outstanding singers and preachers have contributed to the gathering, some local such as Shelby E. Gragg and the mountain parson Alfonso Buchanan, and others with names of international significance such as Dr Billy Graham and Dr Oral Roberts. The unique mix of 'backwoods' amateurism and 'urban' professionalism is all part of the event's appeal. As a performer alongside Arthur Smith and others at several of these gatherings, George says he always enjoyed the exhilarating spectacle of the 'preachin', singin' and shoutin''. It was quite an insight into the traditions and spirituality of his home state.

George's local church when he was a boy in Winston-Salem was a small missionary church. It had seemed less concerned about the size of its own congregation than with more far-flung missionary work. Nonetheless, the church leadership took care to instil the basics of the Christian faith in its members, young and old, and George is grateful for that early grounding. 'Most folk down South would describe themselves as believers. Most are affiliated to a church where they get their spiritual food and drink. Going to church is important, I think. Being with fellow believers boosts you up and offers encouragement. I don't believe it's enough to say, "I can worship the Lord out in the middle of an open field – I don't need to go to church..."'

Raised in such a strong church-going area, George was surprised to find that it was quite different in other areas and other countries. The more interested he became in matters of faith, the more eye-opening his international trips became. Britain, with its low church attendance figures, was one of the places that shocked him most. 'I'd always considered the British Isles to be the cradle of Christian civilization. We North Carolinians always looked to the British Isles as the place where our ancestors originated, so it seemed strange to me that people here in the South's Bible Belt could be so church-orientated, while our cousins back in the home country seemed to be so much the opposite!' Little did George know then that he would later take part in numerous evangelistic events in Britain, performing in hundreds of local church concerts – a man from the New World sharing his faith in the Old Country.

In the early seventies, George's deepening spiritual awareness and more conscious engagement with the faith that had been with him since childhood was not yet evident in his songs. Indeed, the demands of work were once again gaining the upper hand and he found himself in increasing demand. In August 1972 George embarked on his first nationwide UK concert tour for Mervyn Conn. This was soon followed by an invitation from television producer Manny Pittson to do a show which would be televised across Canada from Hamilton, Ontario. The Canadian series was sold on to a number of foreign countries, including Ireland, Great Britain, South Africa and New Zealand.

George consequently found himself with simultaneous television series being broadcast in the UK and Canada, as well as the USA via Arthur Smith's show. Exposure was particularly strong in the British Isles, as both the BBC and ITV networks were screening his shows. Offers to make personal appearances on tour came pouring in as a result, which meant that although George was off the road, he was actually in the air for a considerable amount of time! Flights to Canada and the British Isles became frequent features of his life. So much for the plans to spend more time with his family!

'I guess you could say that I'm a creature of television,' says George wryly. 'My career was jumpstarted both in Canada and on the other side of the Atlantic by way of television. In the seventies, when we were doing the syndicated series from Hamilton, Ontario, the programme was picked up by the ITV network in the UK and shown late at night there. They used to call it "a late-night filler", broadcast after the pubs closed. All the symbolism on that series was Canadian or American, from the props to the material and the guests – who included Mac Wiseman, Doc and Merle Watson, John D. Loudermilk and Skeeter Davis. Our European viewers didn't seem to mind, however, and the show was also screened in Ireland on RTE Television for several years. During that same period, I was doing a television series for BBC 2 Outside Broadcasts. Some of the guests on that series were people like Olivia Newton John, Ralph McTell, the writer of "Streets of London", the McCalmans, Moira Anderson and Albert Lee. We also had some American guests including Skeeter Davis, John D. Loudermilk and Slim Whitman.'

In a repeat of their previous difficulties, the pressures and strains on the Hamiltons' home life in Charlotte started to mount as George's success grew. The children were getting older, and contrary to intentions, the move to North Carolina seemed to mean even more absences from home for George. It was a strange turn of events, but he could not have foreseen how his career would take off in international terms. That possibility certainly had not been at the forefront of his expectations in Nashville. Now here he was, travelling the world, in demand in many countries and enjoying an ever-rising status, all thanks to a break into television. Looking back, however, George does admit that once again those exciting developments took place at some cost to his home life.

George could not stop, though. There was so much to do, so much intriguing music to explore. He was open to new ideas all the time: country, pop, rock, folk, rhythm and blues, gospel – all these musical styles left their mark on him and contributed to the unique style he came to create. George has never been much enamoured with labels, however. 'Just file me under "Country Singer" and I'll be happy!' he says. 'That's all I ever wanted to be, since I first heard Hank Williams' wail on those heavy 78s.'

Most singers exhibit various trends in their style as their career progresses, and George has always prided himself on being an experimentalist. Like every innovator, he has also continually wanted to re-examine what he has already done, to review and evolve, to improve where he can. Over many decades, such experimentation has led George down diverse paths, not least into the riches of contemporary urban folk music. 'It never hurts to re-examine our traditions in order to remain basic, down to earth and honest,' he explains. 'Things are so complicated these days that we often forget there is elegance in simplicity! People are always eager to hear high-quality songs that say something worthwhile. When such lyrics are married to pretty melodies and attractive arrangements, "country" or not, they touch people's hearts.'

In the late sixties and early seventies, Waylon Jennings, Bobby Bare and George Hamilton IV were all part of the 'folk-country' promotion push by RCA Records. George took the chance to record Joni Mitchell's 'Urge For Goin'', which he described as 'a pretty folky and left-of-centre song for Nashville at that time'. It was clearly a winner. George was in the Nashville studio listening to the final mix when Waylon Jennings dropped by. After Waylon heard the freshly recorded version of Joni's song, he came over to George. 'Where'd you get that song, man?' he demanded. 'I hate you!' Fortunately, he was smiling, and George was relieved to see that he meant it in a jokey way. Nonetheless, Waylon was probably not the only one to wish he had secured that special song for himself.

George first met Waylon when he was working with Buddy Holly as his bass player. That was back in 1958 when George toured with Buddy, and he and Waylon developed a good friendship over the years that followed. Waylon was another innovator. 'Waylon, like Buddy, was from Lubbock, Texas. I think they were high-school friends. Waylon and I later did several country music package show tours together. We always hit it off really well. Musically, we were both coming from the same place, both of us with a liking for folk-country music and lyrical songs. Waylon, however, was into way-left-of-centre material like "MacArthur Park" and all that, while almost everyone else in country music was into the styles of George Jones and Buck Owens. Waylon was definitely a trailblazer in terms of the folk-country and country-rock trends in country music.

'Recently I've been impressed by his work on the *Old Dogs* CD release with Mel Tillis, Jerry Reed and Bobby Bare. I think it's a wonderful concept, old country stars kind of making fun of themselves! If I'd known they were working on that CD project, I would probably have invited myself along ... I think it's great how they take a light and humorous look at ageing – we hear so much these days about age discrimination. Certainly, the focus of country radio in the States is narrowed down today to "hot, young country" at the expense of everything else. It's nice to be reminded by Waylon and the boys that old dogs still have some life in them!'

From an artistic point of view, George was always eager to explore fresh musical areas, never content merely to rest on the laurels of previous chart success or the security of the status quo. Style, sound and musical content were all aspects that had to change and grow, and George found great satisfaction in pushing back the boundaries. The urban folksong revival which began in the sixties was a particular boon, and George soon started to record material by Bob Dylan, Peter, Paul and Mary, Leonard Cohen, Joni Mitchell, Barry McGuire and Gordon Lightfoot. As time passed, he found himself moving away from the safe confines of the now-established Nashville Sound to pioneer his own brand of folk-country music.

As part of his development of this 'thinking man's folk-country music', George remembers how he found fresh audiences and a different kind of concert venue at events such as the Newport Folk Festival of 1968. There he appeared alongside such rebel luminaries as Pete Seeger, Joan Baez, Arlo Guthrie and Janis Joplin. His new contacts were an inspiration to him, and he particularly admired Joni Mitchell. 'I remember once when Joni was in Nashville appearing on the Johnny Cash television show. I got a phone call inviting me down to the Ramada Inn where she and some other entertainers guesting on the show that week were staying. When I arrived at her room and knocked on the door,

Joni opened it and I was greeted by a couple of The Monkees – Mickey Dolenz and Michael Nesmith – as well as Graham Nash and Mickey Newbury, plus a young songwriter who was just beginning to make his mark in Nashville but was not very well known yet.

'Everyone was singing songs, playing guitars and leaping about from bed to bed! There was a lot of merry-making, and people seemed to be taking turns to impress each other with their songs. Joni was sort of holding court, sitting in the middle of the room and passing the guitar around. Nowadays in Nashville we'd call it a "guitar pull". Finally, after everyone else had done their thing, Joni spoke to the young, unknown songwriter. "Kris, why don't *you* sing us a song?" she suggested. "Aw no!" came the reply. "I don't have anything that would compare with what these guys have written." Joni encouraged him anyway, insisting that he sing something. Eventually he took out a notebook and sang, literally reading the lyrics off the page: "Busted flat in Baton Rouge, headin' for the trains..."

'The song, of course, was "Me And Bobby McGee" and the youngster with the voice was Kris Kristofferson! I'll never forget how every single person in the room suddenly fell quiet and every eye was riveted on Kris. We all realized straightaway what a phenomenal talent he was. After he'd finished singing, which he'd done very shyly and quietly, the California stars were all in his face, telling him to be sure and give them a call the next time he got to LA!' When Kristofferson's song was finally minted, George's friend, producer and record label head Fred Foster was credited as co-writer.

Apart from Joni Mitchell and her associates, another huge influence on George was Bob Dylan, whose career he had followed from the outset. He has been singing some of Dylan's folk music compositions for many years now. 'I never met Bob Dylan, but I dearly wish that I had because I was always intrigued by him. I went to see him in concert with his band at the Coliseum in Charlotte, and I'll never forget the way he closed the concert with "Forever Young". I was very moved by that haunting song. I saw him perform a few times after that and he always closed the programme with the same song – although, surprisingly, it was never a hit for him, or for anyone else. I always had the impression that the song meant a lot to him and served as a benediction of sorts!'

For George, the song 'Forever Young' is about spiritual youth rather than being physically young or handsome. 'Bob Dylan speaks about being "young at heart" or "young in the spirit". The Bible says that unless we "become as little children", we will never see the Kingdom of Heaven. That's what Bob's song is speaking about too. I guess we've all met people in their eighties and nineties who seem to have impressive spiritual youth and vitality. I dearly hope that can be said of me when I reach that kind of age!'

It may have started slowly, but as the years passed it became increasingly noticeable that the music of George Hamilton IV was beginning to reflect a deepening social conscience and an awareness of the necessity of putting down spiritual roots. Much of the folk material recorded at that time was searching and even mystical in tone and content, reflecting a personal search for eternal, satisfying reality. For George, as for many others, it was more than just an engaging musical style. Deep down, he was beginning to seek for real truths and spiritual fulfilment. It was a search that would ultimately bring him to a deep and lasting faith in Christ, a faith he would go on to share with tens of thousands of people across the globe. Those days of folk music experimentation were times of paddling in the shallows of philosophical thought and spiritual exploration. It would be several more years before George would move out into deeper water and make his life-changing decision.

CHAPTER 9

UK LINKS

> George Hamilton IV reflects the influence of the British traditional and contemporary folk scene. His songs reflect his absorption of the atmosphere of his many visits, conveying the feelings of the towns and cities he has travelled through.
>
> **Ian Grant** (BBC radio producer, London, England)

George's links with Britain, begun in the late sixties, were to become increasingly close as the years passed and his international career went from strength to strength. He has always enjoyed visiting the UK and has a keen appreciation of the history shared across the Atlantic. Years ago, on one of his earliest visits to England, George's friend the BBC broadcaster and country musicologist Bob Powel took him on an autumn sightseeing visit to the Mayflower Pub on the muddy banks of the River Thames at Rotherhithe.

'Did you know,' Bob said to his companion, 'that the old pub there stands on the site of the dock that was once the home port for the Pilgrim Fathers' ship the *Mayflower*?' He went on to explain that across the now bustling street from the picturesque pub was the graveyard where the *Mayflower* captain and some of the crew were buried. George was impressed, but Bob's next piece of information surprised him into laughter. The Mayflower Pub, said Bob, was the only place in England which was legally authorized to sell American postage stamps!

As they walked on, the talk drifted from connections of history and faith to musical links. 'D'you know, Bob,' said George, 'I'm amazed that it was so many years before it dawned on me that our so-called American country music had its roots and beginnings over here in the folksongs of the British Isles. Look at traditional songs like "Barbara Allen" and "Greensleeves", for example.'

'That's right, George,' replied Bob with a chuckle. 'There's nothing new under the sun!'

George, however, was sure there was one thing that Britain and America do not have in common, and was pleased to have the last word. 'Of course, Bob, you good folks in the United Kingdom don't get to see that ol' sun too often, do you…'

George's UK connections started in earnest with Mervyn Conn. The British show-business entrepreneur cut his career teeth during the sixties with an assortment of pantomimes, plays and musicals, as well as the early Beatles' Christmas shows. Introduced to country music via Johnny Cash, he showed great courage and vision in his conception of the annual International Festival of Country Music, held at Wembley from 1969 onwards. Throughout the 20 years of its existence, the festival gave the British public a unique chance to see an array of country talent unsurpassed outside Nashville or Las Vegas. Mervyn's preferred choice for anchorman at his festivals was George Hamilton IV, and the two soon built up a close rapport. Mervyn would ring George regularly to discuss his ambitious plans for the next festival.

The entrepreneur shrewdly judged that George's qualities as an entertainer and a diplomat were perfectly suited to the UK's culture and people. The two men's partnership and friendship continued long after the demise of the International Festivals and included collaboration on a number of other innovative projects, most notably a musical telling the story of Patsy Cline's life. Sandy Kelly played Patsy, supported by Johnny Worthy and Roger Rettig, who provided the musical and stage direction. George played himself and 'narrated' the story. The musical toured successfully throughout the UK over a number of years during the mid-to-late nineties, and enjoyed a run at the Whitehall Theatre in London's West End.

'Some people have been critical of Mervyn Conn,' George observes, 'probably more out of jealousy than anything else, because he's a very successful businessman, albeit a tough one! Marty Robbins, for one, held him in high regard and they were great friends. I remember Marty once had a big backyard barbecue for Mervyn while he was visiting Nashville to line up talent for the Wembley Festival. That was very unusual for Marty, who wasn't normally so gregarious. Whatever his faults may or may not be, Mervyn put his money where his mouth was when he booked the very first International Festival of Country Music at Wembley Arena in 1969. A lot of people were laughing behind his back, but it worked. Many folks talked about promoting country music internationally, but Mervyn Conn was the one who went out and did it!

'Bill Anderson and I were part of that first Festival of Country Music. What a great event! All day long there were booths out in the foyer where the fans could meet all the artistes, get autographs or photos and buy their records. In the evenings there were the concerts. Bill and myself couldn't wait to get back home and tell everyone in Nashville about our British experience.

'At that time we were both on the board of directors at the Country Music Association. At a board meeting soon after Bill and I returned home from Wembley, there was much talk about how fans had been gatecrashing the Nashville country music DJ Convention. Many music industry folks felt that the 'industry-only' event was badly affected by all the fans who descended on Nashville hoping to meet their favourite stars attending the convention. Fresh from the UK, Bill and I suggested some kind of annual fan-orientated event, which might occur in the early summer, six months before the industry convention in the fall. It could be a special event where the industry and the artistes would cater specifically for the fans and the artistes would meet them, sign autographs and appear in photos.

'We described our great personal experiences at Wembley and the CMA folks seemed to like the idea. They started kicking around ideas for a "fan convention", a "fan club gathering", a "festival for fans". Then somebody said, "Yeah, let's have some sort of a fair – a *Fan Fair*!" That name really caught everyone's fancy and some serious planning got underway. The first Fan Fair took place in 1971. There weren't many people in attendance the first time, but it really grew rapidly in the following years. It wasn't long before it was being called the *International* Country Music Fan Fair. Nashville has much to thank Mervyn Conn for – it all began with his new ideas in the UK.

'Jo Walker-Meador, former executive director of the CMA, was always a keen believer in the internationalism of country music. She was the one who invited Jiri Brabec and the Country Beat from Czechoslovakia to perform at the Fan Fair, along with many other artistes from around the world. To me, one of the saddest things of recent years has been the diminished emphasis on internationalism at the fair. I'm hoping that will change.'

There is no denying that George Hamilton IV has done more to help popularize country music in Great Britain than any other artiste. For a start, he has made countless appearances on local and national BBC television and radio, ranging from breakfast shows to variety shows and even documentaries such as the mammoth undertaking *How the West Was Sung*, produced and written by the BBC's Charles Chilton. The Nashville star has made many friends in the Corporation over the years.

In the mid-eighties, your author found himself in the BBC's Shepherd's Bush studios, watching the taping of yet another show hosted by George. During a break in the proceedings, I fell into conversation with one of the technicians, asking him which performers had made the most impression on him while he had been working there. 'You know, Paul,' he told me, 'I've worked here for 12 years, and I can boast that I've seen almost all the superstars at one time or another. But let me tell you this. None of them conduct themselves – in their guarded *and* unguarded moments – consistently as well as that man.' Removing his hand from the camera controls, he pointed in the direction of George, who was well out of earshot and absorbed in his work as show host. I felt it was a telling comment from a hardened professional! George has always avoided putting on show-biz airs and graces, and that technician is not the only one to be charmed by his obvious sincerity and enthusiasm for what he does.

George's television shows showcased many of Nashville's great stars as well as giving exposure to new personalities emerging from the fledgling country music scene in the UK itself. He also gave unprecedented air time to contemporary Christian music, with appearances by the Samuelsons (a fine quartet of brothers from Sweden), Living Sound (a vocal and instrumental combo from Tulsa, USA) and Nutshell (England's own promising trio headed by Paul Field), to mention just a few. Paul Field was the musical mind behind Cliff Richard's 'Millennium Prayer' song that did so well in the pop charts in the final days of 1999. 'Millennium Prayer' was also used as the finale for the musical *Hopes and Dreams*, conceived by Rob Frost.

George is quick to express admiration for the 'phenomenon' of Sir Cliff Richard, an undoubted global superstar. He first saw Cliff in a movie produced for the Billy Graham Evangelistic Association, and subsequently heard much about him from people close to Dr Graham. As a show-business peer and fellow Christian with a deepening faith of his own, George was intrigued by Cliff's combination of Christian witness and pop success. He was eager to meet him face to face.

'While I was in London in the early seventies,' he recalls, 'I managed to get myself invited to the Christian Arts Centre in Kensington. Cliff was conducting some sort of Christian seminar that evening and I was somehow invited to join him earlier for dinner with some of his close friends. Later, at the seminar, I watched amazed as he chatted unashamedly about his faith, just sitting on a stool with his guitar. He was so natural and down to earth.' Cliff's personalized gospel songs and the life story he shared that night might just as well have been delivered to a few friends in his own front room. It was a very casual, very modest affair. George was quite puzzled. The man was a superstar, after all! Clearly he was also a sensible and articulate man who was concerned to tell other ordinary people about what he believed.

'Sir Cliff is still truly genuine in his faith,' affirms George. 'He also has a wonderment about his work, and he remains an enthusiast, neither cynical nor hardened by his years in show business. He's come through, with flying colours, every attempt by the media to tarnish his image and undermine the sincerity of his faith. Many of my buddies back home in Music City can learn something from this guy!'

Cliff Richard is not the only musician to impress George on his visits to the UK. He has met and made friends with many others, some famous, some less well known. One English songwriter in the folk tradition whom George came to admire was Ralph McTell, and he has recorded Ralph's classic song of social consciousness, 'Streets Of London', several times. 'It always reminds me of the fine work of the London City Mission among the needy people in the capital,' he explains. George has visited the Mission on numerous occasions and is an enthusiastic supporter.

George considers that, if Ralph had not written anything other than 'Streets Of London', that one gem of a song would be still a rich and worthy legacy. Ralph, of course, did write other things, and George fell in love particularly with a catchy and patriotic song called 'England'. 'Once, when I was in England watching the BBC's programme *Pebble Mill at One*, Ralph McTell was introduced singing "England" with a group of schoolchildren providing vocal back-up. I was immediately taken up by the song, because it summed up my own feelings about the "mother country"! It deserved to be a classic, and I just had to record it. Ralph will always be one of my favourite English folksingers and songwriters.'

Another English singer-songwriter who caught George's attention was the increasingly popular Charlie Landsborough from Liverpool. Having previously worked as a navvy, a postman and a schoolteacher, Charlie was looking for a breakthrough on the music scene. He is quick to credit George Hamilton IV with helping him on his way. When he was still barely off the starting block, George was warmly recommending Charlie's songwriting and performing ability to anyone who would listen. 'Charlie Landsborough has been an inspiration to me,' George says, 'and we've become close friends. I must have met him for the first time about 15 years ago. He has probably become one of my biggest musical and spiritual influences. I've recorded many of Charlie's songs, including "No Time At All", which I first heard in the mid-seventies.' At the start of the new millennium, Charlie Landsborough is among Britain's leading country songwriters, with many popular compositions to his name, including 'What Colour Is The Wind?', 'My Forever Friend', 'Heaven Knows' and 'I Will Love You All My Life'.

Among the better known figures George met during his time in the UK is Sandy Kelly. Since 1993, Sandy, her husband Michael and their family have been a large part of George's life. Born, bred and based in Ireland, Sandy first met George in 1990 while he was appearing with his son George V on Sandy's RTE television series. Sandy and George IV later toured together with Slim Whitman in March 1993. At that time there was much talk backstage about Mervyn Conn's Patsy Cline musical, which would be launched the following autumn. Sandy Kelly had been chosen to star in the main part. At the end of that March tour, George remembers congratulating Sandy on landing the role, but then says he thought no further about it.

Then somewhere, a few months later, Mervyn Conn, Sandy Kelly and the musical's director were discussing what they were going to do for the part of a narrator. During that meeting, Sandy made her views clear. 'The right man for the narrator role is under your nose,' she told the others. 'George IV! He was a friend of Patsy's and worked with her in the late fifties and early sixties. George could bring a lot of credibility to this musical.' And so it came about that George found himself with a part in a musical, telling Patsy's story to audiences the length and breadth of the British Isles.

'I owe my involvement in the British Patsy Cline musical to Sandy Kelly,' he says, looking back with pleasure. 'We became dear friends during the course of several years as we took the show across England, Scotland, Ireland and Wales. After the road tours we went on to perform in London's West End at the Whitehall Theatre. Mervyn has also taken us and the production back on the road several times since then. I think to date we've done 611 performances of *Patsy Cline – The Musical* in Britain and Ireland! It was an ongoing production from 1993 right through to the summer of 1998.'

Often, during breaks in those tours, Sandy's husband Michael would invite George over to Ireland to participate in concerts with Sandy and her band. 'It's very much a family show. Sandy's son William is the drummer and her sister, Barbara Ellis, also stars and sings in the show. Michael is not only the booking agent, he's also the sound engineer and musical director! It's principally through the Kellys that I've come to know and love Ireland, both geographically and musically. Thanks to Sandy and all the Kellys, I've had the chance to tour all over Ireland and get to know the people and their music.

'It's interesting that during all those years I spent travelling back and forth to the UK – from the late sixties through to the early nineties – I'd only been to the Republic of Ireland once or twice. Then it was mainly just for radio or television work. I'd never really performed in concert there. In the last few years, however, due to my association with the Kellys, I've had the opportunity to explore the country's music and to admire it as a sightseer! I've learned a lot of wonderful Irish folksongs. In fact, the Kellys and I have been working on an album of Irish songs at Tom Kelly's studio (Tom is Michael's brother) in Ballina on the west coast of Ireland.

'I've got a great respect for Sandy's talent. She's got the same spirit, strength, power and fire that made Patsy Cline so special. I've never seen anyone capture the "essence" of Patsy onstage the way Sandy does, and it made that musical something unique. I admire her very much as a person as well. She's a delightful human being and I'm very grateful to Sandy and her family for taking me into their hearts and homes and introducing me to Ireland in a very special way.'

Sandy and the Kelly family may be relatively recent additions to George's circle of friends, but many associations go back rather further. When he first travelled to England in 1967, the first British band he worked with was the Hillsiders from Liverpool. They loom large in his memory as great entertainers and very charismatic characters. 'They were so classy onstage. I remember the first time I met them in 1967, down at the Westbury Hotel in London. I recall hearing that they'd gone to school with the

Beatles in Liverpool. The Hillsiders, of course, went their own way into country music when the Beatles went into rock – though I think the Hillsiders also used to play the Cavern in Liverpool back in the days when the Beatles were there. We did quite a bit of touring together and we even recorded an album for RCA, produced by Ian Grant, former producer of the *Country Meets Folk* BBC radio series.'

Although the Hillsiders have disbanded now, former members Joe Butler and Kenny Johnson remain close friends with George through their continuing work on the British country music scene. George is enthusiastic about developments in Britain over the years. 'I have a lot of respect for the Hillsiders, and for Country Fever with Jon Derek (when we toured together, Albert Lee played lead guitar). The Jonny Young Four is a top-class outfit too. Jonny is one of the finest tenor ballad singers I've ever heard. They're all great British musicians and singers, and I'm proud to have been associated with them. These people have meant a lot to me. They have encouraged and inspired me, as well as teaching me quite a bit about the British music scene.

'Of course, Bill Clarke was lead guitarist and musical director for many of my BBC television series and went with me to Eastern Europe and also New Zealand. Stuart "Luce" Langridge has more often than not been my British drummer. I first met Luce through touring with the Jonny Young Four. He was their drummer when I toured with them in the early seventies. Most recently, he worked with me at the Whitehall Theatre run of the Patsy Cline musical. Both Bill Clarke and Luce Langridge joined me on many UK and European tours featuring my American musician friends Dick Schuyler on bass and Don Ange on piano. Britain's Tony Cervi and Harry McDonald were sometimes on piano when Don Ange wasn't able to travel with us. On tour in Britain, I still try to work as often as I can with Bill, Luce and Nigel Portman-Smith (on bass guitar). In recent years, more and more of my work in the UK has been solo acoustic, but when I do need a band I invariably call on these fine British musicians!'

Another British musical friend George has worked and toured with through the years is Pete Sayers from Newmarket . They first met in Nashville when Pete was a resident there for several years and co-hosted a television show on WSM television. 'Pete is one of the most all-around talented musicians and singers that I've ever known,' George says firmly. 'He was with me on all my early tours for Mervyn Conn in Britain.' George believes he was immensely fortunate in all the people he worked with on his early visits – they encouraged him to keep on coming back! 'I recall two particularly talented friends on my first trip to England, who appeared on the BBC's *Country Meets Folk* programme. Lorne Gibson was a wonderful ballad singer, and Little Ginny Brown is my favourite female British country singer. They say good things come in small packages, and she certainly confirms that!'

During a summer season in Blackpool in 1979, George also worked with Raymond Froggatt. It was the UK's very first all-country-music summer season show. Also appearing at the Winter Gardens Theatre were the aforementioned Little Ginny and Pete Sayers, along with a band called the Mintings. At that time 'Froggie', as Raymond was known, was considered by many in the country music community to be a rock'n'roller, but George is disdainful of such narrow labelling. The point was that Froggie was a brilliant showman and a talented musician. 'Oh yes, many people said he wasn't really country. But all the other performers and I would sit in the wings every night and watch his set at Blackpool with huge enjoyment. Raymond Froggatt is a magical, unique person and a spellbinding performer.'

As well as doing a season in Blackpool, George made other connections with northern areas of the country, as he recalls. 'Malcolm Anthony Bawden was company manager, compere, MC and fellow performer on most of my concert tours for Mervyn Conn over the years. He's now a hotelier in the Lake District, and I think that's my favourite part of England. The rain seems warmer up there... But I'd better not say too much or I'll upset my good friend Tony Goodacre. He comes from Yorkshire, and you might say he's one of England's finest country music ambassadors.'

George also ventured north of the border, of course, and was struck by what he found in Scotland. 'I first met Scottish songstress Moira Anderson on a BBC television show in the mid-seventies. She and Andy Stewart taught me so much about the musical lore and legend of Scotland. I was fascinated, all the more so because I know my distant ancestors were Scottish. Andy Stewart taught me the song "These Are My Mountains", while Moira taught me "Wild Mountain Thyme" and made me aware of what a great songwriter Robert Burns was. Being a practical lady, she also advised me to open a British bank account since I was spending so much time in the UK. "The only bank to be affiliated with," she told me, "is the Royal Bank of Scotland!" To this day I still proudly hold my British bank account with the Royal Bank of Scotland.'

Both Andy and Moira had a great influence on George, as friends and fellow performers. Andy and George did a considerable amount of concert work together, including a couple of weeks at His Majesty's Theatre in Aberdeen. George's very first visit to Scotland was as a guest on Andy's television show *Andy's Party* in the early seventies. On subsequent visits, George made other friends too. 'Colorado is a wonderful Scottish band. We did a lot of work together both in Britain and in Eastern Europe. In more recent years Alastair MacDonald, the great Scottish folksinger, has been a true inspiration to me, and has played a vital part in my education regarding Scottish folk music.'

George's associations and collaborations in the UK have not been limited to his work with other talented individuals. He now has long-standing links with various organizations. Most notable among these are the BBC and the British Country Music Association, and many other creative partnerships and projects have grown from those starting points.

Phil Lewis was the Controller of BBC 2's Outside Broadcasts when George travelled over to the UK to take part in the first Wembley International Festival of Country Music. Phil spotted George early on and thought he might be the right person to host Britain's first country music television series. 'I'm eternally grateful to Phil,' says George. 'He's the man who really gave me a showcase forum and platform in Britain through that television series.'

David Allan was the announcer and compere for the first BBC series George did from the Nashville Rooms in West Kensington back in the early seventies. He was also closely involved in the country music festivals at Wembley. 'Through the years, David and I worked together frequently and became good friends. I have a lot of respect for him. He's not a fair-weather friend; he's always been there for me as an encourager, ready to help with anything. It was David who researched his way through the BBC archives and assembled most of the material for my lecture and concert engagement at Moscow University in March 1974. Apparently, that was the very first time an American country performer had travelled to the heart of the Soviet Union to perform.'

Charles Chilton, former writer and producer for BBC radio and a knowledgeable musicologist, also chipped in with advice and background input for George's visit to Moscow. 'Charles knows more about country music, history and life in general than I'll ever be able to learn,' comments George with admiration. 'He's an expert on country, western and folk music, and he was a good friend of Josh White Senior and Tex Ritter.' George and Charles collaborated on a number of radio series, beginning with *How the West Was Sung*, which Charles had originally intended to put together with Tex Ritter. Tex died before the project could be set up, however, and Charles invited George to do the series with him instead. Other radio series followed, including *The Great American Railroad* and *The History of Country Music*, all carefully constructed with music, stories and background history.

Very early on during his first visits to the UK, George made the acquaintance of a number of people closely involved with the British Country Music Association, and he appreciated the warmth of their welcome and their enthusiasm for all things country. 'Tony Byworth showed me around the country music venues in the London area. Later, as the editor of *Country Music People*, Tony was also very helpful to me. At one time he was in charge of Acuff-Rose's London office, so I had many dealings with him there too. Tony has since made quite a name for himself with the Nashville record labels, thanks to his public relations work with some of country's biggest stars, including George Strait, Garth Brooks and Nanci Griffith.'

George is Honorary President of the BCMA now, and was delighted to be asked to take on the appointment. 'I believe the BCMA has done more to promote the real heart and soul of country music in Britain than any other organization. The officers of the BCMA – Tony Byworth, John Ryan, Ronnie Simper and Mike Storey – and all the members are passionate lovers of country music, and that's great to see. They've always been encouraging towards me, and I'm especially grateful to Jim Marshall, the BCMA President, for his constant support and encouragement over the years.'

George Hamilton IV is one of the very few American artistes of his age who can boast a dedicated, actively supportive British fan club. With members around the globe, it is headed up by the hard-working Sue Marshall from her office in Edinburgh.[1] Sue is firmly devoted to furthering the cause of the Hamilton dynasty, and is an admirer of both Georges, IV and V. She is tickled to find herself operating the fan club from the appropriately named Hamilton Drive! Her sons Tony and Stephen help her out from time to time, and George is always happy to express his thankfulness to Sue and her family.

'I can never express enough gratitude to Sue Marshall for all she has done for me in the UK over the years. We've actually been kicking around the idea of renaming the fan club "George Hamilton IV and Friends Ltd – A Mutual Appreciation Society"! I'm so appreciative of the club members, who've supported me so much over the years, and really, I think I'm a bit long in the tooth now to be having a fan club...'

Asked about her friendship with George, Sue immediately tells a story which for her illustrates the generosity of his character better than anything else. She respects George not only as a country music star, but as a person. In the late spring of 1988, Sue and her sons were mourning the loss of husband and father Allan, who had died just a few weeks before. The phone rang one

1 For further information, write to Friends of George Hamilton IV, 3 Hamilton Drive, Edinburgh EH15 1NP.

evening, and it was the organizer of the local country music club, ringing to give Sue some good news. 'I wanted to tell you something exciting, Sue. George Hamilton IV will be performing at our club on 19 June as part of a charity concert. Put it in your diary!'

Sue was grateful to have something that good to look forward to, and wanted to get involved with the preparations. She was determined to do something, desperate for anything to relieve the grief she felt for Allan. In the succeeding weeks, however, nobody seemed able to tell her anything about the concert, not even the charity it was meant to be for. They did not seem to need her help. Sue became increasingly frustrated and felt unjustly left out of things.

Sue and Allan had first met George in 1982 via Allan's DJ involvement with hospital radio. Over the years George had given interviews for the radio station, sent the family Christmas cards and had generally been very kind. He had been particularly supportive and sympathetic during and after Allan's illness. So why, if George was such a good friend, thought Sue, was he suddenly keeping her in the dark about an event that was happening right on her doorstep? The benefit concert was advertised widely on radio, but the good cause was still not mentioned. When Sue finally tracked George down at his home in the States and asked him over the phone to explain what was going on, he seemed to be just as unclear and vague as everyone else.

Sue was deeply puzzled, but continued to encourage friends and neighbours to buy tickets and go along to the show. Whatever it was for, a concert by George was not to be missed, and Sue was an enthusiastic promoter. When the day came and Sue and her sons arrived at the venue, they found the hall packed out. They took their seats, and the club organizer stood up. 'Do you know why this great man is here, Sue?' he asked.

'Of course I don't!' Sue barked back. 'That's what I've been trying to find out these last three weeks!'

The next comment took the wind right out of her sails. 'He's here for you and the boys, Sue!'

Sue is blind, and consequently did not feel able to take instant flight, although that was her first thought, she says! She was stunned. It transpired that various people, including the local Tucson Country Club organizers and the Scottish Country Music Fellowship, had wanted to do something for the Marshalls while Allan was still living. When he died, they decided to go ahead with the plans for Sue and her sons. The organizers had initially asked George if he could send over some albums to raffle. Instead, however, he brought himself over the Atlantic as the headline artiste. Along with local performers Route 65 and Gerry Ford as support, he gave his services free for the evening, and Sue and her family received all the takings.

'The boys and I didn't know what to say or how to thank everyone,' says Sue. 'But I knew what I wanted to do with the money! I knew that we should go to Nashville, and we went later that year. George and his family hosted us and were absolutely wonderful.'

A few days after the benefit show Sue rang George, who had gone on to tour various venues in England, to express her heartfelt thanks. 'George, why was I kept so much in the dark?' she asked.

'If we'd told you,' George replied, 'would you have let the show go ahead?'

'No,' said Sue after a moment.

'There you are, then!'

As well as having his fan club based there, George has received many invitations to perform in Scotland over the years. Indeed, he often jokes that he has traded on his name when it came to a place to stay, successfully persuading the Duke and Duchess of Hamilton to give a bed to a long-lost clan member! In fact, the Duke and Duchess, along with the Duke and Duchess of Abercorn in Northern Ireland, are long-standing friends and admirers of George IV.

'My association with Angus, the Duke of Hamilton, originated through his mother, the Dowager Duchess,' George explains. 'She invited me to come and take part in some charity fundraising concerts for a campaign by the Lamp of Lothian, a local charity in Haddington, where they live. I had my band with me – Bill Clarke,

Dick Schuyler, Don Ange and Luce Langridge – and one of our perks for the first concert was that we were invited to spend the night at the Duke's residence, Lennoxlove House. That's how the Duke and I first met. We became good friends over the years and in 1997 we celebrated my sixtieth birthday at Lennox Love as guests of the Duke. While we were there, we did a charity concert at St Mary's Church in Haddington, with the proceeds going to the church and a local charity.

'Then the Duke announced that he would like to spend *his* sixtieth birthday in Nashville with us. So in September of 1998 the Duke and Duchess came to Nashville, and we held a celebration for the Duke's birthday. When they arrived, the Duke gave me an interesting piece of Hamilton history. He'd brought with him an antique walking cane, which looked as if it was well over 100 years old and was inscribed with the name "Reverend G. Hamilton". It now stands in a prominent position by our front door!

'I was scheduled to appear on the Grand Ole Opry that weekend, so I invited the Duke to come along with me and appear on TNN's *Opry Backstage* television show. Bill Anderson, the host interviewer, asked the Duke if he liked country music. "Of course I do!" he exclaimed. "I've got a whole collection of country records at my home in Scotland." Then he surprised us all by singing a verse and chorus of Roy Acuff's "Wabash Cannonball". He knew it by heart and sang it with perfect confidence on nationwide television. Now *that's* royalty for you – the Duke of Hamilton singing the King of Country Music's signature song!

'As everyone out there probably knows by now, I'm a proud member of "Clan Hamilton"! And I'll always treasure my friendship with the Duke and Duchess of Hamilton, the Duke and Duchess of Abercorn and their families on "the other side of the pond". They're all very down-to-earth, charming and friendly people. Duke Angus very kindly calls me "Cousin George", as does the Duke of Abercorn, but I'm not certain we're even remotely kin – other than the fact that we share the same last name!'

There is one enduring friendship George made in the UK which has led on to the most unexpected association. Little did he know when he met journalist and schoolteacher Al Moir in 1986 that the friendship would lead to him becoming an honorary governor of an English junior school! George must surely be the only American music star to take up such a position.

It all started in the Staindrop Lodge, a small hotel on the outskirts of Sheffield. Al had been asked to interview George for a magazine feature. He had known of George for some years, having reviewed a number of his albums and shows, but this was the first time he had conducted an in-depth interview with the star. The final question he put to George was designed to tell him something about the singer's perception of himself. 'If, on some unhappy day, I was left with the unenviable task of having to write your obituary,' he said, 'how would you best like to be remembered?'

It was not what George had been expecting, and he raised his eyebrows as he mulled it over. Then he replied hesitantly, 'I guess it would be nice if you could say something like, "He was truly an international ambassador of country music." '

The interview had taken place over breakfast and George returned to his room to pack while Al finished off his meal. Some time later, looking a little flustered and considerably more serious than he had done during the interview, George returned to Al's table. 'Al, I'm so glad you haven't left yet,' he said. 'I've been thinking over that last question you asked and the way I answered it. I hope, after all these years, folk know I've always tried to promote country music wherever I went. But if the time comes and you have to write something about me, I wonder, could you possibly say something like, "God gave George Hamilton the blessed gift of music. In return, George tried his best to be an ambassador for God"?'

Al freely admits that he could lay no claim to being a committed Christian, but looking into George's eyes that day, the seasoned journalist was deeply moved. He liked the idea of such a big star getting his life into that kind of perspective. 'I've rarely come across such genuine humility or sincerity,' he says, looking back. 'Perhaps someday it will be George who writes *my* obituary, and if so, I would be deeply honoured if he would just call me his friend.'

A lasting friendship was indeed born that day. In 1990 Al, along with his brother-in-law Larry Kelly, arranged to visit his married sister in Ohio. Larry was a hard-bitten assembly line worker at General Motors. He was a keen country music fan whose lifelong ambition had been to visit Nashville in the hope of meeting his idol, George Hamilton IV.

By that time, with the success worldwide of the 'Nashville sound', Nashville was becoming more and more the hub of the whole country music industry. In comparison, Charlotte was a quiet backwater and opportunities there were limited and small. George was frequently having to commute to the Grand Old Opry and travel to the UK, Europe and Canada as new opportunities arose. Rightly or wrongly, George also felt that he was missing out, and that it was all happening without him. This feeling, together with his earlier misgivings and the pressure being put on him by his peers and the industry, led him to the decision to move back to Nashville in August 1986.

When Al arrived, he contacted George, but by sheer bad luck, George happened to be away with his family on his annual vacation in North Carolina. Although he could not be there himself, George did arrange backstage passes for Larry and Al at the Grand Ole Opry, and he made a note of the Nashville motel where the two were staying.

They enjoyed the show at the Opry and on the way back Larry stopped off for a meal while Al returned alone to his motel room. When the telephone rang, Al picked it up and was astonished to hear George's voice again. He was even more surprised when he heard what George had to say. Concerned that after almost 55 years, Larry had not got to do the one special thing he had wanted, i.e. to meet him, George had decided to cut short his family holiday. Skipping a night's sleep, he was intending to drive the many hundreds of miles back to Nashville, especially for Larry. Al protested, but George was adamant. A rendezvous was arranged and George suggested that it would be more fun if Larry was kept in the dark about the meeting.

At noon the next day, Al persuaded a puzzled Larry to drive to the appointed place. Five minutes later, George pulled into the car park. He looked weary, but still managed his usual beaming smile. Quite unprepared, Larry failed to recognize the star, who was clad in an ordinary check shirt and jeans, and walked straight past him. He was halfway across the car park before he realized he was on his own. George and Al burst into gales of laughter and Larry retraced his steps, frowning. Then he finally recognized his idol and stopped dead in his tracks, speechless. George went over to greet Larry with his customary hug of friendship.

What an afternoon that turned out to be. For three hours, George ferried Al and the starstruck Larry around little known places in Nashville, off the beaten track to the average tourist. The normally laconic Larry, sitting up front with his all-time hero, was transformed that day into a nonstop chatterbox. Then, much later that night, he sat on the edge of his motel bed and cried like a baby. Al was awed by the difference one person's kindness had made, and it cemented the friendship between himself and George. He could not know what surprises were still in store.

During the course of that afternoon George casually mentioned that his wife Tinky was a kindergarten teacher. Al said with pleasure that he was a teacher too, and jokingly made a proposal. 'Any time you're on tour in Britain, you'd be welcome to drop into my school for a visit! Our children meet for a daily assembly and if you've a mind to, you'll be more than welcome to speak and sing to them. That'll be a feather in your cap for you to tell Tinky about when you get home!' They laughed, and Al thought no more about it.

In November 1990, when the Nashville visit had faded to a happy summer memory, Al's phone rang. 'Hi Al,' came George's drawl. 'I'm in England! I'm sorry to be calling you so late. I've just got back to my hotel after a show in Sheffield. Maybe you know, I'm presenting my Christmas concert in churches round the country. Tomorrow I'm on my way to Leeds and I've been looking at the map. You're about halfway between Sheffield and Leeds, aren't you? Do you remember when you were in Nashville, you happened to mention that your school holds a daily assembly? Well, if it's all right with you, it'll sure be nice to drop in and meet you all!'

Of course it was all right! Al had been teaching at the same school for about 20 years and knew that such a celebrity would be received with open arms. He gave George careful directions to the junior school in the little village of Kirk Sandall on the outskirts of Doncaster, arranged an arrival time, and then let George retire to bed to get some rest in anticipation of the big day.

At nine o'clock the next morning, 200 children aged between nine and 12 filed reluctantly into their classrooms for the start of another day. Not one of them had ever heard of George Hamilton IV, but there was an obvious air of excitement amongst the staff, and it was catching. Head teacher Barney Wordsworth raced down to the local music shop to pick up a sound system. As he loaded the equipment into his car, he told the startled shop owner why he was in such a big hurry. The owner was aghast. 'Get that load of rubbish back in the shop! There's no way I'm going to let George Hamilton IV use that cheap sound stuff!' Wrenching the equipment away from the protesting head, the owner carted it back into the shop, where he personally selected the very best system he possessed. Then he shut up shop, drove back to the school with Barney and made sure everything was set up perfectly. He even stayed for the assembly and refused to accept any payment for the use of his equipment, or for any lost business during his absence from the shop.

On the stroke of 10, George arrived at the school. There was a biting cold north wind carrying a freezing drizzle across the car park. George looked nothing like a superstar, with a bobble hat pulled down over his ears and a woollen muffler tucked into the collar of his overcoat. He was welcomed into the hastily tidied staff room, where he drank a reviving cup of hot black coffee before heading off to the hall to face an audience of youngsters who knew nothing about him or his music.

George knew how to win them over. Poking fun at himself and admiring their bright red school uniforms, he very quickly won over the entire school. He sang to them with just his guitar for company, and in between the songs he told amusing stories. Somehow, he managed to condense his normal 90-minute church presentation of the Nativity story into a shorter time span that kept the children's interest. Al was deeply impressed. 'George may not have been trained as a schoolteacher, but he managed to entertain the children for the best part of an hour. The rapt expressions on their faces said it all. The spontaneous applause at the end was as enthusiastic as any adult audience would give anywhere!' In the end, the assembly overran quite considerably. It did not seem fair to deny the long queue of children wanting George's autograph, and George was ready to talk warmly to each child. 'Somehow,' says Al, 'the thought of a geography or science lesson could not compete against that kind of excitement!'

When it was all over, Al invited George to join the staff and children for the midday meal. 'Though let me warn you, eating here is a somewhat risky undertaking at the best of times!' George, who had no need to rush off urgently, accepted with some curiosity, and refused to be ushered to the head of the lunch queue, waiting his turn with everyone else. When he had collected his meal, George joined the children at one of the tables and lowered his tall frame into an impossibly small plastic chair. Then he examined the food on his plate. 'Roast turkey! Did you folk know it was Thanksgiving Day today? Is this especially for me?'

The children looked at him blankly, so he proceeded to explain. 'In America, we have three major festivals of religious significance: Christmas, Easter and Thanksgiving. Back in 1863, President Abraham Lincoln decreed that the fourth Thursday of November each year should be set aside as Thanksgiving Day, and it was declared a national holiday. Thanksgiving is a time when families get together and share a big meal, and I miss being away from home at this time. Today just happens to be the fourth Thursday of November, and back home my family will soon be gathering to celebrate. When I woke up this morning I thought about that and it seemed I'd be having my Thanksgiving dinner in some motorway café on the M1! But here I am, eating turkey among friends, and I can tell you, this is almost like being with my family back home. I'm just so glad y'all invited me over!'

George tucked into his meal, chatting to the children and two members of staff, Sandy Chappell and Gerry Hickman.

A wide-eyed, tousle-headed boy, well known to the staff as a rascal, had managed to sit himself next to George. When George asked him whether he had been away on holiday, the lad replied in a broad Yorkshire accent, his mouth stuffed with jam roly-poly, yellow custard dribbling down his chin. 'Oh aye!' he said indistinctly. 'Me mam an' me went t'Spain, but it were right boring! Me mate went camping t'Austerfield, and 'e 'ad a right good time! I wish I'd 'ad gone wi' me mate!' It was George's turn to look blank. He had not understood a word. Discreetly wiping custard from his sleeve, he smiled and nodded anyway, and tucked into his own bowl of pudding.

Perhaps hoping not to have to decipher any more of his neighbour's Yorkshire accent, George commented on the pudding instead. 'This is great! This is the best custard I've ever tasted! We just can't get custard like this back home.' Angie, the school cook, just happened to be hovering nearby. When she overheard George's remarks, she scuttled off and returned minutes later with a huge bowl of steaming roly-poly and custard, which she placed smiling before George. Sometimes being the gentleman has its drawbacks. George stoically tackled the second helping of pudding, while the rascal next to him gazed at these riches with resentment, having had his own plea for seconds firmly ignored!

George was not allowed to forget that school visit. About a year later, he appeared at a concert in Glasgow. Al Moir's 80-year-old mother had been desperate to meet George and demanded that her son arrange a meeting. Al got her a ticket for the concert and gave her one of his business cards, on which he scrawled a message to George. He also suggested that she should take along a small packet of custard powder. Al was confident that George would see the significance and make a point of chatting to her.

After the concert Al received a phone call from his sister Margaret, who had accompanied her mother to the theatre. She was very irate. When she arrived at the theatre, she told Al, she had been met by the spectacle of her mother waving the business card and carrying the biggest catering-size tin of Bird's custard powder she had ever seen! George had duly invited them to his dressing room. 'Al,' Margaret said, 'I've never been so embarrassed in my life! Guess who had to stagger behind Mother with that ridiculous tin of custard powder? Me! When George saw it he laughed so much he nearly cried – it was nearly as big as he was! I can't imagine what he'll do with it. But he did think it was funny, and he made a big fuss of Mother, dedicating a song to her during the show. I think Mother has fallen in love!'

Back at Kirk Sandall School on the day the custard saga began, the throwaway comment about Austerfield made by the tousle-headed boy sitting next to George had triggered a thought in Gerry Hickman's mind. After lunch that day the teacher spoke to George about a local landmark. 'George, this young man mentioned Austerfield, and you talked about Thanksgiving Day. I know it's a fairly tenuous connection, but did you know that one of the Pilgrim Fathers, William Bradford, was born in Austerfield? I don't know very much about him, except that he grew up there and sailed on the *Mayflower*.' Sandy Chappell chipped in. She thought William Bradford had been christened in the church at Austerfield, and the village of Scrooby, also nearby, boasted another Pilgrim Father, one William Brewster. George was fascinated. He knew about the Rotherhithe connections with the *Mayflower* down in London, but had not realized that the links came so far north.

Later on Al mentioned Austerfield too. He had an idea. 'You know, George,' he said, 'I would hazard a guess that there are thousands of children here in Britain who celebrate Christmas but have never really learned its true significance. And I bet there are people in America who celebrate Thanksgiving Day without having a clear idea what it's all about. What about doing something similar to the piece Waylon Jennings did about the American Civil War? I don't suppose anyone has done that yet, a presentation for children. It could make a good school project.'

Over the weeks that followed, the idea took root in George's mind. When his Christmas tour finally came to an end, he found himself with a day off before his flight home. He headed towards Austerfield. Strolling around the tiny village, he came upon the small Norman church of Saint Helena. It was a significant moment to stand before the font where William Bradford had been christened so many centuries ago, and extraordinary to think that he had sailed on the *Mayflower* and eventually become Governor of Plymouth, Massachusetts. George then drove on to Scrooby, where he picked up as much information as he could about the life and times of William Brewster. Both Bradford and Brewster had been major players in the Pilgrim Fathers' story.

In the New Year of 1991, George had some unaccustomed spare time on his hands. He used it to pursue his growing interest in the story of the early New World settlers, and he launched into some serious research. Gradually he began to assemble a clear sequence of events, searching out appropriate hymns, biblical texts and poems and writing up a narrative which could be used for a presentation of the whole Thanksgiving story. By the spring of that year George had completed his research and the presentation was ready to go. He then rang me in England to explain the concept of 'Thanksgiving in the Country'. We had already worked together on several projects, including his Christmas church tour of the previous year. I duly made arrangements for George to present his 'Thanksgiving in the Country' programme in churches of all denominations all over the British Isles around the time of Harvest Festival. With Wes Davis in support, the tour was a great success and the churches were packed out with enthusiastic audiences. In 1993 George recorded an album of the whole programme.

That same year George also returned to Kirk Sandall Junior School to host another assembly where he performed his Thanksgiving presentation for the children. Most of the pupils he had met the first time had now moved on, of course. The tousle-haired boy who had provided the first spark of an idea for the project was no longer there, but George paid tribute to him and recalled his first visit with appreciation. He then addressed himself to the sea of new young faces, and they listened absorbed as the tale unfolded and George sang and rhymed his way through tales of escape, rough sea voyages, hardship, death and determination.

The next day, the headmaster was swamped with telephone calls from parents prompted by their children's excitement, asking him if it would be possible for them to see the performance too. George was happy to oblige, and one autumn evening the school hall was filled to overflowing with older versions of the faces he had performed to in the assembly. George was so touched by the enthusiasm of his Kirk Sandall audiences, both old and young, that he presented the school with a collection of his sacred song albums. They have been played at school assemblies every week since then, and each new intake of children soon becomes familiar with the music of George Hamilton IV, singing along with great gusto!

In 1994, the school board invited George to become an Honorary Governor of Kirk Sandall School. By this time George had practically adopted the school and a real relationship had developed. He was more than pleased to accept the offer and has carefully maintained the link, as Al Moir observes. 'Although his normally hectic schedule rarely allows him to attend meetings, George never misses an opportunity to drop in on "his school". Over the years the children have come to love him and regard him as a friend.'

On Thanksgiving Day 1995, George returned to the church of Saint Helena in Austerfield to pay tribute to William Bradford. Every pew in the small church was filled, with many people also standing at the back. By then, George had lost count of the number of times he had played at the Grand Ole Opry, and he had become accustomed to the massive audiences at Billy Graham's rallies. Yet that night he believes he gave one of the best performances of his life, to one of the most appreciative audiences he had ever experienced.

CHAPTER 10

TO CANADA AND BEYOND

> In my estimation, George Hamilton IV has done more for Canadian folk and country music writers than anyone else I know from south of the border.
>
> **Curley Gurlock** (broadcaster, Camrose, Alberta)

MANY PEOPLE in the UK have mistakenly assumed that George Hamilton IV is a Canadian. It is an understandable error: perhaps the first time they saw him was on one of his popular television shows originally filmed in Canada and syndicated to Britain and other countries, or perhaps they were led to the conclusion by the many songs of Canadian origin which George includes in his repertoire. George himself is alive to the elements which connect Canada to both the UK and his home country the US.

'Canada is 100 years younger than my own country,' he explains. 'Therefore it's 100 years closer to our shared European heritage. We in the USA and Canada share a mutual heritage in the folk music tradition of our mother country Britain. What we like to think of as North American country music actually had its roots and beginnings in the folksongs and ballads of the countries which make up the British Isles. Our music's cradle days were witnessed by the old-fashioned troubadours and minstrels.'

George loves the UK, but he has a special feeling for Canada too. 'They call Canada "the big land", and it's certainly that! It's a vast, uncrowded, unpolluted territory full of cool north winds and warm, friendly people. I remember my school geography book about Canada left me with vivid impressions of snow, pine trees, huge mountains and wide open spaces. I've certainly found all that to be true! I've had a long-time love affair with Canada. I guess it started with the Royal Canadian Mounted Police's Sergeant Preston and his wonderful dog, King, the books of Jack London ... and I've always had a soft spot for Canada's Hank Snow, "The Singing Ranger". It was great, of course, to get to know him personally in Nashville.'

George's love affair with Canada reached a significant milestone in 1969 with his first, highly acclaimed album of all-Canadian music, entitled *Canadian Pacific*. In the years that followed he was to record five further studio albums of Canadian material, underlining his assertion that country and folk music is really 'people' music, with a common thread no matter what its place of origin. The broad base he draws on for his material is surely part of his universal appeal as a country star.

In the late sixties George became the first Nashville-based artiste to record the avant-garde material written by 'urban- folk' Canadians such as Joni Mitchell (her song 'The Urge For Goin'' has already been mentioned), Leonard Cohen ('Suzanne') and Buffy Sainte-Marie ('Take My Hand For A While'). First and foremost, however, George credits the music of Gordon Lightfoot as being the first that made him aware of the special pull of Canadian country music.

'I often refer to Gordon Lightfoot as the master, the teacher and the best of them all!' he says. 'Somehow, I could see that Canadian country music was a wonderful blend of the best of the old and new worlds. The stories, messages and metaphors of the folk music have a simple elegance and catchy, sing-along quality that's quite outstanding.' Unashamedly, George admits to being a 'folka-billy' and is proud of it! He has always loved folk-country music and asserts that, to him, Canada in particular was where this art form matured and came of age. 'When I listen to the nineties' music of Nanci Griffith, Kathy Mattea and Suzy Bogguss, I can hear echoes of Gordon Lightfoot, Joni Mitchell and Ian and Sylvia Tyson. Canadian folk-country music has had a major influence on later generations of Nashville singer- songwriters.'

An early trip up north to Toronto, where he was booked to appear at the Jack Starr Horseshoe Club, was the hook that first caught George, after which he became increasingly enamoured of the Canadian folk-country sound. He now considers Toronto to be one of the great music cities of the world. In his lifetime, it has become a booming, bustling music centre, often referred to in country music circles as 'the Nashville of the North'. Two important Canadian country music network TV shows – the *Tommy Hunter Show* and Carl Smith's *Country Music Hall* – originated in Toronto and many enterprising clubs featuring country music also blossomed in one concentrated area of the city. George has always greatly enjoyed his visits, revelling in what he describes as Toronto's 'super-rich vein of Canadian country music-makers'.

Whenever he was booked to tour round Canada, he would travel by plane as far as he could, then take to the car and enjoy the quiet solitude and peace of the region's country roads. It was possible to travel for miles without seeing another person, or even a single house. Such solitude could have its drawbacks, however. Always aware of possible threats from the elements and the wildlife, George would prepare very carefully for his long cross-country journeys, especially during the bitter Canadian winter. Sufficient fuel and emergency provisions were on the automatic checklist, and essentials included a shovel, a blanket, a flask of hot black coffee and some cookies – even if only to satisfy Tinky that he was looking after himself!

In 1972 George was entrusted with his own Canadian television series. *The George Hamilton IV Show*, broadcast from Hamilton, Ontario, ran successfully for seven years and was syndicated to New Zealand, South Africa, Hong Kong, the UK and the Republic of Ireland. Ireland's RTE network was the first to recognize the potential of the Canadian series in other countries. At the height of his television popularity, George had shows being televised simultaneously on the BBC and ITV networks in the UK. That was and still is unique for a country music performer!

George recorded successfully for Chet Atkins' Nashville operation until 1974, when he passed his RCA contract from south to north of the border. RCA Canada was independent of RCA USA, and was left to paddle its own canoe in commercial seas. In the country music genre, they traditionally struggled against the competition of the giants of Nashville. RCA's Canada's country music division had its own homegrown Canadian talent but few had made much impact apart from the yodelling legend, Wilf Carter, and the velvet-voiced Stu Phillips. Stu was poached by RCA USA to replace Jim Reeves when he died.

Securing the signature of George Hamilton IV gave RCA a considerable boost to their modern country music operation, and they went on to profit from his boundless enthusiasm and capacity for work. In turn, the deal gave George increased regional and international opportunities, to the envy of some of his Nashville colleagues. The move also gave George abundant room to experiment with his pioneering brand of country music and, thanks to his long-established status on the country music scene, his subsequent recordings and musical collaborations brought mainstream attention and popularity to scores of talented but internationally unknown Canadian artistes.

One of George's favourite Nashville record producers is his Canadian songwriter friend Ray Griff. Born in Vancouver in 1940, he made his name in Calgary, Alberta and only later became part of the Music City scene. George is deeply grateful to Ray for the song 'Canadian Pacific', featured on his album of that name. It became a hugely successful international number for George and still retains its popularity today, thanks to what he calls its 'evergreen folk quality'.

George admits that he does not always get things right with his choice of songs, but was happy to be proved wrong on the one occasion when he mistakenly assessed a composition by Ray as being below par. '"Something Special" was a song by Ray Griff that I recorded back in the sixties,' he explains. 'I honestly didn't think it was very commercial, so we put the song on the flip side of John D. Loudermilk's "Break My Mind". I always thought that "Break My Mind" would be the biggest and most memorable hit of the two, but over the years countless folks have requested Ray's "Something Special" instead. That's one song I badly misread!'

Another song that was not allowed to get away was a great number written by young Buffy Sainte-Marie. 'Her classy song,

"I'm Gonna Be A Country Boy Again" has doubled at times as a theme song for me,' George comments. An outstanding talent and an undeniably colourful character, Buffy Sainte-Marie was a Cree Indian from Fort Queppelle, Saskatchewan. George says that Chet Atkins and John D. Loudermilk always described her as 'a gas', and George himself admired her enthusiasm, humour and zest for life. 'She was a passionate, outspoken fighter for the rights of the Native Canadian Americans,' he recalls. 'She was also a skilful and inspirational songwriter. Chet Atkins wanted me to record Buffy's song "Take My Hand For A While" and he told me, "If you'll record the song, I'll play lead guitar on it." He played a Dobro, an acoustic guitar with a metal resonator inside it, and the sound was something special. Oddly enough, I don't recall him playing lead guitar on any of my other records, and it was absolutely gorgeous!'

Other great songs from Buffy's pen included 'The Universal Soldier', a big hit for Donovan in the seventies, 'Soldier Blue' from the movie of the same title, and 'Up Where We Belong', the world-famous hit for Joe Cocker and Jennifer Warnes. 'Up Where We Belong' shot to fame as one of the pop classics of the eighties, hitting the Top Five in charts across all the major continents. George came to admire and respect very highly Buffy Sainte-Marie's artistry, recognizing her quality songwriting before many others and accordingly doing much to circulate and popularize her work.

One of the greatest Canadian influences on George, however, was Gordon Lightfoot. Back in December 1965, George flew to Toronto with John D. Loudermilk to appear on Carl Smith's television show *Country Music Hall*. As preparations for the show got underway, George was delighted to have an opportunity to meet Gordon Lightfoot, whom he had long admired as a supreme folk-tunesmith from north of the border. The two men shook each other enthusiastically by the hand and got chatting about their work, oblivious of the bustling backstage crew, who were scrambling around the singers trying to arrange the lighting and sound ready for the recording of the show. George and Gordon agreed to meet after the show for a drink and an informal jam session at the

Canadiana Motor Hotel. Ronnie Hawkins, the Arkansas-born rock 'n' roll legend, would also be there. After a tiresome day, it was something to look forward to!

During the course of the evening, the musicians enjoyed sharing ideas and experiments, and in the process consumed a whole case of what George described at the time as 'good Canadian nectar'. That night Gordon also taught George a song he had written called 'Steel Rail Blues'. George rightly recognized the modern 'train ballad' as a future hit, and it did indeed go on to become a classic. For George, of course, its attraction was not just the undoubted quality of the music. It also brought back fond and vivid memories of his long-departed railroading grandfather.

Some time later, at George's invitation, Gordon flew to Nashville to supervise and pick guitar (a flat-top Martin in this case) when George recorded the song on 7 February 1966. Also in on the recording were Chet Atkins and Felton Jarvis, who was Elvis Presley's producer at that time. Both George and Gordon were highly delighted to see it hit the Country Top Ten that year, and the song went on to become one of George's greatest successes. There was a hairy moment in the studio, however, which might have come close to derailing the whole project, as George explains.

'We were in the studio recording "Steel Rail Blues". Gordon Lightfoot had come down to Nashville specially. He was playing acoustic guitar for the recording and was doing a great job. It sounded really good to me. After one of the takes, I think it may even have been the first, Chet came over the speaker. "That's a keeper," he said. Everybody was about to put their instruments down and go into the control room to listen to the playback, when Gordon Lightfoot answered in a loud voice, "The hell it is!" There was a long pause while we all waited to see what response was going to come back from "control central" where Chet was sitting. Then we heard Chet's voice over the speaker again. "I beg your pardon?" he said. He sounded rather startled!

'Gordon's retort was quick and to the point. "This is *my* damn song," he exclaimed. "I came all the way down here from Toronto to help you get it right, and we're gonna get it right or else we're not gonna get it!" Well, there was another long pause. All the other musicians were just waiting for the moment when Mr Atkins would come storming out of the control room and lay down the law. Nobody had ever heard *anyone* talk back to Chet that way in a recording studio! After the longest pause, we heard Chet speaking again. "O-kay..." he said very slowly. So we buckled down and did another take, and sure enough, it was noticeably better. Gordon was right, I guess! It's to Chet's everlasting credit that he had enough humility to let the guy who wrote the song have his way and take another shot at it.'

While he was in Nashville, Gordon spent the night at George's home and thoroughly charmed Tinky and the children. He also shot pool with John D. Loudermilk's wife Gwen – although it is sad to have to report that Gordon dishonoured himself by losing! 'Well, buddy,' said George to the loser in mock seriousness, 'you've written some great songs ... but I guess you can't be good at everything. Keep practising!'

Gordon was raised in Orillia, Ontario (the name Lightfoot is deceptive: he is not a Native Canadian American as one might assume). He cut his teeth early in Canadian country music, playing along to the radio and his 45 record collection in his bedroom. He later studied music in California and served his apprenticeship amongst the tough audiences of the Toronto coffee houses. He eventually emerged to be Canada's top folksinger while still under 30 years of age. George is quick to acknowledge his own debt to Gordon for the evolution of his musical ideas. 'In the mid-sixties, I guess it was true to say that Gordon influenced my musical life more than any other individual, except possibly for Chet Atkins and John D. Loudermilk. Looking back, I still look on Gordon as the master of the art of folk-country music. "Early Mornin' Rain", for example, is a Lightfoot classic. We recorded it on 24 January 1966 and it went on to reach the Top Ten. It has remained a country music favourite for my audiences. I have to thank Gordon for that!'

Gordon was also arguably the main trigger behind a larger project George undertook in the late sixties. 'Having met Gordon Lightfoot in the mid-sixties and being by then well on the way to becoming infatuated with Canadian folk-country music, largely through Gordon's inspiration, I started pestering Chet Atkins to let me record a whole album of Canadian folk-country songs – the music of people like Gordon, Ian and Sylvia, Leonard Cohen, Joni Mitchell and such. Eventually, we started compiling songs and Chet got interested in the idea, but it took a while to come about.

'In the end it was Chet who suggested that we come up with a "theme song" to capture the spirit of the album. It was to be entirely Canadian music, songs from the north country, the land of the maple leaf, conjuring up ideas of snow, mountains and pine trees. Chet recommended that we contact Ray Griff, the Canadian songwriter who by then had come to Nashville to work on new material and become part of the music community there. Chet wanted to approach Ray and commission him to write a song specifically as the title track for the album, which we eventually recorded in 1969. It was the first album of all-Canadian music recorded by an American country singer – I'm proud of that fact!

'Ray duly wrote "Canadian Pacific" for us, specifically with the thought of capturing the spirit and the feel of his home in the north. There was never any intention of making a hit single out of it. It was just the theme track, the title track of the album. Ironically, however, it become one of our best known and most requested songs in Canada, the British Isles and the rest of Europe. I think that may have been triggered off by a radio show called *Family Favourites* on the BBC World Service, which of course is heard internationally. Someone, for example, would write in to the show to request that a song be played for a Canadian relative. The show's controllers would play "Canadian Pacific" to fulfil the request. Alternatively, folks would request a song to be dedicated or played for a British relative to remind them of their Canadian family members, and again they'd play "Canadian Pacific"! So, although the song was never a hit in the States, it did become a signature song of sorts for me in other places, all thanks to that great institution, the BBC World Service.

'It also helped, no doubt, that 1967 was also the year of the very first International Festival of Country Music at Wembley, and it was the year of my first tour of the UK with the Hillsiders and Albert Lee on an RCA package. Consequently, songs from the

Canadian Pacific album were the first songs I was seen and heard performing on tour in the UK and at the Wembley Festival. These songs from the *Canadian Pacific* album, in particular "Early Mornin' Rain", "Steel Rail Blues", and "Canadian Pacific" itself, were the first that the British people associated with me. Later, I added other Canadian songs to my performing repertoire including "Four Strong Winds", "The Urge for Goin'" and "Suzanne" by Leonard Cohen. All this Canadian material led to some confusion: to this day, I still get people in Britain, Ireland and continental Europe asking me, "What town in Canada are you from?" It's an honour, of course, but not quite right!'

One world-famous chart-topper who hailed from Canada back in the swinging sixties and seventies was Joni Mitchell. George is an ardent admirer and describes Joni as 'Her Royal Highness, the Beautiful Magic Flower Lady of Folk Music'! Born in McLeod, Alberta in November 1943, Joni later studied art in Calgary and was always colourfully and fashionably turned out. 'I'm sure that every guy who ever saw her perform fell in love with that enchanting girl,' George says. 'As her song "Both Sides Now" illustrates, she was also a mistress of word pictures and poetic imagery. And, of course, she kindly agreed to let me record "Urge For Goin'" in 1967, and although it seemed very radical for the country music market at the time, it became a Top Ten hit. I'll always be grateful to Joni for that.' Revered as one of the greatest urban-folk music innovators in the seventies, Joni Mitchell was typical of the left-wing generation that spawned the hippie movement – such a contrast to the right-wing, conservative stance of the older generation typified by Hank Snow, who was also, interestingly, Canadian-born.

The seventies were also a successful decade for the talented duo Ian and Sylvia Tyson. They were well admired by George even before he recorded Ian's song 'Summer Wages' in 1969. George owned all their albums and respected them both as performers and people. 'One of the most pleasant evenings I ever spent was in their Toronto home,' he recalls. 'Sitting cross-legged on their living room floor, I ate chilli and enjoyed listening to their latest recordings!'

There was so much creative talent coming out of Canada in those and later years, and George acknowledges them all as having influenced him in one way or another. One great singer-songwriter from the Canadian provinces who particularly caught his eye was Dick Damron. Born in Bentley, Alberta, Dick paid his dues in country music on radio and television stations in Red Deer before moving to Edmonton. In his time he was also an oil-rig worker in rural Alberta. Like so many other songwriting greats – not least Hank Snow – Dick knew how to use his hands in a day of hard labour, be it in industry or the fields, and such experiences seemed to add a special seasoning to these artistes' musical creations, somehow sharpening their observations and expressions. George describes Dick Damron as a real country gentleman who richly deserved the awards he received for his hit songs. As a Christian, George was particularly enchanted by Dick's devotional song 'Jesus, It's Me Again', a plaintive prayer with movingly humble lyrics. George recorded the song on his *High Country* album in the late nineties.

Many people would say that one of George's own most notable qualities is humility, yet he prefers to highlight songwriter Gene MacLellan as someone who possessed humility in abundance. He describes Gene as one of the frontrunners of the so-called 'Maritime Mafia', among whom were also Anne Murray and Brian Ahern. The 'Maritime Mafia' was the affectionate nickname that George loved to use of the growing group of singers, musicians and songwriters from the Maritime Provinces. At the time, they developed their own unique folksy sound and personalities, independent of the overpowering influences of the USA musical scene. During the years of George's involvement, the group matured in their unique Canadian artistry and self-belief.

Hailing from Prince Edward Island off the coast of New Brunswick and Nova Scotia, Gene MacLellan bequeathed to the world such gems as 'Snowbird' and 'Put Your Hand In The Hand'. 'Snowbird' became a classic when it was popularized by Canadian superstar singer Anne Murray. 'Put Your Hand In The Hand' became a popular modern-day spiritual, with multiple recordings by artistes ranging from Elvis to George IV himself. George remembers Gene MacLellan warmly. 'Gene was a kind gentleman from Canada's "down east" who wore his success humbly. He genuinely viewed the world with sensitivity and his fellow citizens with respect.'

Although fiercely loyal to his beloved Carolinas and very much a Southern gentleman, George is also strongly determined and passionate in his stand for 'all things Canadian', particularly the Canadian musical heritage. Down the years he has recorded countless songs that pay tribute to the majestic beauty of Canada's wilderness and to its small but warm-hearted population. When he tucked himself into bed in Winston-Salem as a young boy and pored over his atlas with a torch after 'lights out', exploring the details of the northern land which seemed so huge and full of exciting possibilities, he would never have imagined that one day he would be travelling the world, promoting Canada's musical heritage to audiences in the USA and far beyond. For George ended up with a truly international career, and because he had absorbed so much from Canadian material and influences, that particular heritage has often seemed to be at the forefront of his work.

Since his first dizzy visit to Australia in 1959 in the company of Chuck Berry and Bobby Darin, George had travelled quite a bit, though this became a far greater feature in his schedule from the late sixties onwards as he established a name in the UK and his fame spread to many other countries through the medium of television. The more he journeyed abroad, the more he says he learned first-hand that country music was a genuinely international experience. Wherever he performed, it seemed, the music communicated very effectively with his audiences, getting feet tapping and tugging heartstrings all over the world.

Wesley Rose, of the Nashville-based Acuff-Rose Publishing and the Acuff-Rose Artist Corporation, was manager to Roy Orbison and George IV for many years. George remembers that Wesley was the first person to suggest that he should travel to England. 'In 1967 I was going over to Germany to tour the American military bases. I'd been over there a few times before, but on this particular tour, which had been organized by Acuff-Rose, Wesley suggested that I stop off in London on my way back in order to visit the Acuff-Rose offices there. That was my first visit to England, made in November of 1967. While I was there I did Wally Whyton's *Country Meets Folk* radio programme from the old BBC Playhouse Theatre down on the banks of the River Thames, and the show was broadcast in December that year.'

It proved to be the start of an international career success unique in the world of country music. During the last three decades of the twentieth century, in terms of the international scene George IV enjoyed an almost continuous upwards journey in his career. The level of his fame and status outside the USA has generally been much greater than has been the case with most of his Grand Ole Opry comrades. He seems to have a powerful kind of communion with his audiences, a musical togetherness which he shares with the thousands of people who have been to see him perform in far-flung places and cultures far removed from Nashville. Always an enthusiast for his art, George considers that his role as the 'International Ambassador of Country Music' has also involved a practical, statesmanlike application.

'In my own way, I like to think that I've helped to destroy many walls and build a few bridges instead. I'm very grateful for the acceptance I receive for my music internationally. Bob Powel, the UK music journalist and radio presenter, was one of the first people to refer to me as "the International Ambassador of Country Music". I think he started to use the phrase, originally coined by *Billboard Magazine*, half-jokingly, when I'd returned from my trip to the Soviet Union and Eastern Europe in March 1974. Bob also compiled and wrote the book which is included in my RCA box set from 1976, *The George Hamilton IV Story*. He now lives in Thailand, but Bob has been a dear friend and keen supporter since my early days in England. Originally from Quebec, he possibly had a soft spot in his heart for me because so much of my repertoire was Canadian. We hit it off from the beginning. I always saw Bob as a real musicologist and historian. He really knows about music, country music in particular.'

George's trip behind the Iron Curtain in 1974 was a fascinating experience for him, and it also won him a valued accolade back home. In New York on 14 January 1975 George was delighted to receive a Trendsetter award from *Billboard* magazine, one of America's foremost music journals. His performances in the Soviet Union in the spring of the previous year were acknowledged by *Billboard* as an outstanding achievement. George had penetrated previously uncharted territory for an American country artiste.

Six years before his Soviet Union adventure, in 1968, George had toured the Far East, appearing on the Osaka Grand Ole Opry in Japan. He even stayed long enough to record a single in Japanese entitled '*Hoshi No Komoriuta*', which means 'Memories Of Mama'. The following year he was part of RCA's 'Goodwill Tour' to the UK, Denmark, Holland, Germany, Sweden, Norway and Finland. George's UK visit that year kicked off a cycle of more than annual returns to the old country which continues to this day. For the next couple of decades, of course, a highlight of those visits were the International Festivals of Country Music held at Wembley. (Incidentally, other countries later followed suit and held their own International Festivals, inviting George to act as MC – Sweden in 1976, Finland in 1977, Holland and Norway in 1978, Germany in 1979, France and Switzerland in 1980 and Austria in 1984.)

International recognition continued to build as the years passed, developing very rapidly indeed as the sixties came to an end and the new decade began. In 1970/71 George was the first of the USA's country artistes to record an entire album – *North Country* – in Canada using all-Canadian material, musicians and personnel. Never content to stand still, within months of completing that northern album, George returned to the UK for a similar project with the Liverpool band the Hillsiders. The result of this creative collaboration was the happy meeting of American and British country music cultures on the album *George Hamilton IV with the Hillsiders: Heritage.*

It soon became clear that as well as charming fans worldwide, George was acquiring professional recognition for his overseas endeavours. In 1971 he was voted by the USA's *Billboard* magazine and the UK's *Record Mirror* as Britain's 'Number One Country Artiste'. The following year he received the Juno Award for Outstanding Contributions to Canadian Country Music, the first US artiste to be recognized in this way by the Canadian journal *RPM Weekly*. That same year, at the fourth International Festival of Country Music in London, George was formally (and uniquely) designated by *Billboard* and *Record Mirror* as the 'International Ambassador of Country Music'.

The next year, 1973, found him back in Canada receiving the BMI Canada Special Award for Outstanding Contributions to Canadian Country Music. By this time George's passport was beginning to look somewhat dog-eared, with all the fingering and stamping it received during his packed travel schedule! That year he was also awarded the UK's Top USA Male Country Singer award at the fifth International Festival of Country Music. At the same time he accepted the position of Honorary President of the British Country Music Association, a position which he still proudly occupies today.

In 1974 George embarked on a six-week concert tour of the British Isles. It included a lecture on the history of country music at the American Embassy in London's Grosvenor Square. That was followed in the spring by his concert tour through countries behind the Iron Curtain. Accompanying him on that groundbreaking trip was his UK-based agent and friend, Mervyn Conn. George played four concerts to 28,000 people in Prague, accompanied by the Czech band Jiri Brabec and the Country Beat. From there he journeyed on to Hungary and Poland, and then to Moscow where he gave several lectures and concerts that traced the history of country music. George has been travelling ever since.

Constant travel may have led to huge international success, but George is the first to say that the experience has not always been a positive one. It has carried with it a very hefty personal price tag. 'A lot of fans seem to think that an entertainer's travelling lifestyle is one great big piece of cake. How wrong can they be?' he says. 'If I ever sit down and try my hand as an author, my first book will be called *Home Is a Holiday Inn*!' Long years of experience means that he knows now how to settle in quickly and feel immediately at home in any hotel. It is a disciplinary routine that George knows by heart. 'I'm a gypsy of sorts, I guess, and I've accepted my lifestyle. I've learned to live with it, and even love it, but it's not easy!

'Well-meaning folks have often said to me, "Why don't you bring your wife and kids along?" Can you *imagine* what that would mean for the poor wife and kids of an entertainer? You do a show, get to bed late and sleep a few hours, and then early next morning you get up to pack and go on to the next town. Once there, although you may be tired out, you have to put your mind into interview mode, because the radio and television stations expect that and it's all part of the necessary promotion. After that you prepare for the next show. That's the routine, day after day after day. I can tell you from experience – and I'm sure Tinky would back me up – that it's no fun for a poor spouse who has nothing much to do except sit in the wings of one theatre or another, or in a car seat on yet another trip to an unfamiliar town. There certainly isn't much time for togetherness on a concert tour. Believe me, it's best doing it on your own!'

Ever since the beginning of his career, and despite his huge international success, George Hamilton IV has invariably considered himself to be nothing special as a singer, technically speaking. That is why, he says, it has always been so important for him to identify with the songs he sings. Lacking the power and ability of a great virtuoso singer, he feels he concentrates instead on the meaning of each song. If he feels passionate about what he is singing and believes in it enough to give something of himself in the performance, then he can still communicate most effectively with his audience.

'Many times,' he explains, 'I've been asked whether it's really possible to sing moving songs night after night and remain true to their meanings. I've discovered that, over time, what happens is that songs evolve and change. When I sit back now and listen to songs I recorded years ago, I'm often surprised to find that I don't sing them in the same way any more. Instead, the songs seem to have grown or evolved alongside me as *I've* grown into maturity. And because of that, they have retained their meaning and have stayed personal and fresh, no matter how many times I may have sung them.'

This is undoubtedly the key to his popularity all over the world. George is a communicator *par excellence*. Whatever the situation, whatever the culture of the people to whom he performs, George's enthusiasm seems to dissolve any barriers to understanding, and everyone simply ends up enjoying the music and the experience of the show. This communication with audiences, however large or small, is more important to George than other, more measurable indicators of success. He is genuinely unworried now about achieving chart successes back home in the USA. Indeed, he considers it a very sad fact that these days in his home country more and more emphasis is being put on chart success at the expense of other considerations. The charts, he maintains, are not the only, or even the most accurate barometer of who is of value in the country music scene, and it is wholly wrong to set them up as such.

'I'm pleased and proud to say that I've been one of many classic artistes who are well loved all over the world. I haven't been represented in the charts in America in recent years, however, but that "chart syndrome" only seems to be true in my own country! In the UK, for example, one can hear a wider variety of music on the radio stations. There is much more to music than just the Top Thirty!' To illustrate his point, George tells the story of two country-music-loving friends of his from England who visited the USA for a month. He met up with them again in England when they returned, and George asked how the trip had gone. 'You must have had a wonderful time in America,' he said. 'I bet you heard a lot of country music on the radio. Did you get your fill?' His friends gave a telling reply. 'No, George,' they said, 'we didn't hear all that much country music on the radio ... but we memorized 20 songs from the country charts!'

George's travel experiences were not entirely limited to an endless stream of hotels, theatres and airport lounges; nor was the development of his international country music career always the sole consideration. Sometimes he had the opportunity to explore further afield, and some journeys took on a wider personal significance. One very special, life-changing trip occurred for George in

1973, when he was invited to join Arthur 'Guitar Boogie' Smith and his musical troop for a tour of the Holy Land. Like many other visitors to the land where Jesus lived, George found himself challenged in a profound and spiritual way as he took the chance to see some of the places significant to stories recorded in the Bible.

The result of that extraordinary trip was the filming of two television specials for the *Arthur Smith TV Show*, as well as a keepsake album made for Pat Boone's Lamb and Lion label. The first-hand experience of the country of the Bible also left George deep in thought about his faith, and prompted him over subsequent years to explore more fully his relationship with God.

In March 1999 George returned to the Holy Land with Tinky, on a tour organized by pastor Des Morton from Bristol, England. Arriving at Tel Aviv Airport, they stepped off the plane into the warm Israeli sunshine and climbed onto a bus to be taken to their hotel. Both George and Tinky say they were struck by the beauty of Tel Aviv, now a large modern city, set against the deep blue of the sea. Particularly viewed from the air, it seemed to them to hold a huge weight of history, and they felt awed by the reminder that this country represented so many centuries of significance.

The next day, the holiday party set off for the northern Galilee area of Caesarea Philippi. They stopped at an ancient amphitheatre and there, under the warm sun, two actors who were travelling with the group played out scenes from the Gospels. Then George sang his testimony song, 'Acres Of Diamonds', and the rest of the party joined in with the choruses. It was a profoundly meaningful and emotional time. George admits he had to hold back his own tears, and the whole group seemed affected by that shared moment of communication.

Tinky recalls the trip with joy. 'We didn't leave a stone unturned during those 12 days. It was wonderful to stop at all those fascinating sites and to have the relevant Scriptures read to us. It just seemed to make the stories come alive. Beverly, our tour guide, added details about the Jewish history that surrounded each place, and our understanding of the whole situation improved by leaps and bounds! And I'll never forget the songs George sang in each different site. Our visits to the Mount of

Olives and the Garden of Gethsemane were the most moving. Especially the Garden, where the actors Mike and Kim performed the scene when Christ prayed before being led away to his trial and crucifixion by the Roman soldiers. It was unbearably poignant.'

George has his own special memory from the trip. 'I think my most meaningful stop was Golgotha, where Christ died, and the Garden Tomb where they laid his body. It was wonderful to stand there and think over all that it meant to us, and then to realize that of course he was no longer there, but risen! Our visit was made on a Sunday morning and I was invited to sing and share at an open-air church service by the Garden Tomb. I sang "I Come To The Garden Alone", which was my mother's favourite song, and "Nailed Scarred Hands". Then the pastor spoke, and his words seems to go straight to the heart. It really was something special.'

CHAPTER 11

THE GROWING LIGHT

And he hath put a new song in my mouth, even praise unto our God: many shall see it, and fear, and shall trust in the Lord.

King David, Psalm 40:3

IT WAS A BEAUTIFUL, fresh spring day in London's Hyde Park. Sitting in his hotel bedroom overlooking the park, George Hamilton IV was busy preparing himself for the start of another International Festival of Country Music at Wembley in the early 80s. Playing in the background, BBC Radio 4's *Thought for the Day* programme had an Easter theme. Frank Topping was telling the Easter story in very simple terms. 'I wasn't really listening carefully to what he was saying,' George recalls. ' I was thinking mostly about myself ... what was I going to sing at the concert at Wembley ... would the audience like me ... would I go over as well as my peers ... would I get an encore ... the usual show-biz preoccupations.'

Frank Topping went on to explain the significance of Maundy Thursday, the day before Good Friday. George had never thought much about it before, and was more interested just then in changing a guitar string. Maundy Thursday, said Frank Topping, was the day, almost 2,000 years ago, when Jesus Christ had held his Last Supper. Christ sat down at a table with the best of his friends and shared a simple meal with them. What he said next grabbed the whole of George's attention, and pretty much took his breath away. 'Before the dramatic night was over in Jerusalem, some of Christ's so-called dear friends were to deny that they ever knew him. Indeed, one of them was directly responsible for the arrest that led to his execution on the cross. Wasn't that a terrible thing?'

George had never considered the actions of Jesus' friends in that way before. 'Why, yes!' he thought, suddenly understanding. 'Those guys were the best friends Christ ever had. That's disgusting! Why should they deny they ever knew him? If anyone should have known him, it was the disciples. How could they *do* that? I would never do something like that!'

He was incensed when Frank Topping went on to say, 'You're guilty of that, and so am I!'

George was shocked into retorting aloud. '*What*?' he snapped at the radio. 'You've got to be kidding, man! I wasn't even around 2,000 years ago!' How on earth could someone try to implicate him in the crucifixion? What a ridiculous idea. And besides, he had been a good Christian all his life. He was a regular member of a smart, fashionable church back home, where he could sing almost every hymn by heart, and he had always taken part in all the traditions of his church. '*I'm* okay, buddy, thank you very much!'

But the radio voice continued. 'You have denied Jesus, and so have I – by your actions and your words, by your life, and by the things you've said and done ... and not done.'

George had had enough. He leaned over the bed to switch off the troublesome voice. He could not, however, shut off the voice of his conscience. Was that all there was to Easter? Mere tradition? *Was* he missing something? His sense of indignation began to struggle with insistent doubts. Perhaps he was an inadequate Christian after all. Perhaps he was *not* 'okay, thank you'.

'Looking back,' George says now, 'it was all part of the coming together of my realization that I needed to get to grips with myself about spiritual matters. I didn't need to learn more in terms of facts and background. I needed to learn to live what I believed, to act my faith. It was a question of priorities. Musical styles and earthly successes come and go with every changing wind of fashion, but God's truth endures for ever. That's where my treasure was truly to be found.'

> For all flesh is as grass, and all the glory of man as the flower of grass. The grass withereth, and the flower thereof falleth away: But the word of the Lord endureth for ever. And this is the word which by the gospel is preached unto you.
>
> 1 Peter 1:24–5

The old-time country music duo Don Reno and Red Smiley used to sing a song called 'I'm Using My Bible For A Road Map'. It is a song George has known from childhood, and it now forms part of his own repertoire. Its words speak truth for him: 'My advice to anybody struggling in the Christian faith is to get their Bible out and read it. It gives us many answers and it's a living, breathing thing. I don't agree with some folk who say that calling the Bible a "road map" is sacrilegious. Through my own experience I've found it to be *the* essential guidebook on the road of life.'

George is ready to admit now that he spent most of his life coasting along in 'token Christianity' and never really woke up to that fact until his visit to Eastern Europe in 1974. 'I awoke then to realize that I had been a backsliding Christian who didn't live up to the faith he professed. I wasn't alone. There were many among my peers who said they were Christians but really didn't live it out at all.'

George was lovingly and diligently raised in that part of America which many people call the Bible Belt. To say that it is a region which is ultra-religiously orientated is no exaggeration. Such an environment, and the way a child is brought up by his parents, tends to have a lasting impact on the adult that child becomes. 'Train up a child in the way he should go: and when he is old, he will not depart from it' (Proverbs 22:6). George was therefore raised in an environment where church-going and Sunday School attendance were the norm. His parents led by example and went along too. In their turn, George and Tinky raised their three children along the same lines. They sang in the church choir, went to the Training Union on Sunday nights and to church suppers on Wednesdays. George remembers those Wednesday evenings with pleasure – largely because the sermon from the pastor was invariably preceded by a delicious meal!

George was also raised to believe that it was healthy to question and re-examine traditions and practices from time to time, in order to retain awareness of their basic meanings, and to remain down-to-earth and honest in connecting beliefs to actions. This should not be limited to matters of church life either, George believes. He has often said that, although life in the latter part of the twentieth century seemed immensely complicated, people should never forget there is still elegance and fulfilment in simplicity. It is so easy to lose sight of essentials.

'My years in show business have taught me that a man's ego is something that easily becomes corrupted,' he explains. 'All around me, I hear cries of "Me, Me, Me". Tex Ritter understood the problem very clearly. He once remarked to me, "George, do you know what the trouble with this world is? The trouble is that there are too many people starring in their own movie. It's real hard to communicate with other entertainers because they all want to star in their own movies!" How right he was. We all need to look up from our self-obsession. People are so quick to be distracted by the glitter of things that are not important in the eternal scheme.'

Down the years, George's songs have fed him not only poetry and music, but also philosophical wisdom and even theology. He sees that his main duty is to entertain audiences and and make sure they receive their money's worth – he is always conscious of the danger of disappointing those who have come to see and hear him – yet he also feels he has an essential message to communicate. He wants to paint a picture and tell a story. This has always been the case, but the older he got, the more concerned he became: 'It was easy to see that values and standards were deteriorating all around me. The world was getting sicker and sicker. There was more and more pornography in the movies and on the newsstands. The dirt and filth steadily mounting in society was sickening. Like others, I was beginning to want to react to all of those negative influences. I wanted to do my part in returning the world to a less decadent time. Not just in the Bible Belt, but among good-living people everywhere, there was a sense of growing intolerance to the seamier side of life which was evident wherever we looked.'

In his heart, George recognizes now, he was yearning to turn back to the deeper values that he had been taught as a child. One verse of Scripture kept coming back to him time and time again:

> Finally, brethren, whatsoever things are true, whatsoever things are honest, whatsoever things are just, whatsoever things are pure, whatsoever things are lovely, whatsoever things are of good report; if there be any virtue, and if there be any praise, think on these things. Those things, which ye have both learned, and received, and heard, and seen in me, do: and the God of peace shall be with you.
>
> Philippians 4:8–9

George's wish to turn back to God, and to live the kind of life Jesus had advocated, grew steadily during the seventies. By then he had spent 20 years on the road as an entertainer, and when he carefully re-examined himself in the light of what he knew to be true, he felt a sense of condemnation. 'My biggest problem as a Christian in show business was not what I believed, but being able to *live up to* what I believed!' he says.

'Through the years, I had been well taught. Nonetheless, it was one thing to know and believe something, and even to feel it deeply, but it was something else to put it into daily practice. I had very deep Christian beliefs, and I held onto those very firmly, but I could not pretend to be a saint. I knew I'd made mistakes, all sorts of them, and I'd probably go on doing that. The important thing that I was realizing was that I had to be real with my God. As an entertainer, however, I feared the trap of making a show of my religion. I knew that if I declared my Christianity openly, there would be a searchlight trained on me from then on! People would be watching me to see when I tripped up.

'I felt I couldn't say that I was a righteous person, yet I still longed to be one, and I was desperate to know how I could achieve it. Then Christian friends told me it was necessary for me to come personally to God in repentance and faith. It wasn't a question of my good works, it was a matter of God's grace. As I came to understand this, it was like standing in a growing light. I didn't deserve God's grace, but he was ready to give it to me, to rescue me as a personal gift.

'The words of one of my favourite gospel songs kept going round in my mind: "Must Jesus Bear The Cross Alone?" He had died for the sins of the whole world and I had to come to terms personally with such grace. Christ had made himself a sacrifice and endured crucifixion for me as an individual. In the face of this, all my life I had been at best apathetic and at worst ungrateful. How could I refuse such a gift? How could I continue to be so off-hand about the way I responded to God? Hank Williams' song "How Can You Refuse Him Now?" asked exactly the right question. I'm convinced it was no coincidence that Hank's song was the first gospel song I ever recorded. Arthur Smith's beautiful song "I Saw A Man" also haunted me with its message about Christ: "If I be lifted up I will draw all men unto me." This became more than just a beautiful line in a song. It became a truth that I was experiencing in my deepest being. Like a magnet, Christ was drawing me to himself. I could feel it.'

Providentially, just as George was thinking his way increasingly seriously through such central matters of faith, he found his contacts with committed Christians proliferating, particularly within the music industry. Country artistes A.G. and Kate, for example, were a Dutch duo George originally met at the Wembley Festivals. 'They have been a great influence on my Christian musical life,' George says. 'We've become dear friends and have performed together too, occasionally in the UK and quite often in Holland.'

The singing preacher Jerry Arhelger, from Weewahitchka in Florida, was one of several key Christian influences on George from the Music City Christian Fellowship. Other members have included Connie Smith, Billy Walker, Skeeter Davis, Emily and Sam Weiland, Joe Babcock, Vernon Oxford, Linda Hargrove Bartholomew, Donna Stoneman and the Fox Brothers. A first-class Christian communicator, Jerry was someone for whom George had a great deal of respect. His singing and songwriting style was not what you might expect from a Christian singer, but was more along the lines of Waylon Jennings, a style George describes as 'a kind of country rock, a trucking-jukebox sound'. Alongside George, Jerry was part of the *Sunday Morning Country* programme. (Every year, at the Fan Fair and the DJ Convention, the Music City Christian Fellowship organized special *Sunday Morning Country* get-togethers for the fans during which each performer would sing a couple of songs.) It gave George an opportunity to observe Jerry close up and listen carefully to his unabashed testimony. Jerry and the others in the Fellowship were an inspiration to George, and they played a large part in encouraging him through his own journey of faith.

The people George worked and sang with were not the only influences emanating from the musical world. There was also the music itself. One of the greatest contributions to George's spiritual development has been made by hymns and gospel songs, absorbed even as a very young boy, and acknowledged as increasingly meaningful in later years. George grew up hearing songs on the radio such as 'What A Friend We Have In Jesus', performed by singers at the Grand Ole Opry:

> What a friend we have in Jesus,
> All our sins and griefs to bear.
> What a privilege to carry
> Everything to God in prayer...
>
> Are we weak and heavy-laden,
> Cumbered with a load of care?
> Precious Saviour, still our refuge,
> Take it to the Lord in prayer.
>
> Joseph M. Scriven, trad.

One very early influence on George was the country crooner Red Foley, Pat Boone's father-in-law, who was a master interpreter of gospel songs. George says he will never forget Red Foley's rendition of 'Peace In The Valley' and other gems.

George is enduringly grateful for the influence of such inspirational songs in his life. In cultural terms, he also finds it fascinating to see how these songs have blended into the country music world, mixing Christian values with entertainment. 'You'll often find this ol' country boy settling down in his favourite armchair at his Nashville home and relaxing to the uplifting and inspiring sounds of gospel music,' he says. 'It's the kind of soothing music I like to hear after the evening's television newscast has told me the worst of the daily headlines. Gospel music dispels the depression and the worry and puts new tread on my tyres!'

Gospel music comes in many different forms, but there is at least one common denominator: quality songs are handed down from one generation to another. The Afro-Americans perhaps offer the most familiar example of music and tradition being passed down over successive generations. Their rich inheritance of 'black spirituals' developed from the hardships endured during the dark days of slavery in the Old South. Now many of these simple expressions of Christian truth have been adopted by other cultures too, and entertainers and evangelists have blended them into the mainstream of popular music and hymnody. Such cross-pollination has been a constant factor – between black and white, north and south, even west and east. George himself drew on all these diverse traditions and cultures to form his own repertoire.

Nowadays gospel music has secured a prominent position in the musical arena. Like George IV, many professional artistes, both black and white, have adopted the genre into their personal musical repertoire. The Grand Ole Opry and other music shows, as well as radio and television, have all helped to give exposure and add to the popularity of gospel music. On some occasions, however, George has met with some opposition, as he explains. 'As a Christian entertainer, I know I have upset more than a few of the stiff-necked, serious-minded religionists who are fearful of mixing ministry with entertainment. Most contentious of all is the vexed issue of the commercialization of a free gospel. Nonetheless, I remain undeterred and will continue to spread the Christian message via popular song. Yes, there *is* a fine balance to be struck between ministry and entertainment, but it isn't a balance that's impossible to strike. I may have failed sometimes, in fact I'm sure I have, but I just try to keep my eyes fixed on God and do my best to find that right balance.'

Vast family audiences have been entertained, uplifted and challenged by George's message in song. He says that he wants his talents to stir even the most apathetic or hard-hearted; he wants to reach those who would remain unmoved by powerful preaching from a pulpit. Different methods of communication reach different people, and George is simply grateful that he now has an opportunity to play his part in spreading the good news about Jesus by doing what he does best.

Other influences outside music and people from the music industry also had a huge effect on George and his deepening beliefs, particularly during the seventies and beyond. When he and Tinky returned from Nashville to live in their home state of North Carolina, for instance, they soon discovered that they were close neighbours with Billy Graham's brother-in-law, the Canadian-born Leighton Ford. George says he was always fascinated to listen to Leighton describing his latest travels, more often than not another great mission with Dr Graham and his team. As Leighton recounted the adventures and achievements of his travels for God, George found himself feeling something bordering on envy for his friend's obvious sense of fulfilment. George loved his entertaining career, yet something was missing. He longed to have the opportunity to share his music in a more fruitful and productive way.

One memorable day in the early seventies, George was shocked to receive a letter from the White House in Washington DC. It contained an invitation to a Presidential Prayer Breakfast, to be led by Billy Graham himself. 'To me, such an invitation could never be treated as commonplace, even though I'd met so many famous people in the course of my musical career. It wasn't a cosy little get-together with the President – there were several hundred other people at the event. Nevertheless, it was a thrill to see President Nixon, to hear his speech and his introduction of Dr Billy Graham. Dr Graham gave a challenging talk, and then my RCA Victor colleague Connie Smith sang "How Great Thou Art".

After the breakfast, George met Dr Graham for the first time. They only had a brief chat, but George was struck by his imposing personality. It made a lasting impression on him. Nonetheless, at the time it seemed too much to hope for that one day he might actually be able to join in with the work of Billy Graham and Leighton Ford.

George was therefore astonished and delighted when some time later he was invited by Cliff Barrows, Dr Graham's choir leader and musical director, to be a guest soloist for the Billy Graham crusade due to be held in Anchorage, Alaska in the mid-80s. 'I can remember very clearly how nervous I was!' George recalls. 'But the crusade's main singer, George Beverly Shea, kindly took me under his wing. When I arrived at the hotel which was our base, he invited me down to the coffee shop for a chat, and throughout the crusade meetings he often gave me the thumbs-up sign, just to let me know I was doing okay. I was deeply grateful for the sincerity of his encouragement.'

After Alaska, Cliff Barrows asked George IV if he would join the Graham team as a guest soloist for the series of meetings planned for the UK under the banner of 'Mission England' in 1984. George was somewhat awed at the prospect. He had long been an admirer of Cliff Barrows, and was always impressed by the quality of the music and singing at Billy Graham's rallies. 'How can anyone forget the wonderful, majestic sounds of praise that characterized the Billy Graham missions?' he says. 'I don't believe that the twentieth century ever saw a more powerful song-leader than Cliff Barrows. With his skills in gospel music and his dedication to the task of worldwide evangelism, he has undoubtedly left his mark. He has never been one to crave the limelight, though, and never seemed to want praise for himself. He would often repeat the words of one of his favourite hymns: "To God be the glory, great things he has done!"'

When George came to know him, he found that California-born Cliff Barrows had a happy-go-lucky exterior that belied his deep sensitivity and discernment. He was far more than just a genial host and song-leader for the Billy Graham missions. A figure of authority, at every rally he was the person in charge of the whole event until the evangelist himself stepped forward to deliver his message. Cliff was born in 1923 and became a committed Christian at the age of 11, determined to go into some kind of full-time Christian service. Just after the end of World War II he met the young preacher Billy Graham in Asheville, North Carolina. They teamed up, and a new chapter in Church history began. A firm believer in the power of music to communicate great truths, Cliff once said, 'Every great moving of the Spirit of God has been accompanied by great singing, and I believe it always will be.'

George agrees. 'Cliff Barrows is a first-class songwriter and an excellent preacher. He's an individual of many skills, but on every continent around the world it's as a song-leader that he will be remembered first and foremost. He has motivated thousands to lift their voices in song to praise God. For me, it's a foretaste of what we might expect to hear in heaven!'

The opening week of Mission England was based in Bristol. George was really excited, and impatient to get started. He joined an outstanding group of guest soloists that included Sir Cliff Richard, Sheila Walsh and Graham Kendrick. Those colourful days made a deep impression on George. 'Mission England and later Mission Scotland were times that proved to be full of great blessings for me, even though I feel I played a very small part. At every meeting we held, I listened carefully to what was said and I learned so much. The experience undoubtedly helped me grow as a Christian. I saw my involvement with those missions as a very personal thing – it was part of my service to God, nothing to do with my career. I tried to ensure that I kept those issues as separate as possible. In my humble view, Dr Graham was God's man for our generation. It was a joy to play my part, especially knowing how well my music had already been accepted in the UK. I genuinely felt that I was putting something back into the pot and not merely adding to my ego!'

Also present at Mission England, and in George's view the finest gospel singer of the twentieth century, was George Beverly Shea, a central figure on all the Billy Graham crusades. He is a gentle giant of a man, and George thinks of him as a mentor, role model and friend. He is also a masterful songwriter, of course, and his much loved compositions include 'I'd Rather Have Jesus' and 'The Wonder Of It All'. George outlines his friend's career with admiration. 'Bev Shea can be described accurately as the most influential and popular gospel singer of the last century. His name and rich baritone voice are known worldwide as a result of his 50-year association with Dr Billy Graham, which took him to every continent on earth. Together with Cliff Barrows, those men forged a powerfully effective partnership in evangelism.'

Bev Shea rose from a position as an obscure clerk in a little insurance office to become the world's best known gospel singer. Born in February 1909, he was the son of a Methodist preacher and was the fourth of eight brothers and sisters. He was raised in Winchester, near Ontario, Canada, and his first public singing occurred in his father's church, where his mother played the piano. He progressed into radio work, and an opportunity came in 1944 to share in a popular hymn programme called *Songs in the Night*, which also featured an unknown pastor then based in Western Springs, Illinois. That pastor was Billy Graham, and so began a lifetime's partnership, augmented not long afterwards by the arrival of Cliff Barrows.

George Beverly Shea has given his life to the task of singing the gospel. Like his preaching and song-leading partners, he has made an invaluable contribution to the task of spreading the Christian message round the world in recent times. It was Bev Shea who introduced the majestic hymn 'How Great Thou Art' to the world stage. He told George that he had first heard it in 1954 during Dr Graham's crusade in London. Like Dr Graham's crusades, 'How Great Thou Art' has an international background. It was first written in Sweden in 1885, by a preacher called Carl Boberg. It travelled to Russia, where it was translated and used for some years before being translated on into English by a missionary named Stuart K. Hine in 1948. Under the auspices of Tim Spencer, of Sons of the Pioneers fame, the song went on to be published and popularized worldwide, not least by George Beverly Shea.

George says he cannot speak too highly of the great gospel singer. 'Bev Shea is truly world famous as a result of his long association with Dr Billy Graham. Having already been going for over 50 years, that remarkable partnership remains alive and well today! Bev is also highly respected by traditional country performers as a quality songwriter as well as a performing artiste with scores of albums to his credit. Who can forget Jim Reeves' interpretation of the Shea classic "I'd Rather Have Jesus"? For myself, I was particularly proud of my version of Bev's "The Wonder Of It All". In 1999 I was delighted that Word Entertainment in the UK released a collector's album in honour of Bev's ninetieth birthday. *Golden Jubilee* has an amazing host of performers on it, including Pat Boone, Wanda Jackson, Wes Davis, Paul Wheater, Bill Gaither, Amy Grant, Stuart Hamblen, Sir Cliff Richard, Jerry Arhelger, Arthur "Guitar Boogie" Smith, Sheila Walsh, Kurt Kaiser and myself. It felt right to do something special for such an amazing guy!'

During Mission England, George went with Cliff Barrows and Bev Shea to visit several sites full of significance in terms of Church music history. 'It was a great thrill,' he says, 'to strum my guitar and sing along with Cliff and Bev Shea through the magnificent hymns "Rock Of Ages" and "Amazing Grace", so near the sites where they were actually penned!'

'Rock Of Ages', a timeless classic, was written in 1776 as the reformist minister Rev. Augustus Toplady took refuge from a violent storm in the cleft of a huge rock in Burrington Combe, near Cheddar, England. It was a special moment for the three men to sing the well loved hymn within sight of the place of its composition.

> Rock of Ages, cleft for me,
> Let me hide myself in Thee,
> Let the water and the blood,
> From Thy riven side which flowed,
> Be of sin the double cure,
> Cleanse me from its guilt and power...
>
> Augustus Montague Toplady, trad.

The trio also travelled 50 miles north of London to the historic town of Olney. In the corner of the parish church graveyard is the memorial stone of the eighteenth-century cleric John Newton, writer of the autobiographical 'Amazing Grace'. Standing next to Bev Shea and Cliff Barrows in the Olney church, George says he was deeply moved by the significance of the words he was singing.

> Amazing grace! How sweet the sound
> That saved a wretch like me!
> I once was lost, but now am found,
> Was blind, but now I see...
>
> John Newton, trad.

'I will never forget the thrill of singing that great hymn in John Newton's own parish church!' says George with sincerity. 'It was a moment of true sentiment, not cheap sentimentality.'

George has a deep respect for those marvellous old hymns, and appreciates their place in the history of popular, congregational Church music. Neither time nor music stood still with the great hymnwriters of previous centuries, however, and Christian music has been changing and developing ever since. It was in August 1983 that George became aware for the first time of the power of contemporary praise and worship songs. Prior to that, he says, he had not realized the distinction between them and the majestic old hymns of the Church and the toe-tapping, Southern gospel numbers he knew so well. Always ready to explore new ideas and experiment with musical sounds, he was inspired by the discovery.

George was spending the week in De Bron, Holland, at Leen La Riviere's European Christian Artists Seminar. It was a chance to meet artistes from literally all around the world and each day before lunch everyone gathered in the main hall for a time of worship, music and ministry. 'It was an uplifting occasion with a little preaching and a little praying, along with a whole lot of contemporary praise and worship songs,' George explains. 'The atmosphere was electric. One really had a sense that God was close, that the Holy Spirit was at work. The worship was led by Karen Lafferty [writer of 'Seek Ye First'], Dave Bilbrough [writer of 'Abba, Father'] and Graham Kendrick [writer of 'Meekness And Majesty'] and I think everyone received blessing and encouragement through their musical ministry that week!'

Later, during Billy Graham's Mission England services of 1984–5 and at Amsterdam '86, George noticed that the choir director Cliff Barrows was leading the audiences in singing many of the same praise and worship choruses that he had first heard in Holland. The triumphant song 'Majesty', written by Californian pastor Jack Hayford, virtually became the theme song of Mission England and went on to become a standard in churches around the world. Since then, George says that he has better appreciated the power and beauty of this modern-day form of gospel music.

For many years now George has toured extensively in the UK with the contemporary Christian artiste Wes Davis. They continue to perform together in hundreds of venues ranging from concert halls, churches and prisons to the dizzy heights of the American Embassy in London! A West Londoner, Wes Davis was converted through the ministry of the Argentine evangelist Luis Palau during a rally at the London soccer stadium of the Queens Park Rangers team. He is a talented arranger and producer, and is well known for his instrumentation on album tracks by Pat Boone, Jerry Arhelger, Cliff Barrows, Jane Gibbs, the Living Stones, Paul and Laura Ewers and Anita and Ed McGirr, among others.

George is quick to attest to the talents of his colleague and friend. 'Wes Davis has been a great friend and an inspiration over the many years that we've toured up and down the British countryside together, giving Christmas, Easter and Thanksgiving/ Harvest Festival concerts. Among the new generation of Christian songwriters and performers, he's certainly one of the finest! Wes is a gentle spirit and a great musical ambassador for God.'

Wes's qualities as a songwriter are clear to see in his moving ballad about the blind hymnwriter Fanny Crosby, *His Story, Her Song,* which has been recorded by such distinguished artistes as Pat Boone and Jerry Arhelger, as well as George IV. In recent years, George has recorded a couple of albums of original Fanny

Crosby material and has become quite a fan of her and her musical legacy. 'No sacred songwriter enjoyed a higher reputation in the nineteenth and twentieth centuries than Fanny Crosby,' he says. Born in 1820, Fanny showed a talent for poetry early in life. Her first poem appeared in print when she was just eight years old. She was blind from the age of six weeks, but her 'spiritual eyes' remained far-sighted throughout her long life. She died in February 1915, just 40 days before her ninety-fifth birthday. She left an extraordinary legacy of 9,000 hymns and poems, including 'Blessed Assurance', 'To God Be The Glory' and 'Jesus Keep Me Near The Cross'.

Her gospel songs were initially popularized by Ira Sankey, the first internationally recognized performer of such material. The Crosby and Sankey repertoires together became the foundation of all the gospel music which followed. Wes Davis and George IV have retold the Fanny Crosby and Ira Sankey story in words and music in hundreds of venues now, and audiences never fail to be enthused and inspired by what they hear. George tries to explain why this is. 'The power of sacred song comes through convincingly in the stories of these two historical heroes. In their Victorian days untold multitudes of people were melted and swayed by their simple, plaintive gospel songs. Since then, their songs have become well loved, enduring classics, not only for church congregations, but for mainstream country singers too. It has been a great joy for me to pay this tribute to Crosby and Sankey. Since their time, many people, including me, have successfully fulfilled our gospel-singing undertakings because of these pioneers!'

As the years pass, George IV remains keenly aware of the necessity to remain fresh, real and relevant in his Christian life and ministry. 'The psalmist David gave us a challenge when he declared, "O sing unto the LORD a new song" (Psalm 96:1). We should never be satisfied with yesterday's Christian experiences. I believe that each day should bring a better understanding of God and a growing relationship with Christ, and that's a real challenge for me. I try to express my daily spiritual experiences in fresh words of testimony and prayer. We should also never stop writing and singing new songs of faith and worship!'

> Make a joyful noise unto the LORD, all ye lands.
> Serve the LORD with gladness: come before his presence with singing.
> Know ye that the LORD he is God: it is he that hath made us, and not we ourselves; we are his people, and the sheep of his pasture.
> Enter into his gates with thanksgiving, and into his courts with praise: be thankful unto him, and bless his name.
> For the LORD is good; his mercy is everlasting; and his truth endureth to all generations.
>
> Psalm 100

CHAPTER 12

THE AMBASSADOR TAKES STOCK

> A good name is rather to be chosen than great riches, and loving favour rather than silver and gold.
>
> **King Solomon**, Proverbs 22:1

TODAY GEORGE HAMILTON IV is one of the longest-surviving members of the Grand Ole Opry, and a towering figure in the country music community. Few would dispute that he thoroughly deserves the patriarchal role he fulfils as the International Ambassador of Country Music. Along with a small, select band that includes Great Britain's Cliff Richard, George is one of the very few active survivors from the fifties' pop charts. Despite having been in the music business since 1956, however, George has no immediate intention of becoming even semi-retired. Instead, he retains a keen interest in and dedication to the cause of country and gospel music and simply goes on performing, just doing what he does best.

For the last half-century, the name of George Hamilton IV has been synonymous with quality country and gospel music and he has received a host of awards during his career. Respect has come not only from the public but also from professional peers and other parts of the music industry. He has not allowed success to turn his head, however, and always remains firmly focused on the job in hand and on his plans for the future. He has everything clearly prioritized: more important to him than fame or fortune are his family and his faith – and nothing will ever change that, he says.

City-born and raised, George was perhaps an unlikely country music star, and he feels he has his parents and grandparents to thank for a secure family life which ultimately gave him the confidence to follow his interests. His father died in 1976 and his mother in 1978. He was on tour in St John's, Newfoundland when his father died, and in London, England when his mother passed away. On that occasion, the BBC flew George back to America on Concorde so that he could be home in time to attend his mother's funeral. Both his parents are buried in Old Salem's Moravian cemetery, along with other family members. Inscribed on his father's gravestone are the final words of the chorus to the song 'Life's Railway To Heaven': 'Weary pilgrim, welcome home!' George's younger brother Cabot still lives in North Carolina. After a highly successful business career, he retired early and now lives in the mountains at Beaver Creek, where the Hamilton family once owned many acres of land.

While his brother and his eldest son Peyton may not have followed George into the country music business, his second son, George Hege Hamilton V, has done just that. Now there seems to be something of a Hamilton dynasty developing in the country music field. George V was born in 1960, the same year that George IV joined the Grand Ole Opry. Perhaps, he laughs, that was some kind of sign, a warning that another Hamilton was destined for stardom! George clearly remembers the day when his seven-year-old son (usually called Hege to avoid confusion with his father) presented himself at the breakfast table with his first guitar, asking his busy father to show him some basic chords. Pressed for time, George scribbled three chords down on a scrap of paper, then carefully placed his son's fingers under his own onto the strings, to show him how it was done. 'Ouch, Dad! That hurts!' said Hege, but he soon forgot about that when George got him to strum and he produced some real notes for the first time. The next thing George knew, Hege had rushed off to his own room to practise alone. That, says George, was really his most important contribution to his son's musical future.

Looking back several decades later, George recalls that event with heartfelt regret. When Hege was young, George spent an inordinate amount of time on the road, touring or heading off to concerts in far-flung places. It had been unavoidable, really, but George is sorry now that he never had the chance to spend much time together with his children, even just to toss a ball back and forth in the back yard. What a joy it is now, he says, to get together musically with Hege. They have a lot of fun 'picking and singing' along together as often as they can. Many weekends, when their touring schedules allow, father and son can be found onstage together at the Grand Ole Opry.

Always concerned to be sensible and pragmatic, Tinky and George were sure about not wanting to be obsessive backstage parents. They tried not to encourage Hege in any pushy way to follow in his old man's footsteps. They need not have worried, however, because although he did follow George, he made his own footprints! As the years went by, Tinky and George heard increasingly adventurous and ambitious guitar sounds coming from their son's bedroom. Basic chords turned into tunes, then Hege's voice joined in. At first the songs were other people's compositions, then suddenly it became apparent that Hege was creating his own material. He made rapid progress and was clearly gaining in musical maturity. In due course he chose to demonstrate his musical coming of age by deciding to play only his own compositions.

When George went to England to record his television shows, Hege sometimes travelled along with him. As a child and a teenager, the young Hamilton also enjoyed seeing his musical heroes backstage at the Grand Ole Opry and at the famous RCA recording studios in Nashville. On one memorable occasion he even managed to persuade Chet Atkins to sign his guitar.

Thanks to his exposure to many different styles of music, Hege began to forge a style that was all his own. He found his footing by performing at universities and colleges to begin with, and then progressed to playing in country clubs. His innovative country music style incorporating a real rock twist rapidly gained him popularity. Hege recalls how his initial country club performances broke new ground in quite a radical way. Some loved it, but others were not so happy. 'I remember back in 1990, I was working with the English band Nashville Fever. We were said to be "outlaws" who "broke away from the norm". Well, I agreed, and I was proud of it! But many people thought we were too "rocky" for country music.' In fact, George V's new style of country was four or five years ahead of its time. There is no doubt now that he was genuinely ahead of the field, leading others into new territory.

In 1987 George V chose to use the name 'Hege V' when he led his university 'punkabilly' band in recording his original compositions for the *House of Tears* album, produced by REM producer Mitch Easter in Winston-Salem. Ironically, Mitch Easter's uncle John Shields had been a drummer in George IV's high-school band. (John Shields became an Episcopal priest, and later officiated at the wedding ceremony of George V and Lillian Hamilton in 1990.) *House of Tears* landed on many year-end Top Ten lists in the USA, alongside bands of the calibre of U2, Bruce Springsteen and REM. The album also received an abundance of airplay on 'alternative' and university radio stations nationwide and even yielded a music video on MTV – 'Burial Ground of the Broken Hearted'. As part of the promotional activities, Hege and his band toured 10,000 miles across the USA in a Cadillac hearse, the so-called 'Hearse of Tears'. His record label, MTM, allowed Hege to release his first country single, 'She Says', in 1988. The single performed well in *Billboard* magazine's 'Country 100' chart, and a new album was in progress at the time of MTM's demise in late 1988.

By the mid-nineties, George Hege Hamilton V's music was considered by Music City's true-blue conservatives to be 'too dangerous for country music' – largely because they feared change. Yet there was also a growing body of opinion in Nashville which recognized that everything was now tending to sound the same. Some musicians, of course, had been saying that for a long time and had been pleading and searching for an alternative to what they called 'conveyor-belt country music'. Perhaps George IV's son would be the one to lead them out of the uncreative quagmire.

Since 1988, George V has written for Nashville's most prestigious music publishers, including BMG, Sony/Tree and Curb

Music Publishing. He toured round the UK 13 times between 1990 and 1999, and earned the distinction in 1996 of being the first American artiste to tour fully nationwide in Poland. He has also toured in Australia, New Zealand, Japan, Brazil, Germany, Ireland and France. There is even a hotel named after George V in Brighton, England – the George Hamilton V Hotel!

He cut his first solo demo recordings in Charlotte, North Carolina at the Moody Brothers' studio, and it was at the same studio that he later put together the duet acoustic album *Homegrown*, featuring both Georges IV and V. Both Hamiltons gratefully acknowledge the invaluable input of the Moody Brothers. Without their help, they say, the notion of the *Homegrown* album would never have taken root. The nineties proved to be a decade of exciting album releases for George V, all displaying a growing sense of confidence and competence. *Country Classics*, produced by Gordon Lorenz for EMI, was a wonderful reworking of some great hits, including a few more duets with George IV.

George V's self-penned and self-produced *Roll With The Punches* album, recorded with his band The Nash Vegas Nomads, received rave reviews in Australia and New Zealand on its release in 1995. Later the album was retitled *Ghost Town* and released in 1996 by the French Dixie Frog label to appreciative French and European reviews. It was distributed in the UK by Topic to similar accolades. CMT-Europe rated the *Ghost Town* video, filmed in Poland, among its Top Five videos at the end of 1997. His follow-up European release, *Garden of Love*, appeared on the Dixie Frog label in 1998 and has more than matched the international success of its predecessors.

When he is asked about being the son of a famous figure, George V is keen to put the record straight and scotch the idea that it has been an easy ride. 'People say that it's been easy for me because of my father's name, but it hasn't been easy at all! More is expected from someone like me. Just look at how Hank Williams Junior was treated initially. People always ask me why I use the name George Hamilton. Am I trying to gain an advantage? Well, the answer's simple – I use it because that's my name! My father is

George Hamilton IV, I'm George Hamilton V, and there were three others before my father ... I did consider using my middle name for a while, just to be different, but I decided not to continue as "Hege V". Too many people had a hard time pronouncing "Hege", and most press folks always referred to me as "George Hamilton V" anyway.'

He looks remarkably similar to his father, a tall, slim figure. George V, however, has grown his hair long and often wears ragged blue jeans in keeping with his 'rockabilly' style. By contrast, George IV's image has always been that of the clean-cut, all-American college boy, complete with pressed trousers and smart blazer. Father and son each fit the style of their own generation and their own style of music. Like his father, George V has an active international fan club which issues regular newsletters giving the latest information about his tour dates and album successes.[1]

George IV respects the fact that his son is his own personality in artistic terms and no clone. Deep down, it is clear that he takes great personal pride and satisfaction in this creative diversity. 'I definitely would not describe George V as a chip off anybody's block!' he laughs. 'But Tinky must take full credit for our son's guidance and inspiration. Without her, none of his great success would have been possible, and I'm sure he would agree. She taught him to dream big and keep on believing!'

George asserts that of all the 70 or so albums that he has recorded in the last half-century, the duet album with his son, *Homegrown*, is his greatest favourite. They both see it as a family heirloom. 'It's funny to recount,' George IV adds, 'that with George V as my record producer, he was teaching me songs and showing me how to play the difficult guitar chords ... I couldn't help but reminisce about that breakfast table in the kitchen of our North Carolina home so many years ago, and the three guitar chords I scribbled on a tiny scrap of paper. It may not have seemed much at the time, but it was enough to get the ball rolling!'

1 For more information, contact 'George V News', 3 Hamilton Drive, Edinburgh, Scotland EH15 1NP. George V also has a website: www.VivaNashVegas.com

George, of course, is no less proud of his other children. Given half a chance, he waxes lyrical in praise of them all. 'When we had our first son, Peyton, we named him after Tink's father, Edwin Peyton. At that time, we weren't sure we really wanted to carry on the number tradition. But when our second son was born, I think it was my mother who finally convinced us that we should name him George V. I'm glad we did, and I don't think Peyton minds!' The Hamilton's youngest child, Mary Dabney, was born five years after George V.

Mary lives in Charlotte, North Carolina now. She graduated with a degree in journalism from the University of North Carolina and worked for a time for an equestrian magazine called *Saddle Horse Report* in Shelbyville, Tennessee. Later she was the public relations co-ordinator for the American Saddlebred Horse Association at the Kentucky Horse Park in Lexington. She is now an executive at the Bank of America in Charlotte, serving on the bank's board of directors for the Forum for Investor Advice.

Mary was the most horse-mad of the three children, and she had her own pony when the family lived in North Carolina. Peyton was dragooned into helping Tinky and Mary take the pony to shows in George's absence, and he became an enthusiast despite himself. Peyton's real interest, however, was in reptiles, and his pets as a boy included a boa constrictor. George remembers one time when the family came home from a beach holiday. The boa constrictor had somehow escaped out of its cage and disappeared. George clearly remembers Tinky sitting down in the kitchen with a broom in her hand. 'I'm going to sit right here until you find that snake,' she announced, 'and I'm *not* moving!' Eventually, George recalls, they found the snake in a most unlikely place. 'We found that snake inside the record player! It was the last place we thought to look...'

Peyton was always an outdoors type, as his father had been in his younger days. He liked all kinds of animals, but snakes remained a firm favourite. He went off to university to study biology and his parents thought he would go on to become a biologist, biology teacher, game warden or at least something to do with animals and the outdoors. They were still rather surprised, however, when he chose to become a horse trainer. It was a long way from snakes! Peyton and his wife Anne own a thriving stable near Fort Mill, South Carolina, where they breed, train and sell American Saddlebred horses. They have a son, Peyton McAlester Hamilton, George and Tinky's first grandchild.

Despite the inevitable ups and downs of life, George and his wife Tinky have been successful survivors and they are proud of their children's achievements in such diverse arenas. Like their parents, Mary, Peyton and George V are individuals of high integrity and faith, displaying no mean talent when it comes to their own individual pursuits. But what did the children think of their father's musical talents as they grew up? When they were younger, George acknowledges that it probably did not mean that much to them in itself. Life was not always easy, largely as a direct result of his success. 'I think the kids mostly thought it was just my job,' says George. 'Perhaps they saw it as something that kept me away from the family for a lot of the time. Sometimes I've even thought there was a little bit of resentment in the family about my job, rather than enthralment or enchantment. It has been, after all, "the best of times and the worst of times", as Tinky said, and there has been an awful lot of separation.'

The older he gets, the more George says he realizes how important heritage, roots and family are to him. His long-surviving marriage to Tinky, which passed its 40-year milestone in 1998, is rare in any department of show business, including country music. It is a testimony to their faithfulness and sheer determination to see every problem through to the end. Always supportive, Tinky has been content to stay at home, raising their three children and managing the administration of George's affairs. With the children now long grown up and with lives of their own, Tinky and George are happily ensconced in the small suburb of Franklin on the outskirts of Nashville. They are now proud grandparents twice over, to Peyton's son Mac and George V's son George Hege Hamilton VI.

George admits that it was all down to Tinky to hold the fort at home throughout the years he spent travelling around the globe. Such lengthy and frequent periods of absence could not have been a happy experience for her. In George's view, all the wives who stay at home caring for their families while their show-biz husbands are on the road deserve far more credit and admiration than they seem to receive. When Tinky is asked how she coped with her husband being away from home so often during their marriage, she tends to borrow the answer Ruth Graham gave to the same question about her husband Billy and says that she would rather be with George part of the time than with anyone else all of the time.

Since their own children grew up and reached independence, Tinky has taken the opportunity to travel with George sometimes. She is not always thrilled by the prospect of hitting the road, however, and in all honesty has always preferred to remain at home, developing her own circle of friends both in North Carolina and Tennessee. She has always been active in her local church and in charity work too, and could never be taken merely for 'Mrs George Hamilton IV'. She still teaches at the pre-school nursery for three-to-five-year-olds run by Walker Memorial Baptist Church near her home in Franklin. George takes every opportunity to tell people how proud he is of his wife, and they are clearly devoted to one another.

George says he has few really burning personal regrets for anything that has happened in the past, and he does not feel he has any vital hills still left to conquer. His life and career have been rich, enjoyable and fruitful, and he is more than satisfied. Then he pauses, smiles, and says he does have one niggling little regret, and it has to do with a very interesting song called 'One Day At A Time', written by Kris Kristofferson and Marijohn Wilkin.

Marijohn's home state of Texas strongly influenced her songwriting style and in the second half of the twentieth century, as a producer, arranger, songwriter and artiste, she could be described as one of the 'myth-makers' of Nashville. Her songs have been recorded by Johnny Cash, Joan Baez, Stonewall Jackson, Ray Price, Pat Boone, Wanda Jackson, Walt Mills, Porter Wagoner and many more. In 1974 she experienced a profound spiritual renewal, from which flowed many fine songs. The most successful of all these was 'One Day At A Time'. It is an enormously inspirational song, premiered in many parts of the globe by George IV and made into a hit around the world by a number of local singers. George is not surprised by the song's popularity, yet he says that before it became a hit he had an impossibly hard time trying to persuade the powers-that-be that it was indeed a potential winner!

George always believed it to be a quality song. For years before it became a hit, he was frequently featuring it in his concerts. He sang it on successive television shows, year after year. Yet he was never able to persuade the record companies to release the song as a single. 'It's not commercial!' he was told over and over again. 'People don't want to hear that kind of message on the radio!' George did not succeed in recording it as a single, although it went on to be a hit for Lena Martell and Cristy Lane and eventually became established as a standard part of the repertoire. 'One Day At A Time' is a clear example of a song that has contradicted the perceived trends, and scotched the theory that gospel music is neither commercial nor even viable in the secular market place. George asserts that many people identified immediately with what the song said. It speaks about basing your life on Christ's words, and in George's view, there is no better philosophy of life than to live on the principle of 'one day at a time'.

The fact that he did not have a hit with that special song is a very small regret, however, taken in the context of a long and glittering career. At the start of the new millennium, George is fast heading for his 'golden jubilee' in country music. Although he made his first recordings as far back as 1956, in Chapel Hill, North Carolina, he honestly says that even now, after all those years, it is still fun. It has always been difficult for him to think of country music as work. George has simply been pursuing a lifelong love affair, ever since he first heard the Grand Ole Opry on the radio as an impressionable child sitting on his grandfather's knee in Winston-Salem. That love affair is as alive as ever today.

'I perform at the Grand Ole Opry pretty much anytime I'm in town – which still isn't very often,' he says. 'These days, with over 70 members, the Opry's biggest problem is getting everybody on the show. They never have to worry about not having enough talent on any given Saturday night, so there's no pressure on me to do the Opry unless I want to. Of course, all the Opry members want to, because you might say it's the "Mother Church of Country Music"! Most of us, when we're in Nashville, plan to do the Grand Ole Opry if we can.'

He is still full of excitement and enthusiasm for future plans, and he is deeply grateful for the fact that he has been able to make his profession and his living from something that is really a hobby. His long career has been a joy – although it has meant some sacrifices, and the touring and travelling was undeniably exhausting work. Indeed, the difficulties that have been overcome only serve to make his achievements even more worth cherishing. George considers the whole experience to have been a rare privilege.

His hopes for the future include aspirations for the stars who will follow him, and there are some things in the industry which he sincerely hopes will change. Down through the years, George has been intrigued to hear the comments about country music made by so-called experts. He has come to the conclusion, he says, that nobody likes country music except the public! The 'experts' in the music industry often treat his genre as a poor relation, a Cinderella of no consequence, and look down on country music as something of a minority taste.

Judging from his wide travels, however, George cannot believe that to be the case. Time and time again, he has heard people say they would love to buy more country recordings but cannot find them in the shops. He remains amazed that so many of the top country acts in America never have their product released overseas. He puts the responsibility for this squarely at the door of record industry executives. They have, in his view, blatantly overlooked some great talent and have ignored the wishes of the public at large. The solution is obvious to George, and he says he can only hope that things will improve. 'If only country music was marketed properly, with a little more enthusiasm, what a difference that would make! Perhaps the worldwide chart successes of Shania Twain, the Mavericks, Leann Rimes, Steve Earle and others like them will continue to conquer new territory, persuading the industry that it *is* worth making country music more available to the mainstream public.'

In July 1997, George was presenting his *Sunday Morning Gospel Show* at Chris and Bev Jackson's Americana Festival in Newark, England. It was the week of his sixtieth birthday. Midway through the show, to George's astonishment, a large group of his 'adopted' children from Kirk Sandall Junior School filed onto the stage in their bright red uniforms. Once they were lined up behind him, they began to sing 'Give Thanks', the opening song from his 'Thanksgiving in the Country' programme.

Caught completely by surprise, George was visibly moved, and he was not the only one. The vast audience, made of up tough-looking motorcyclists, 'weekend' cowboys, teddy boys, ageing hippies and a host of ordinary, everyday people, all seemed to be reaching for their hankies too. It was a sight to behold, as Al Moir observed. 'If George had never actually uttered the words, "Suffer little children..." then the manner in which he welcomed and accepted the humble gift of song offered by those youngsters demonstrated beyond the slightest shadow of a doubt that if anyone deserved the title "Ambassador for God", it was surely this man!'

For many years now, George has been travelling the world not only on behalf of country music but also on behalf of God, and ('the good Lord willing') he anticipates that he will continue to follow this path well into the new millennium. His enthusiasm for the task has certainly never waned. Some people, keen for their own reasons to try to undermine his unique role, have mocked George by calling him a 'holy hillbilly'. George takes all this in his stride, and quotes a verse or two from Matthew to explain his gracious reaction to such criticism: 'Blessed are ye, when men shall revile you, and persecute you, and shall say all manner of evil against you falsely, for my sake. Rejoice, and be exceeding glad: for great is your reward in heaven ... Let your light so shine before men, that they may see your good works, and glorify your Father which is in heaven' (Matthew 5:11–12,16).

George considers himself most fortunate to have been able to represent Music City USA in so many parts of the world.

However, that privilege, he says, pales into insignificance compared to the joy he finds in representing the Kingdom of Heaven. 'When one comes to Christ in repentance and faith, one becomes a citizen. The Bible says that citizenship is of the Kingdom of God. That's what it means to become a Christian. We no longer look at life in the same old way we did in the past. Our new relationship with Christ brings us into a new relationship with the world and its inhabitants. It's all there in the Bible,' he says, and quotes from Paul's letter to the Corinthians:

> Therefore if any man be in Christ, he is a new creature: old things are passed away; behold, all things are become new. And all things are of God, who hath reconciled us to himself by Jesus Christ, and hath given to us the ministry of reconciliation … Now then we are ambassadors for Christ, as though God did beseech you by us: we pray you in Christ's stead, be ye reconciled to God. For he hath made him to be sin for us, who knew no sin; that we might be made the righteousness of God in him.
>
> 2 Corinthians 5:17–18,20–21

George explains further. 'It's awe-inspiring to know that we not only become citizens of heaven but also new creations. Because of that, we also gain a new view of the people around us. We stop seeing them just as friends, foes or fans, and start seeing them as people in need – and we know we have a message for them, a life-changing message about Christ.'

He tells the story of a fledgling country singer waiting to take his turn on stage at one of Nashville's heavily hyped country music showcases. Just as he was about to step out of the wings, the singer's slick, money-minded manager barred his way and pointed to the small gold cross on the lapel of the singer's jacket. 'You'd better get rid of that, boy. People will think you're a religious nut!'

But the singer responded coolly, 'Why should I take it off? It represents what I hold most dear in life. I need to remember that even my fans need my witness. They're sinners like me – what can be more important than telling them about Christ?'

Like George Hamilton IV, the young singer took his stand that day as an ambassador for Christ. In the ranks of country music, there have been quite a few like him and George knows he does not stand alone in his desire to share his faith. Yet George has become something of a spokesman for this fraternity, and many of his peers now look up to him as a leader. Ever since he became firm and clear about his own beliefs, George has certainly nailed his colours to the mast. In doing so, in standing out for what he believes, he has drawn many fellow artistes to follow his example.

There have been times when George's mission as an ambassador for God has taken him into dangerous situations. One such incident occurred while he was in India on an evangelistic mission with Dr Robert Cunville, an Associate Evangelist with the Billy Graham Evangelistic Association, and his wife. Late at night after a successful meeting in Jowai, the tired but elated team were heading through the mountains back to Shillong, Megalahya. It turned out to be a hair-raising journey, as George explains. 'We were passing through a little village and it seemed that the people in the car in front of us were somewhat inebriated. Their car was weaving from side to side and the driver of our car tried to go around them. Just as we were passing, the other car swerved and hit us.'

Not wanting to get into an altercation with a car full of drunk people, the team's driver just carried on and headed out to the main highway. The other car, however, followed at increasing speed. It pulled up beside the mission team's damaged car, still moving fast, and the driver and passengers screamed viciously through the open windows. 'They tried their best to run us off the road, and eventually succeeded. I don't think they had any weapons, but they did seem very upset! When the cars screeched to a halt, it was evident that they'd had too much to drink. They threatened to torch our car. During all the heated discussion, our local driver was hiding underneath our car, frightened for his life. He was the one they were most mad at – they were wanting to do serious physical harm to him, for sure.'

For the Christian team, not knowing what was to happen and obviously feeling themselves to be in some peril, it was time for urgent, silent prayer. Just at that moment, rescue appeared in the form of some tough-looking Indian soldiers, who appeared very suddenly out of the darkness. Dr Cunville calmly explained the circumstances, and the soldiers made sure that the inebriated men, who came from the village down the road, turned round and went back home. Breathing a sigh of relief, the team thanked the soldiers and continued on their way.

That was not the end of the issue, however, as George recalls. 'The drunk people in the other car simply did a U-turn once the soldiers had gone and came back after us. They continuously bumped into our car on the mountainous road, then they ran us into the ditch again. One of them produced a jagged rock and threatened Dr Cunville's wife with it. It was very dark and our hearts were pounding with fear. The men's objective seemed to be to get hold of the driver of our car. Dr Cunville remained very gentle, a true Christian example! He managed to calm the anger down, then asked them how much the damage to their car would cost to repair – even though they were the ones who had hit us, and our car was more damaged than theirs. They seemed to be satisfied with the amount of cash he gave them.' The aggressive drunks left, still shaking their fists and shouting obscenities at the local driver. It was a terrifying experience for the shaken Christian team, as they were finally free to continue their journey in peace, thanking God for keeping them safe. It had been a close call, and George reckons they were lucky to escape unhurt and alive.

It is sometimes far from easy to bring peace to a situation, especially when there is such passionate hatred being expressed. George is nonetheless convinced that it is right to try. 'As Christians, we are ambassadors of Christ in a world at war with God. The world is like an enemy province as far as God is concerned – he sends his ambassadors out to declare peace not war. That's the reconciliation we Christians represent.'

Being such an ambassador for God – in more everyday, peaceful situations just as much as in tight and dangerous corners like the one described above – calls for courage and confidence. To George it is a privilege and an honour to have the responsibility, but he has not always found it easy. 'I must admit that at first I did experience some embarrassment and get hot under the collar whenever I was called upon to show the colour of my faith to all and sundry! Then it occurred to me one day that I didn't need to be shy about it: it was something to be proud of. Not everyone gets to be an ambassador for a king, so the privilege is all the greater to be representing the King of Kings.

'We see all around us the painful, desperate situations in a world full of turmoil and rebellion, a world apparently tearing itself apart. Christ and his Church are seeking to bring everything back together again, to bring peace instead of war to individuals and to whole nations. That's what reconciliation truly is, and that's the basic task of the ambassador. We're needed more than ever today, and we have Christ's Great Commission to follow: "Go ye, therefore, and teach all nations, baptizing them in the name of the Father, and of the Son, and of the Holy Ghost: Teaching them to observe all things whatsoever I have commanded you: and, lo, I am with you alway, even unto the end of the world. Amen" (Matthew 28:19–20). This Commission has been entrusted to every Christian – I'm only one among many. And I can tell you that there's no greater joy than to know we're pleasing God, and to see others making their personal peace with him. Certainly it's the most important thing I've ever done.'

I am a stranger here within a foreign land,
My home is far away upon a golden strand;
Ambassador to be of realms beyond the sea,
I'm here on business for my King!

E.T. and F.H. Cassel

DISCOGRAPHY

ALBUMS BY GEORGE HAMILTON IV

1957

GEORGE HAMILTON IV ON CAMPUS
(UK – HMV CLP1202; US – ABC PARAMOUNT ABC220)
Clementine/Ivy Rose/When I Grow Too Old To Dream/Tell Me Why/Carolina Moon/You Tell Me Your Dream/Aura Lee/Girl Of My Dreams/Let Me Call You Sweetheart/Love's Old Sweet Song/Drink To Me Only With Thine Eyes/Auld Lang Syne

1958

SING ME A SAD SONG – A TRIBUTE TO HANK WILLIAMS
(UK – HMVCLP1263; US – ABC PARAMOUNT ABC251)
House of Gold/I Can't Help It/How Can You Refuse Him Now?/I Could Never Be Ashamed Of You/Half As Much/(I Heard That) Lonesome Whistle/Your Cheatin' Heart/I'm So Lonesome I Could Cry/Take These Chains From My Heart/Wedding Bells/Cold Cold Heart/You Win Again

1959

BIG 15 (COLLECTION)
(US – Paramount ABVS461)
A Walk On The Wild Side/That's How It Goes/Before This Day Ends/Little Tom/Why I'm Walkin'/Even Tho'/Gee/I Know Where I'm Going/The Wrong Side Of The Tracks/It's Just The Idea/Tremble/Why Don't They Understand?/The Steady Game/One Heart/Loneliness All Around Me

1961

TO YOU AND YOURS (FROM ME AND MINE)
(US – RCA VICTOR LSP2372)
To You And Yours (From Me And Mine)/The Wall/Where Did The Sunshine Go?/East Virginia/Rainbow/I Want A Girl/Three Steps To The Throne

(Millions Of Miles)/I Will Miss You When You Go/Those Brown Eyes/If You Don't Somebody Else Will/Baby Blue Eyes/Life's Railway To Heaven

1963

ABILENE
(UK – SF/RD 7595; US – RCA VICTOR LSP2778)
The Roving Gambler/China Doll/(I Want To Go) Where Nobody Knows Me/The Everglades/Oh So Many Years/Come On Home Boy/Jimmy Brown The News Boy/Abilene/The Little Lunch Box/If You Don't Know I Ain't Gonna Tell You/Tender Hearted Baby/You Are My Sunshine

1964

FORT WORTH, DALLAS OR HOUSTON
(UK – SF/RD7727; US – RCA VICTOR LSP2972)
Fort Worth, Dallas Or Houston/A Rose And A Baby Ruth/If You Want Me To/The Little Grave/Roll Muddy River/There's More Pretty Girls Than One/Truck Driving Man/Linda With The Lonely Eyes/That's All Right/Kentucky/Candy Apple Red/Fair And Tender Ladies

1965

MR SINCERITY – A TRIBUTE TO ERNEST TUBB
(US – RCA VICTOR LSP3371)
It's Been So Long Darlin'/Half A Mind/Letters Have No Arms/You Nearly Lose Your Mind/Rainbow At Midnight/Thanks A Lot/Driftwood On The River/I Will Miss You When You Go/Fortunes In Memories/Walking The Floor Over You/Soldier's Last Letter/Let's Say Goodbye Like We Said Hello

COAST COUNTRY – WEST COAST
(US – RCA VICTOR LSP3510)
Slightly Used/Excuse Me, I Think I've Got A Heartache/You Better Not Do That/Long Black Limousine/Under Your Spell Again/Above And Beyond/I Don't Believe I'll Fall In Love Again/Keep Those Cards And Letters Coming In/Together Again/Under The Influence Of Love/Big Big Love/Foolin' Around

1966

STEEL RAIL BLUES
(US – RCA VICTOR LSP3601)
Early Morning Rain/Changes/Steel Rail Blues/My Face/Tobacco/I Ain't Mad (I'm Just Leaving)/A Nice Place To Visit (But I'd Sure Hate To Live There)/Remember M, Remember E, Remember Me/Write Me A Picture/I've Got A Secret/The Late Mr Jones/Mine

FOLK COUNTRY CLASSICS
(US – RCA VICTOR LSP3752)
As Long As The Winds Blow/Anita, You're Dreaming/I'm Not Sayin'/Four Strong Winds/I Get The Fever/The Great El Tigre/Time/That's A Chance I'll Have To Take/Bad Seed/If I Were A Carpenter/The Deepening Snow/Long Time Gone

1967

A ROSE AND A BABY RUTH
(US – RCA CAMDEN CAS 2200)
A Rose And A Baby Ruth/Truck Driving Man/The Last Letter/The Wall/You Are My Sunshine/Walking The Floor Over You/(That's What You Get) For Lovin' Me/The Roving Gambler/I Will Miss You When You Go/The Ballad Of Widder Jones (And Her Twenty Five Acres Of Sand)

FOLKSY
(US RCA VICTOR LSP3854)
Go, Go Round/Colours/Urge For Going/Gentle On My Mind/And You Wonder Why/Darcy Farrow/My Body's At Home (But My Heart's On The Road)/Ballad Of The Yarmouth Castle/Break My Mind/Ruby, Don't Take Your Love To Town/Man Of Constant Sorrow/I'll Be Gone

1968

THE GENTLE COUNTRY SOUND OF GEORGE HAMILTON IV
(US – RCA VICTOR LSP3962)
The Circle Game/Little World Girl/Canadian Railroad Trilogy/Ballad For The Sixth Love/Be Careful With That Little Drink Before Dinner Do You?/Something Special To Me/It's My Time/*Hoshi No Komoruita* (Memories Of Mama)/Song For A Winter's Night/For Baby

GEORGE HAMILTON IV IN THE 4TH DIMENSION
(US – RCA VICTOR LSP4066)
Back To Denver/Suzanne/Lunch Time/It's More Than Honey That I'm After/Take My Hand For Awhile/No Regrets/Wonderful World Of My Dreams/A Truer Love You'll Never Find/Everything Is Leaving/Did She Mention My Name?/You Never Understood Me

1969

CANADIAN PACIFIC
(US – RCA LSP4164; UK – SF8062)
Canadian Pacific/I'm Gonna Be A Country Boy Again/Shake The Dust/Together Alone/Steel Rail Blues/Both Sides Now/Sisters Of

Mercy/Early Morning Rain/My Nova Scotia Home/Summer Wages/Long Thin Dawn/Home From The Forest

THE BEST OF GEORGE HAMILTON IV VOLUME 1
(US – RCA LSP4265; UK – LSA 3005)
Abilene/Fort Worth, Dallas Or Houston/Break My Mind/A Rose And A Baby Ruth/Before This Day Ends/Why Don't They Understand/Early Morning Rain/Steel Rail Blues/Take My Hand For Awhile/Urge For Going/Three Steps To The Phone (Millions of Miles)

1970

BACK WHERE IT'S AT
(US – RCA LSP4324; UK – CDS1126)
Back Where It's At/She's A Little Bit Country/Reason To Believe/Then I Miss You/Three Cheers For The Good Guys/Carolina In My Mind/Just The Other Side Of Nowhere/Greyhound Goin' Somewhere/The Nature Of Man/Anyway

DOWN HOME IN THE COUNTRY
(US – RCA LSP4435; UK – CDS1126)
There's No Room In This Rat Race (For A Slowpoke Like Me)/Everything Is Beautiful (with Skeeter Davis)/The Best That I Can Do/Me And Bobby McGee/*Natividad* (The Nativity)/Sunday Mornin' Comin' Down/If You Don't Know I Ain't Gonna Tell You/Less Of Me/I've Got A Secret/The Little Grave

1971

LIGHTFOOT COUNTRY
(RCA CANADA CAS2379; released as *Early Morning Rain* in USA)
Early Morning Rain/Steel Rail Blues/Go Go Round/Ballad Of The Yarmouth Castle/Song For A Winter's Night/The Canadian Railroad Trilogy/Home From The Forest/I'm Not Saying/Did She Mention My Name?/Long Thin Dawn

DOWN EAST COUNTRY
(RCA CANADA CASX2558)
My Nova Scotia Home/Prince Edward Island Is Heaven To Me/Apple Blossom Time In Annapolis Valley/Maritime Farewell/Take Me Back To Old New Brunswick/Ghost Of Bras D'or/Squid Jiggin' Ground/Atlantic Lullaby/Isle Of Newfoundland/Farewell To Nova Scotia

NORTH COUNTRY
(US RCA VICTOR LSP4517)
I'm Not Sayin'/Countryfied/Love Is Still Around/North Country/Snowbird/It's All Over/My North Country Home/Goin' Down The Road/Moody Manitoba Morning/Put Your Hand In The Hand

GEORGE HAMILTON IV WITH THE HILLSIDERS
(HERITAGE RCA UK LSA3043)
Streets Of London/Fairy Tale Lullaby/The Leaving Of Liverpool/Dirty Old Town/Come Kiss Me Love/Teach Your Children/(Hillsiders) Georgia Woman/I Will Show You A Fool/Going Back Home/The Loving Kind/It's Not That Simple/The Game Of Love

1972

OUT WEST COUNTRY
(RCA CANADA CASX2613)
Williams Lake Stampede/Mountains And Maryann/Saskatchewan/Nothing Changes But The Seasons/Alberta Bound/The Calgary Song/Into The Mountains/Old Bill Jones/Dirty Old Man/My Rocky Mountain Home

THE COUNTRY SOUNDS OF GEORGE HAMILTON IV
(UK MUSIC FOR PLEASURE MFP50295)
A Rose And A Baby Ruth/Your Cheatin' Heart/Loneliness All Around Me/You Win Again/I Can't Help It/Even Tho'/I Heard That Lonesome Whistle/One Heart/A Walk On The Wild Side/Cold, Cold Heart/Tremble/Half As Much/I Know Where I'm Going/Take These Chains From My Heart/I'm So Lonesome I Could Cry/Carolina Moon

COUNTRY STYLE
(US – ABC PARAMOUNT GA266D)
Take These Chains From My Heart/A Walk On The Wild Side/Clementine/Loneliness All Around Me/One Heart/Tell Me Why/Tremble/Aura Lee/Little Tom/Love's Old Sweet Song/Your Cheatin' Heart/Drink To Me Only With Thine Eyes

YOUR CHEATIN' HEART
(US – ABC HS11379)
House Of Gold/I Can't Help It/How Can You Refuse Him Now?/Half As Much/I Heard That Lonesome Whistle/Your Cheatin' Heart/I'm So Lonesome I Could Cry/Cold, Cold Heart/You Win Again

WEST TEXAS HIGHWAY
(US – RCA LSP4609; UK – LSA3060)
Tumbleweed/Sweet Baby James/10 Degrees And Getting Colder/A Little Bit Of Sunday Every Day/I Don't Think About Her No More/West Texas Highway/What's Fort Worth/That's The Way I Talk/Plain Ole Three Chord Hurtin' Country Song/All My Highways

16 GREATEST HITS
(US – ABC ABCX750B; UK – AAABCL5178)
A Rose And A Baby Ruth/Your Cheatin' Heart/Loneliness All Around Me/You Win Again/I Can't Help It/Even Tho'/A Walk On The Wild Side/Cold Cold Heart/Tremble/Half As Much/ I Know Where I'm Going/Take These Chains From My Heart/I'm So Lonesome I Could Cry/Carolina Moon

COUNTRY MUSIC IN MY SOUL
(US – RCA LSP4700; UK – LSA3092)
My Carolina Home/The Child's Song/Colorado/You Wanted Me To Tell You Like It Is/Just Biding My Time/Country Music In My Soul/Ain't Life Easy/If You've Been Wondering/Streets Of London/Twist Of The Wrist

TRAVELIN' LIGHT
(US – RCA SLP4772; UK – LSA 3124)
Travelin' Light/High Lonesome Sound/It Was Time For Me To Move On Anyway/Maritime Farewell/Keep On The Sunny Side/Don't It Seem To Rain A Lot/I've Never Sung A Staying Song Before/Beaver Creek/Alberta Bound/The Call

FAMOUS COUNTRY MUSIC MAKERS COAST TO COAST
(UK – RCA DPS2034/2; double album set)
Disc 1: I Don't Believe I'll Fall In Love Today/Big Big Love/Slightly Used/ Under Your Spell Again/You Better Not Do That/Keep Those Cards And Letters Coming In/Above And Beyond/Long Black Limousine/The Isle Of Newfoundland/My Nova Scotia Home/Prince Edward Island Is Heaven To Me/Take Me Back To Old New Brunswick/Ghost Of Bras D'Or/Squid Jiggin' Ground/Atlantic Lullaby/Apple Blossom Time In Annapolis Valley
Disc 2: Thanks A Lot/You Nearly Lose Your Mind/Driftwood On The River/Half A Mind/I Will Miss You When You Go/Walking The Floor Over You/Rainbow At Midnight/Soldier's Last Letter/It's Been So Long Darling/ Fortunes In Memories/Letters Have No Arms/Let's Say Goodbye Like We Said Hello/Farewell To Nova Scotia/Foolin' Around/Excuse Me I Think I've Got A Heartache/Together Again/Under The Influence Of Love

1973

INTERNATIONAL AMBASSADOR OF COUNTRY MUSIC
(US – RCA USP 4826; UK – LSA 3169
Blue Train (Of The Heart Break Line)/Suzanne/Release Me (And Let Me Love Again)/Christian Island (Georgian Bay)/Farewell To Nova Scotia/ Canadian Railroad Trilogy/Green Green Grass Of Home/People Call Me Country/The Leaving Of Liverpool/*Hoshi No Komoruita* (Memories Of Mama)

CANADA WITH LOVE
(RCA CANADA – KPLI7006)
Alberta Bound/Old Bill Jones/Early Morning Rain/Canadian Pacific/My Nova Scotia Home/Steel Rail Blues/Dirty Old Man/Countryfied/North Country/Squid Jiggin' Ground/Moody Manitoba Morning/Song For A Winter's Night

SINGIN' ON THE MOUNTAIN
(US – RCA CAMDEN ACLI0242)
Singin' On the Mountain/Old Camp Meeting Days/The Old Country Church/Family Bible/Amazing Grace/Acres Of Diamonds/He's Everywhere/Life's Railway To Heaven/Wings Of A Dove/I'll Fly Away

1974

BLUEGRASS GOSPEL
(US – LAMB & LION LL1015; UK – 112012)
I'm Using My Bible For A Road Map/Old Time Religion/When It's Prayer Meetin' Time In The Hollow/I Shall Not Be Moved/Father's Table Grace/ Will The Circle Be Unbroken/Shake My Mother's Hand For Me/O Come Angel Band/Where Did All The Good Folks Go?/Build Me A Cabin In Glory/Precious Memories/Gathering Flowers For The Master's Bouquet

GEORGE HAMILTON IV GREATEST HITS
(US RCA APLI0455)
Blue Train (Of The Heart Break Line)/She's A Little Bit Country/Canadian Pacific/Break My Mind/A Rose And A Baby Ruth/Early Morning Rain/West Texas Highway/Abilene/Steel Rail Blues/Urge For Going

THE BEST OF GEORGE HAMILTON IV VOLUME 2
(UK – RCA LFLI7504)
Canadian Pacific/Dirty Old Man/Blue Train (Of The Heart Break Line)/ Suzanne/10 Degrees And Getting Colder/Anyway/She's A Little Bit Country/ Streets Of London/Countryfied/Let's Get Together (with Skeeter Davis)/ West Texas Highway/Second Cup Of Coffee/Back Where It's At/Country Music In My Soul

BACK TO DOWN EAST COUNTRY
(UK – LSA3200; CANADA – KCLI0051)
Back To Down East Country/Cape Breton Lullaby/Pictou County Jail/Fiddler's Green/Where The Blue Waters Foam/Peter Amberlay/Lismore Lady/T.C. Carry Me/The Little Boats Of Newfoundland/Shores Of Prince Edward Island

1975

TRENDSETTER
(UK – LSA3229; RCA CANADA – KPLI0002)
Bad News/The Ways Of A Country Girl/Let My Love Shine/Where Would I Be Now/The Good Side Of Tomorrow/My Canadian Maid/The Wrong Side Of Her Door/Time's Run Out On You/The Isle Of St Jean/The Dutchman

GEE
(Hilltop Records by arrangement with Pickwick Records, ABC Dunhill ABCJS6161)
Gee/I'm So Lonesome I Could Cry/Cold Cold Heart/Why Don't They Understand?/Your Cheatin' Heart/Half As Much/House Of Gold/I Heard That Lonesome Whistle/I Can't Help It

1976

BACK HOME AT THE OPRY
(UK – PL10192; US – RCA KPLI0192)
Headed For The Country/Streets Of Gold/Winterwood/Blue Jeans, Ice Cream And Saturday Shows/Follow Me/Bad Romancer/Crystal Chandeliers/Sleeping Through Goodbye/It's Almost Tomorrow/Leaving London
THE GEORGE HAMILTON IV STORY
(UK – DPS1001; double album plus book and George's life story narrative on record)
Disc 1: A Rose And A Baby Ruth/If You Don't Know I Ain't Gonna Tell You/Why Don't They Understand/Abilene/Before This Day Ends/Take My Hand For Awhile/Break My Mind/Steel Rail Blues/Urge For Going/Three Steps To The Phone (Millions Of Miles)/Fort Worth, Dallas Or Houston/ Blue Train (Of The Heart Break Line/She's A Little Bit Country/My North Country Home
Disc 2: Countryfied/Canadian Pacific/Dirty Old Man/Early Morning Rain/Nothing Changes But The Seasons/Truck Driving Man/Alberta Bound/Streets Of London/Travelin' Light/*Natividad* (The Nativity)/Follow Me/The Dutchman/Fiddler's Green/Singin' On The Mountain

1977

FINE LACE AND HOMESPUN CLOTH
(ANCHOR UK/DOT USA/GRT CANADA – ANCL2022)
Everlasting Love/In The Palm Of Your Hand/No Time Left For Lovin'/May The Winds Be Always At Your Back/I Wonder Who's Kissing Her Now/ Cornbread Beans And Sweet Potato Pie/I Had A Horse/The Wonderful Soupstone/Till The Fiddle Comes Off That Wall/John's

GEORGE HAMILTON IV – THE ABC COLLECTION
(US – ABC AC30032)
A Rose And A Baby Ruth/You Win Again/Before This Day Ends/Half As Much I Could Never Be Ashamed Of You/Tremble/That's How It Goes/ *Memphis Tennessee/Your Cheatin' Heart/A Walk On The Wild Side/I'm So Lonesome I Could Cry/Cold, Cold Heart/It's Just The Idea/*She Wasn't Like That When She Used To Be Mine/*So Small/*You've Lost That Loving Feeling
(* recordings by George Hamilton the actor, not George Hamilton IV)

HOMEWARD BOUND
(K TEL INTERNATIONAL LTD CANADA – Kelo Music LPWC343)
Abilene/Let My Love Shine/She's A Little Bit Country/Break My Mind/Urge For Going/Crystal Chandeliers/The Ways Of A Country Girl/Before This Day Ends/Three Steps To The Phone (Millions Of Miles)/If You Don't Know I Ain't Gonna Tell You/Early Morning Rain/Canadian Pacific/Peter Amberlay/Shires Of Prince Edward Island/Back To Down East/The Little Boats Of Newfoundland Follow Me/Truck Drivin' Man/Dirty Old Man/ Fort Worth, Dallas Or Houston

1978

HITS OF GEORGE HAMILTON IV
(UK – RCA PL42335)
Travelin' Light/10 Degrees And Getting Colder/Urge For Going/Second Cup Of Coffee/Back To Denver/Anyway/Alberta Bound/Take My Hand For Awhile/Truck Driving Man/Everything Is Beautiful (with Skeeter Davis)/ Claim On Me/Carolina On My Mind/She's A Little Bit Country/Write Me A Picture/West Texas Highway/It's My Time

THIS IS GEORGE HAMILTON IV
(UK – DHYK 0008)
Snowbird/Remember M, Remember E, Remember Me/Ballad Of The Yarmouth Castle/My North Country Home/Little World Girl/Back To Denver/Put Your Hand In The Hand/I Get The Fever/Williams Lake Stampede/Write Me A Picture/Everything Is Leaving/Anita, You're

Dreaming/Truck Driving Man/The Wall/Tobacco/It's My Time/Into The Mountains/Where Did The Sunshine Go/As Long As The Winds Blow/ Did She Mention My Name/The Circle Game/Wonderful World Of My Dreams/East Virginia/I Ain't Mad (I'm Just Leaving)

FEEL LIKE A MILLION
(UK – ANCHOR ANCL 2026; US – DOT USA/GRT Canada 9308 2 26)
Why Should I Cry Over You/All I Want (Is My Old Fashioned Girl)/Only The Best/Take This Heart/Some Day My Ship Will Sail/(Who Are You Mocking) Mocking Bird/Before I'm Fool Enough (To Give It One More Try)/One Day At A Time/It Amazes Me/Oh So Many Years/You Ain't My Kind Of Country Woman/Feel Like A Million

1979

FOREVER YOUNG
(UK – MCA RECORDS MCF3016)
Forever Young/I'll Be Here In the Morning/Wild Mountain Thyme/Two Ships That Passed In The Night/'Rangement Blues/I Never Loved A Woman Like You/Spin, Spin/Catfish Bates/Someone Is Looking For Someone Like You/Common Ground/Mose Rankin/We Go Back

REFLECTIONS
(LOTUS RECORDS, in association with ANCHOR and RCA for K-TEL UK only – WH5008)
Abilene/Canadian Pacific/Early Morning Rain/I'm Gonna Be A Country Boy Again/Put Your Hand In The Hand/Green Green Grass Of Home/Both Sides Now/Streets Of London/Travelin' Light/Crystal Chandeliers/Take These Chains From My Heart/Everlasting Love/You Win Again/I Wonder Who's Kissing Her Now/Feel Like A Million/Cold Cold Heart/Why Should I Cry Over You/Your Cheatin' Heart/Why Don't They Understand?/ A Rose And A Baby Ruth

1980

COUNTRY CLUB – THE HITS OF GEORGE HAMILTON IV
(RCA CANADA – KELI8106)
Williams Lake Stampede/Dirty Old Man/Follow Me/Crystal Chandeliers/Fiddler's Green/Abilene/Bad News/Peter Amberlay/The Ways Of A Country Girl/Into The Mountains/Cape Breton Lullaby/Break My Mind/Shores Of Prince Edward Island/Canadian Pacific

1981

GEORGE HAMILTON IV CUTTING ACROSS THE COUNTRY
(UK – RCA PL 18106 CT PK 18106)
Williams Lake Stampede/Dirty Old Man/Follow Me/Crystal Chandeliers/Fiddler's Green/Abilene/Bad News/Peter Amberlay/Ways Of A Country Girl/Into The Mountains/Cape Breton Lullaby/Break My Mind/Shores Of Prince Edward Island/Canadian Pacific

GEORGE HAMILTON IV 20 COUNTRY CLASSICS
(UK – WARWICK MCWW5101; joint production with Mervyn Conn Ltd)
Country Music In My Soul/Amazing Grace/Early Morning Rain/Abilene/Release Me/Break My Mind/Old Flames (Can't Hold A Candle To You)/Medley: I Saw The Light, I'll Fly Away/Oh So Many Years/Have I Told You Lately That I Love You/You're My Best Friend/Mountain Dew/One Day At A Time/Jambalaya/Forty Shades Of Green/I Love Music/Forever Young/Wild Mountain Thyme/Paradise/The Last Farewell

GEORGE HAMILTON IV
(UK – MUSIC FOR PLEASURE MFP5786)
Canadian Pacific/Dirty Old Man/Blue Train (Of The Heart Break Line)/Suzanne/10 Degrees And Getting Colder/Anyway/She's A Little Bit Country/Streets Of London/Countryfied/Let's Get Together (with Skeeter Davis)/West Texas Highway/Second Cup Of Coffee/Back Where It's At/Country Music In My Soul

1982

GEORGE HAMILTON IV THE COUNTRY AMBASSADOR
(CARNABY USA IV 8161; not a compilation – all tracks are re-recordings)
Country Music In My Soul/Release Me/I'm Gonna Be A Country Boy Again/Old Flames (Can't Hold A Candle To You)/Early Morning Rain/Green Green Grass Of Home/I Saw The Light/The Last Farewell/A Rose And A Baby Ruth/Jambalaya/Break My Mind/Have I Told You Lately That I Love You/Forty Shades Of Green/You're My Best Friend/Streets Of London/Abilene/Mountain Dew/Amazing Grace/I Love Music

ONE DAY AT A TIME
(UK – WORD WST9618)
One Day At A Time/I Shall Not Be Moved/Forever Young/The Shadow Of A Cross/Someone Is Looking For Someone Like You/Where Did The Good Folks Go?/Some Day My Ship Will Sail/You Are The Finger Of God/Feel Like A Million/Old Time Religion/Mose Rankin/I'm Using My Bible For A Road Map

GEORGE HAMILTON IV, JIRI BRABEC AND COUNTRY BEAT
(SUPRAPHON 1113 3090 ZA – import)
One More Country Song/Travelin' Light/My Little Friend (dedicated to Filip)/Break My Mind/Let's Get Together/Me And Bobby McGee/Glad To Come Around/Darling Corey/Streets Of London/Bad News/Jambalaya/ Country Music In My Soul

SONGS FOR A WINTER'S NIGHT
(UK – RONCO RTL2082 CT 4CRTL2082)
Song For A Winter's Night/Mull Of Kintyre/When We Are Gone (I Will Love You)/When I Dream/I Believe In You/Castles In The Air/Lucille/A Bunch Of Thyme/Me And The Elephant/England/Only Love/The Way Old Friends Do/Waiting For The Sun To Shine/Teach Your Children/Four Strong Winds/Blue Eyes Crying In The Rain

1984

20 OF THE BEST
(UK – RCA NL89371 CT NK 89371)
Three Steps To The Phone (Millions Of Miles)/To You And Yours/If You Don't Know I Ain't Gonna Tell You/Abilene/Fort Worth, Dallas or Houston/Truck Driving Man/Walking The Floor Over You/Write Me A Picture/Steel Rail Blues/Early Morning Rain/Urge For Going/Break My Mind/Little World Girl/Back To Denver/Canadian Pacific/Blue Train (Of The Heart Break Line)/She's A Little Bit Country/Back Where It's At/ Anyway/West Texas Highway

MUSIC MAN'S DREAMS
(UK – RANGE 7004)
Music Man's Dreams/Double Or Nothing/It Must Be Love/Growing On Me/Would You Still Be Mine/The Man I Used To Be/Keeper Of The Moon/ Back Around To Me/The Water Is Wide/The Life I Love/Are The Good Times Really Over/'Til I Gain Control Again

1985

HYMNS COUNTRY STYLE
(UK – WORD WST9656 CT WC9656)
What A Friend We Have In Jesus/Bringing In The Sheaves/I'd Rather Have Jesus/It Is No Secret/Tell Me The Old, Old Story/How Great Thou Art/Rock Of Ages/Alleluia/I Love To Tell The Story/The Old Rugged Cross/In The Garden/Majesty/Abide With Me/Wings Of A Dove/Blessed Assurance/The Lord's My Shepherd

GEORGE HAMILTON IV
(UK – DOT MCF3314; US – MCA39033 CT USMCAC39033)
Abilene/Forever Young/You're The Best Thing/Till I Gain Control Again/Can't Remember, Can't Forget/Early Morning Rain/I Will Love You All My Life/Break My Mind/Good Ole Boys Like Me/Cornbread, Beans And Sweet Potato Pie

1986

THE VERY BEST OF GEORGE HAMILTON IV (AT THE COUNTRY STORE)
(UK – STARBLEND RECORDS LTD CST030 CT CCSTK 030)
Canadian Pacific/Early Morning Rain/Streets Of London/Green Green Grass Of Home/Fort Worth, Dallas Or Houston/Break My Mind/She's A Little Bit Country/Both Sides Now/Release Me (And Let Me Love Again)/Abilene/Country Music In My Soul/Leaving Of Liverpool/Travelin' Light/Sunday Morning Coming Down

GIVE THANKS
(UK WORD WSTR9697 CT WSTC 9697)
I Love You, Lord/Give Thanks/All Heaven Declares/Meekness And Majesty/Jesus Name Above All Names/Our God Reigns/The Wonder Of It All/Freely, Freely/Seek Ye First/Abba Father/Spirit Of The Living God/He Is Lord/Benediction

1989

AMERICAN COUNTRY GOTHIC (WITH THE MOODY BROTHERS)
(UK – CONIFER CD CDRR304 CT MCRR 304)
If I Never See Midnight Again/My Hometown/This Is Our Love/Little Country County Fairs/Farmer's Dream Plowed Under/Never Mind/I Will Be Your Friend/More About Love/Heaven Knows/Back Up Grinnin' Again/Carolina Sky/I Believe In You

A COUNTRY CHRISTMAS
(UK – WORD CT WSTC 9707)
C.H.R.I.S.T.M.A.S./Christmas Legends And Facts/Away In A Manger/Isaiah 9:2, 6:7 and 7:14/Natividad/John 1:1–5 and 13:34–35/The Christmas Guest (reading)/Matthew 25:34–40/Joy To The World/Christmas In The Trenches/Love Is The Reason/The Prayer Of St Francis/The Little Grave/Ready For Christmas (reading)/Origin Of Silent Night/Silent Night/A Christmas Thought (reading)/Morning Star/A Christmas Prayer and Benediction/Joy To The World (reprise)

1990

A COUNTRY CHRISTMAS
(UK – WORD CD WSTCD 9707)
I Wonder As I Wander/C.H.R.I.S.T.M.A.S./Christmas In The Trenches/See Amid The Winter's Snow/The Friendly Beasts/Joy To The World/The Little Grave/Silent Night/Away In A Manger/Natividad/Morning Star (with the London Emmanuel Choir)/In The Bleak Midwinter

HOMEGROWN – GEORGE HAMILTON IV AND V
(US – LAMON CD LRCD 10225 2 CTLRI 10225)
Homegrown (IV & V)/These Days (IV)/Love Games (V)/Daughter Of McLeod (IV & V)/It's My Time (IV & V)/Medley: Using My Bible For A Road Map; Build Me A Cabin In Gloryland (IV & V)/Tumbleweed (IV & V)/A Couple More Years (IV)/No Time At All (IV)/Spin, Spin (IV & V)/ Precious Hand (V)/Don't Let Me Come Home A Stranger (IV)

1991

GEORGE HAMILTON IV ABILENE
(COUNTRY HARVEST USA ER103; cassette only)
(A collectors' item made from a series of live radio programmes recorded by the US Navy to encourage recruiting. Dates of actual recordings unknown)
Abilene/A Rose And A Baby Ruth/Walkin' The Floor Over You/Canadian Pacific/Life's Railway To Heaven/Truck Drivin' Man/Gentle On My Mind/If You Don't Know I Ain't Gonna Tell Ya/Write Me A Picture/Early Morning Rain

EASTER IN THE COUNTRY
(UK – WORD CT WSTC 9716)
John 3:16/The Best Of Hands/Isaiah 53:1–6/The Wonder Of It All/Origins Of Easter (reading)/How Can You Refuse Him Now?/John 10:11, 14–16, 27–29/Jesus Makes My Heart Rejoice/Trouble In The Amen Corner (reading)/Rock Of Ages/Less Of Me/One Solitary Life (reading)/ Philippians 2:5–8/Matthew 16:24–26/Seek Ye First/Mark 11:1–2, 7–10/ Meekness And Majesty/The Best Of Hands (reprise)/Matthew 28:1–6/In The Garden/He Is Risen/Although Jesus Was The Son Of God (reading)/ Let Your Love Flow Through Me/I Simply Argue (reading)/Medley: Spirit Of The Living God; He Is Lord/Hebrews 12:1–3/Because He Lives/An Easter Thought (Benediction)

COUNTRY CLASSICS – GEORGE HAMILTON IV & V
(UK – EMI Music For Pleasure CDMFP5933/CDP & 98351 CT MFP 5933)
Abilene (IV & V)/I Can't Stop Loving You (V)/Distant Drums (IV)/Wayward Wind (V)/My Truly, Truly Fair (IV)/Raining In My Heart (IV)/It Doesn't Matter Anymore (V)/An American Trilogy (IV)/Sixteen Tons (V)/Canadian Pacific (IV & V)/Release Me (IV)/Welcome To My World (V)/The Last Thing On My Mind (IV)/I Walk The Line (V)/Try A Little Kindness (IV)/Green, Green Grass Of Home

OLD COUNTRY CHURCH
(DAYBREAK CT DC 137)
That Old Camp Meeting/What A Friend (with Mary McKee and Crawford Bell)/Acres Of Diamonds/Life Is Like A Mountain Railroad/The Wings Of A Dove/Once In Royal David's City (with Mary McKee and Crawford Bell)/The Old Country Church/Where Did All The Good Folks Go?/The Family Bible/I'll Fly Away/The Pilgrim (with Mary McKee)/Someday My Ship Will Sail

1992

LASSOES AND SPURS
(CANADA – CD BMG MUSIC 06192 17274 2)
My Nova Scotia Home/Squid Jiggin' Ground/Farewell To Nova Scotia/Canadian Pacific/Early Morning Rain/Both Sides Now/Home From The Forest/Together Alone/The Isle Of St Jean/Time's Run Out On You

1993

COUNTRY GENTLEMEN
(UK – CT MASTER MUSIC DT 007)
Country Music In My Soul/Release Me/Abilene/Mountain Dew/Old Flames (Can't Hold A Candle To You)/Early Morning Rain/Green, Green Grass Of Home/Medley: I Saw The Light; I'll Fly Away/The Last Farewell /Jambalaya/Break My Mind/Have I Told You Lately/Forty Shades Of Green/You're My Best Friend/Streets Of London/I'm Gonna Be A Country Boy Again/Amazing Grace

THANKSGIVING IN THE COUNTRY – A HARVEST FESTIVAL CELEBRATION
(UK – WORD CD WSTCD 9740 CT WSTC 9740)
Come Ye Thankful People Come/*Welcome To Thanksgiving In The Country/Bringing In The Sheaves/*The Mayflower/If My People (2 Chronicles 7:14)/Give Thanks/*Harvest History/Praise God From Whom All Blessings Flow/*Psalm 95/How Great Thou Art/*St Francis' Quote/The Wonder Of It All/The Diary Of A Church Mouse (recitation)/The Pilgrim

(with Mary McKee)/*The Pilgrim Fathers' Persecution/The Dutchman/*The Pilgrim Fathers' Journey/Must Jesus Bear The Cross Alone/The Way Old Friends Do/*The Pilgrim Father's New Home/We Gather Together/*A Pilgrim Ballad/Robert Burns' Quote/For The Beauty Of The Earth/Rejoice In The Lord (Philippians 4)/The Old Country Church/Mary Had A Little Lamb/*The Great Provider/Rock Of Ages/Alleluia/*Gratitude/Sowin' Love/*Ephesians 5:19–20/National Day Of Prayer/You Laid Aside Your Majesty (with Wes Davis)/*Random Thoughts/The Old Camp Meeting Days/*Dean Of Derry Prayer/I'd Rather Have Jesus/*Happy Thanksgiving Everybody/May God's Blessing Surround You Each Day
(*narrations composed or arranged by George Hamilton IV/New Music Enterprises)

1995

CANADIAN COUNTRY GOLD AND UNMINED TREASURES
(CANADA – BROADLAND INTERNATIONAL CD BRI CD 0195 2 CT BRI CS0195 04)
Homefolks (with Larry Mercey)/The Farmer's Song (with George Hamilton V)/Paper Rosie (with Dallas Harms)/Navajo Rug (with Ronnie Prophet)/The French Song (with Lucille Starr)/Canada (with Ray Griff)/R.R#2 (with Gary Buck)/Working Man (with Ronnie Prophet, Glory Ann, Stu Phillips, Stephanie Hunter, Eddie Eastman, Susan Jacks, Gary Buck)/Your Distant Arms (with Colleen Peterson)/North Country (with Myrna Lorrie)/Carpenter Of Wood/Jesus It's Me Again/Children Of The Street (with Gary Fjellgaard)/The Moon Is Out To Get Me (with Sandy Kelly)/Good Friends (with Sandy Kelly)

TREASURED KEEPSAKES – INSPIRATIONAL RECITATIONS
(UK – ALLIANCE MUSIC CD ALDO19 CT ALC019)
The Mother Watch (*Just a Closer Walk With Thee)/Father's Table Grace (*Hold To God's Unchanging Hand)/Touch Of The Master's Hand (*Softly And Tenderly)/Footprints (*Great Is Thy Faithfulness)/If Jesus Came To Your House (*Sweet, Sweet Spirit)/Old Doc Brown (*Love's Old Sweet Song)/Laughter And Worry (*Smile)/The Slave Trader (*Amazing Grace)/The Funeral (*Jesus Is All The World To Me)/Cowboy's Prayer (*Red River Valley)/To A Sleeping Beauty (*Beautiful Dreamer)/Should You Go First (*Until Then)/The Old Homestead (*Long, Long Ago)/Old Age Grace (*You Make Me Feel So Young)/Ragged Old Flag (*Battle Hymn Of The Republic)/Mama Sang A Song (*Whispering Hope)/The Cross In My Pocket (*Near The Cross)/Trouble In The Amen Corner (*I'll Meet You In The Morning)/Strangely Warmed (*Rejoice The Lord Is King)/Going Home (*I'm Bound For The Promised Land)
(*backing music)

THE MEEKNESS AND MAJESTY OF CHRISTMAS
(NELSON WORD TIME CDD012 CT C012)
Joy To The World/Majesty/You Laid Aside Your Majesty (with Wes Davis)/Away In A Manger/Meekness And Majesty/The Heart Of Christmas/Once In Royal David's City/The Saviour Of The World/In The Bleak Midwinter/The Christmas Guest/C.H.R.I.S.T.M.A.S./The Little Grave/I Wonder As I Wander/Silent Christmas Eve/Silent Night/Christmas In The Trenches/See Amid The Winter's Snow/The Cowboy's Christmas Prayer/Natividad/The Friendly Beasts/Ready For Christmas/Morning Star/That's Why He Came/Spirit Of The Living God

TO YOU AND YOURS FROM ME AND MINE
(BEAR FAMILY RECORDS CD BCD 15773 FK; six box set)
CD1: Beer Wine And Whiskey (Hank Hamilton)/Sleeping At The Foot Of The Bed (Hank Hamilton)/Caribbean/Satisfaction Guaranteed/A Satisfied Mind (The Serenaders)/Serenaders Swing (The Seranaders)/It's My Way/I'll Always Remember You/Jalopy Jane/Driftin' (version 1)/Daniel Boone/Driftin' (version 2)
CD2: I've Got A Secret/ A Rose And A Baby Ruth/If You Don't Know I Ain't Gonna Tell You/If I Possessed A Printing Press/Only One Love/Everybody's Body (master)/High School Romance/Everybody's Body (take 10)/Why Don't They Understand/Little Tom/Even Tho'/You Tell Me Your Dream/Carolina Moon/Let Me Call You Sweetheart/When I Grow Too Old To Dream/Tell Me Why/Aura Lee/Girl Of My Dreams/Drink To Me Only With Thine Eyes/Love's Old Sweet Song/Auld Lang Syne/Ivy Rose/Clementine/One Heart/May I/Now And For Always/House Of Gold/I Can't Help It
CD3: How Can You Refuse Him Now?/Your Cheatin' Heart/Half As Much/I Could Never Be Ashamed Of You/I'm So Lonesome I Could Cry/Cold, Cold Heart/(I Heard That) Lonesome Whistle/Wedding Bells/Who's Taking You To The Prom?/I Know Where I'm Goin'/You Win Again/Take These Chains From My Heart/So Soon/When Will I Know/Lucy, Lucy/House A Car And A Wedding Ring/The Two Of Us/The Steady Game/Last Night We Fell In Love/Can You Blame Us/Love Has Come To Our House/Gee/One Little Acre/I Know Your Sweetheart/Tremble/Why I'm Walkin'/Loneliness Is All Around Me/Before This Day Ends/The Wrong Side Of The Tracks/It's Just The Idea/A Walk On The Wild Side Of Life/That's How It Goes
CD4: Can't Let Her See Me Cry/To You And Yours (From Me And Mine)/Three Steps To The Phone (Millions Of Miles)/The Ballad Of Widder Jones/I Want A Girl/Those Brown Eyes/Where Did The Sunshine Go?/Baby Blue Eyes/Life's Railway To Heaven/East Virginia/The Wall/If You Don't, Somebody Else Will/Rainbow/I Will Miss You When You Go/Life Is Too

Short/China Doll/Tender Hearted Baby/Commerce Street And Sixth Avenue North/If You Don't Know I Ain't Gonna Tell You/(I Want to Go) Where Nobody Knows Me/The Roving Gambler/Oh So Many Years/Jimmy Brown The Newsboy/The Little Lunch Box/Come On Home Boy/The Everglades/You Are My Sunshine/The Last Letter/If You Want Me To/Linda With The Lonely Eyes/In This Very Same Room

CD5: Abilene/Mine/Oh So Many Years/Remember M, Remember E, Remember Me/There's More Pretty Girls Than One/You're Easy To Love/Fort Worth, Dallas Or Houston/Fair And Tender Ladies/Kentucky/Candy Apple/Tag Along/The Little Grave/Texarkana, Pecos Or Houston/Truck Drivin' Man/A Rose And A Baby Ruth/Roll Muddy River/That's All Right/Driftwood On The River/Let's Say Goodbye Like We Said Hello/Rainbow At Midnight/It's Been So Long Darlin'/Letters Have No Arms/Walking The Floor Over You/I Will Miss You When You Go/Half A Mind/You Nearly Lose Your Mind/Fortunes In Memories/Soldier's Last Letter/Thanks A Lot/A Nice Place To Visit (But I Sure Hate To Live There)/Twist Of The Wrist

CD6: A Nice Place To Visit (But I Sure Hate To Live There)/(You Don't Love Me) Anymore/The Late Mister Jones/Write Me A Picture/Something Special To Me/I've Got A Secret/Slightly Used/Under Your Spell Again/Above And Beyond/Excuse Me (I Think I've Got A Heartache)/Wishful Thinking/I Don't Believe I'll Fall In Love Today/Foolin' Around/Another Day, Another Dollar/Keep Those Cards And Letters Coming In/Under The Influence Of Love/Big, Big Love/You Better Not Do That/Long Black Limousine/Together Again

1996

COUNTRY BOY ... BEST OF
(BMG RECORDS (UK) LTD CD CAMDEN 74321 393402)
Abilene/Break My Mind/Early Morning Rain/Steel Rail Blues/Urge For Going/Canadian Pacific/Second Cup Of Coffee/Anyway/I'm Gonna Be A Country Boy Again/Both Sides Now/My Nova Scotia Home/Travelin' Light/10 Degrees And Getting Colder/Streets Of London/Everything Is Beautiful/Carolina In My Mind/She's A Little Bit Country/West Texas Highway/Together Alone/A Rose And A Baby Ruth/Crystal Chandeliers/Country Music In My Soul

WHISPERS OF LOVE (FANNY CROSBY SONGBOOK)
(ALLIANCE MUSIC UK CDALD016 CTALC016)
To God Be The Glory/All The Way My Saviour Leads Me/I Am Thine O Lord/The Blind Girl/Whispers Of Love/Tell Me The Story Of Jesus/Blessed Assurance/Near The Cross/Pass Me Not/Rescue The Perishing/He Hideth

My Soul/Praise Him, Praise Him/The Valley Of Silence/Close To Thee/Jesus Is Tenderly Calling Thee Home/Safe In The Arms Of Jesus/Saved By Grace/ My Saviour First Of All/Will Jesus Find Us Watching?

1997

HEAVENLY SPIRITUALS (ARTHUR SMITH SONGBOOK)
(HOMELAND USA CD HD9713 CT HC9713)
Acres Of Diamonds/Miss Elsie's Place/Trusting In Jesus/One Of A Kind/ One More Mountain To Climb/A Man Such As I/Singin' On The Mountain/Not My Will/Stepping Stones/Shadow Of A Cross/I Look Up

GEORGE HAMILTON IV ABILENE
(COLLECTABLES USA COL-5875; CD only)
The Roving Gambler/China Doll/(I Want To Go) Where Nobody Knows Me/The Everglades/Oh So Many Years/Come On Home Boy/Jimmie Brown The Newsboy/Abilene/The Little Lunch Box/If You Don't Know I Ain't Gonna Tell You/Tender Hearted Baby/You Are My Sunshine/A Rose And A Baby Ruth/Why Don't They Understand?/Now And For Always/ High School Romance

1998

HIDING IN THEE (IRA SANKEY SONGBOOK)
(WORD UK CD TIMEDO28 CT TIMECO28)
What A Friend We Have In Jesus/Ira Sankey Story/Rock Of Ages/Alleluia/ The Old Homestead/Come Ye Thankful People Come/Name Them One By One/Bringing In The Sheaves/The Farmer And The Lord/The Lord's My Shepherd/In The Cross Of Christ I Glory/The Cross In My Pocket/Must Jesus Bear The Cross Alone/My Glory All The Cross/I Love To Tell The Story/Peace Attendeth My Way/Tell Me The Old, Old Story/He Will Make It Plain/For The Beauty Of The Earth/The Lord Brings Back His Own/ Praise God From Whom All Blessings Flow/Her Story His Song/Blessed Assurance/All Things Well/Abide With Me/Safe To The Rock

HIGH COUNTRY
(BROADLAND INTERNATIONAL CANADA CD BRICD0398 CT BRICT03984)
CD1: A Rose Between Two Thorns/What Colour Is The Wind/God Is Alive/Lord, Turn Me Around/Just As Soon As The Lord Opens The Door/Sittin' Home On A Sunday/Jesus Makes My Heart Rejoice/Where I'm Goin'/Christmas In Heaven/I've Never Seen An Armoured Car Following A Hearse/Lord, I'm Glad That You Are God/Circle of Wood/Wings Upon The Wind/Carpenter Of Wood

CD2: If You Get Across Jordan/It Ain't That Way/When God Closes A Door/My Forever Friend/Jesus, It's Me Again/A New Love In My Life/My Home Was My Training Ground For Life/Something We Can Hang On To/A Path That Never Fades/Hand Me Down/The Golden Rule/Leave It To Me/We Will Meet Again/Circle Of Wood (with Opry cast)

STARS OF THE GRAND OLE OPRY – GEORGE HAMILTON IV
(FIRST GENERATION USA CD FGCD 111)
(Previously released in 1984 as *Music Man's Dreams* on vinyl with two additional tracks)
Music Man's Dreams/It Must Be Love (with Melba Montgomery)/Growing On Me/Would You Still Be Mine/The Man I Used To Be/Back Around To Me/The Water Is Wide/The Life I Love/Are The Good Times Really Over/ 'Til I Gain Control Again (with Melba Montgomery)

1999

STREETS OF LONDON
(WORD UK CD INCLD007)
More About Love/Something Beautiful/Heaven Knows/Broken And Spilled Out/Streets Of London/Behold Me Standing At The Door/No Time At All/The Ballad Of Ira Sankey/Faith Is The Victory/Because He Lives/Shall We Meet Beyond The River/I Believe In You/There Is Something About That Name/When My Life's Work Is Ended/Breathe On Me Breath Of God/ Jesus Makes My Heart Rejoice/The Good Shepherd/In Heavenly Love Abiding/Alleluia/Gentle Shepherd

COUNT YOUR BLESSINGS (IRA SANKEY MEMORIES)
(NEW MUSIC ENTERPRISES UK CD NMCD999)
Wonderful Words Of Life/Ballad Of Ira Sankey/The Ninety And Nine/Now The Day Is Over/Bringing In The Sheaves/Alleluia/Name Them One By One/Count Your Blessings/Can We Say We Are Ready/The Old Homestead/ Home On The Range/Praise God From Whom All Blessings Flow/Safe To The Rock/Hiding In Thee/When My Life's Work Is Ended

BLESSED ASSURANCE (FANNY CROSBY MEMORIES)
(NEW MUSIC ENTERPRISES UK CD NMCD998)
Tell Me The Story Of Jesus/All The Way My Saviour Leads Me/I Am Thine O Lord/The Blind Girl/Whispers Of Love/Rescue The Perishing/Should You Go First/More Of Thee/Blessed Assurance/The Valley of Silence/Close To Thee/To God Be The Glory/The Mother's Watch/Safe In The Arms Of Jesus/Her Story, His Song/The Silver Cord

2000

BEYOND THE RIVER
(TKO MAGNUM CDSD 087)
Shall We Gather At The River?/Shall We Meet Beyond The River?/For The Beauty Of The Earth/Safe To The Rock/Hiding In Thee (with Bud Tutmarc)/Praise Him, Praise Him/Faith Is The Victory/Hold The Fort/ Ballad Of Ira Sankey/Wonderful Words Of Life/When My Life's Work Is Ended/The Good Shepherd/Saviour Like A Shepherd (with Bud Tutmarc)/ Bringing In The Sheaves/The Lord Brings Back His Own/The Ninety And Nine/Now The Day Is Over/Must Jesus Bear The Cross Alone?/Peace Attendeth My Way/It Is Well With My Soul/Alleluia/Hiding In Thee (with Bud Tutmarc)/Come, Thou Long-expected Jesus (with A. G. and Kate)/The Slave Trader/Amazing Grace

THE VALLEY OF SILENCE
(JASMINE JASCD 379)
When My Life's Work Is Ended /Her Story, His Song/The Silver Cord/ Blessed Assurance/Behold Me Standing At The Door/He's Calling Today/ Tell Me The Story/All Things Well/All The Way/My Saviour Leads Me/To God Be The Glory/The Mother's Watch/Safe In The Arms/I Am Thine/In The Cross Of Christ I Glory /The Cross In My Pocket /Near The Cross(with Bud Tutmarc) /Rescue The Perishing/The Valley Of Silence/Close To Thee/ Can We Say We Are Ready?/The Blind Girl/Whispers Of Love/ Precious Memories(with A.G. and Kate)

George Hamilton IV was a voice, a persuasive voice,
That travelled the world-wide through.
His country songs flew on beams of light,
Speaking to folk with a gentle might,
Old and young pointed to paths of the true.
The International Ambassador's sound
Traversed over land and sea,
To human hearts he brought the key,
Telling his story and singing his song,
Praising the right and blaming the wrong.

Paul Davis, Wes Davis

INDEX